THE SCARLET T

ADVENTURES

IN WARTIME ESPIONAGE

BY

DONALD DOWNES

WILDSIDE PRESS

CONTENTS

TO THE MEMORY

OF THE EIGHTEEN BANANA BOYS

MALAGA 1943

And thou meanderest forever
At the bottom of my dream
THOREAU

INDEBTEDNESS

TO

Joshua and Rahab

TO

Bob who made the beginning possible

TO

George and Art who tried to keep knives out of my back

TO

David, and Allen, and Lane for their
extraordinary confidence in me

TO

André, Gordon, Arthur, Carl, Ricardo, Lee,
Bill and the rest of the band

BUT ABOVE ALL:

TO

Big Bill for his patience, trust, affection,
and inspiration

INTRODUCTION

1451 BC

The earliest record of an espionage mission is probably the story of Rahab and the Spies in the Book of Joshua.

'And Joshua the son of Nun sent out of Shittim two men to spy secretly saying, "Go view the land, even Jericho." And they went, and came into an harlot's house, named Rahab, and lodged there.'

Then apparently some alert counter-intelligence agent of the Kingdom of Jericho spotted the Israelian agents and tipped off the King. The King even knew that the spies were in the house of Rahab the harlot because he sent her orders:

'... and bring forth the men that are come to thee ... for they be come to search out all the country.'

But Rahab had heard of Israel, its ally Jehovah, the miracles of the crossing of the Red Sea and the Manna provided in the wilderness. She was greatly impressed, so she hid the agents under flax stalks which were drying on her roof and claimed that the young men had already fled.

'... whither the men went I wot not; pursue after them quickly; for ye shall overtake them.'

The King's men pursued the spies who were still safely on Rahab's roof. When the hue and cry had died down, Rahab went up to the roof to make her deal with the Israelian agents. She was helping them, she said, because Jehovah was God, and because Israel was strong enough to have destroyed the kingdom of the Amorites and the cities of Sinon and Og.

'Now therefore, I pray you, swear unto me by the Lord, since I have shewed you kindness, that ye will also shew kindness unto my father's house and give me a true token:

'And ye will save alive my father and my mother, and my brethren, and my sisters, and all that they have, and deliver our lives from death.'

The young men agreed to this pact, and gathered the information to take back to Joshua. Precisely what this information was, the security-minded Author of The Old Testament does not tell us, but He does give us a clue by driving home the fact that Rahab's house

xi

was 'upon the town wall', and He repeats, 'She dwelt upon the wall'.

Their work done, Rahab let the men down outside the walls of Jericho by a scarlet cord or rope. Standing below her window under the walls, the spies repeated their oaths to save Rahab, her family, and their possessions when Israel should destroy the city. She was given detailed instructions.

'... thou shalt bind this line of scarlet thread in the window which thou didst let us down by; and thou shalt bring thy father, and thy mother, and thy brethren, and all thy father's household home unto thee ... and if thou utter this our business, then we will be quit of thine oath....'

The young men returned to Israel and reported to Joshua.

What they had to say is not told in the Book of Joshua. But on the strength of their information the armies of Israel moved against Jericho, secure in the knowledge that the walls of the city were sensitive to the blowing of trumpets and the shoutings of a multitude. Joshua attacked with trumpets and shouts and the walls fell down. The information reported by her espionage service and properly exploited by her armed forces had brought victory to Israel.

Very often in history, as in the case of Israel and Jericho, the fate of nations has depended on the success of a small anonymous group, who have taken their lives in their hands to carry out an espionage mission to save their homes or to serve an ideal – the Word of Jehovah or the Democracy of Jackson.

What is unusual in this story is that Israel kept the promises made by her spies to Rahab.

'And they utterly destroyed all that was in the city, both men and women, young and old, and ox, and sheep, and ass, with the edge of the sword....

'And Joshua saved Rahab the harlot alive, and her father's household, and all that she had: and she dwelleth in Israel even unto this day....'

From 1451 BC to AD 1953, three thousand four hundred and four years, the basic pattern of the espionage mission has not changed – its object is still to *go view the land*. But the good faith of Israel is almost the only recorded instance of a government keeping the promises made by its secret agents. The history of the broken promises is long, uniform, and disillusioning.

*   *   *

Fresh from the life of a New England schoolmaster, I became a 'young man', first for the Britain of Joshua Churchill and, later, for the United States of Joshua Roosevelt. I went myself and sent others 'to spy secretly' much further than 'even Jericho'.

My espionage travels took me once around the world, to all the continents except Australia, over most of the great mountain ranges and across most of the great rivers. At various times I followed the routes of Captain Cook, Sinbad the Sailor, T.E.Lawrence, Magellan, Vasco da Gama, Marshal Lyautey, and Admiral Livy.

In telling some of the stories of those years, I plead the precedent of the Author of the Old Testament in being security minded, and I hope to be excused for leaving a number of things untold and a number unexplained.

Rome,
March 1953.

CHAPTER ONE

BEACHHEAD I

9 SEPTEMBER 1943

Gravity can unmake a fox-hole in beach sand almost quicker than you can say 'Dive Bomber'.

The negro boy in the next sand ditch had said, 'What are you white folks coming over to our beach for ? You'll spoil our natural night-time camouflage'.

Neither the negro beach engineers, with whom the Major and I slept, nor the 142nd infantry of the 36th division, who were holding the line about a mile inland, had ever been under fire before; humour is better than alcohol in such moments.

Personal pride and humour are what hold you together when ice sharp fears are eating at your insides. Everybody is afraid, each body thinks he is the only body afraid and it is his pride which carries him through. If he were alone he would vomit or cry, or both.

The hole was on the Salerno beachhead, to be exact on the beach of the village of Paestum, and it was the night of 9 September, 1943.

Two days before, Colonel Smith, headquarters commandant of 5th Army, had come to me on deck of the *Duchess of Bedford* and said:

'The old man wants to get ashore as soon as possible and wants an easily camouflagable wooded area reserved for his HQ. You're wanted as an expert on the terrain. How about it ?'

My mouth said 'yes'.

'OK fellow, landing craft number 368 – listen for it on the loud speakers – 3 – 6 – 8 – '.

Then when Smithy had gone below my mind awakened and began to weigh the matter.

Pro: (almost all irresponsible and personal reasons).

1) Go ashore on the first hours of the first invasion of Europe.

2) Hadn't I said that I and my outfit would serve 5th Army in any way? Wasn't that why I had the only OSS outfit actually with and an integral part of an American Army in the field ?

3) As an amateur classicist I was lured by the fact that the landing would be in full sight of the most glorious ruins of ancient Greece –

1

the temples of Paestum, and at landing hour they would be pink and gold in the light of a September sunrise.

Con: 1) I had two pairs of socks and one clean shirt in my bulging musette-bag. The rest was a big six figures of Uncle Sam's money in occupation lire and good U.S. gold seal dollars. It would cost my uncle a lot of cash to have me knocked off and cash isn't some light worthless article with which to burden someone else, who also has to land through the surf. Besides, I had signed for it and I was stuck with it.

2) I was going ashore as an expert on the countryside. I had been here exactly three times to see the temples, once I had bathed on the wide, uninhabited, white beach. True had I looked at a lot of aerial photos in Africa, but who hadn't? Expert indeed!

3) I had won nearly $2,000 in that last wild poker game. It might be fun to live to spend it.

4) I had an infected toe, having lost a nail running barefooted away from something anonymous two nights before when we were being bombed. I would not walk too well in the sand with the hole cut in the toe of my shoes.

5) I had never been down a landing net. I was fat and old by Army standards – forty.

6) G-2, and in particular Art Blom and Colonel Howard, had been extravagantly generous in what they had let me load on a D-day convoy despite the logistical squeeze. Twenty men, four jeeps, two weapon carriers, two radio base-section trucks, and about twenty big cases of equipment – from special sabotage explosives to false Italian documents – strong evidence that they must want the outfit.

My big mouth had said 'yes'.

The old *Duchess of Bedford* had been rejected once for this convoy as 'too high in profile' which made her an easy bomb and torpedo target. It also made my take off spot on the boat deck seem five nautical miles above the water.

To get the landing barge you climb down a rope net with meshes about a foot square. If the sea is rough (and it was), the landing barge shoots up five or ten feet, bangs against the side of the ship and drops down again.

While your carbine, gas mask, revolver, and grenades are catching in this swinging net, and while a heavy man above is stepping on your fingers, and while the net, on each roll of the ship, hangs free away from the side, and then, heavy with men, bangs back against the steel plates, you are supposed, with more than sixty pounds of junk hanging on you, to jump lightly into the barge at the crest of one of its upward catapultings . . . .

Some of us had known that the Italians had been talking armistice before we had left Africa. In the afternoon before D-day the loudspeakers announced that General Eisenhower would make a special broadcast that evening 'to be heard on this public address system'.

The effect of the Italian surrender was hysteria. By now everyone knew our destination was the Italian mainland – even the least bright private. The end of Eisenhower's speech couldn't be heard for the dancing, kissing, backslapping and roaring of the troops. 'The war's over – the war's *over* – the *war's* over'.

To all of us who knew what a big gamble, even bluff, this landing was to be, who knew how thin was our margin of supply and transport and how many green and untried troops were going to learn the hard way, the hysteria was frightening and ghoulish.

Little knots of HQ officers gave nervous and embarrassed glances at one another. I saw a young British Captain boil over. He turned on the soldiers nearest him.

'Stop it, you bloody fools, stop it. The war isn't over. This will only make Jerry fight harder. Don't laugh your fool heads off, you'll probably be dead on some beach tomorrow' – red in the face and ashamed, he walked quickly away, beating his leg cruelly with his own swagger stick. The episode did our nerves no good. A few officers wondered if the Italian Army would fight with us, against us, or just melt away.

The evening dragged on with no poker. There was ginger ale, with nothing stronger available, and the sweat of nervousness. About midnight our hundreds of lightless ships came to a dead stop. After the throbbing and the engine sounds the silence was a symbol of insecurity.

I recognized, far to the north, the silhouette of the mountains between Agerola and the Chiunzi Pass, above Amalfi and Maiori; they were outlined against a bombing of Naples, green flashes in the dull red overglow of fires, which relighted memories of Naples on other summer days. And now the sadness of seeing an old and dear friend hideously, relentlessly punished – poor, hot, dusty, bittersweet Naples!

Old mother Sgazetta was probably jelled with terror under her peroxided hair in some crowded shelter in Piedigrotta, and what had

3

she ever done to be so punished except to be like Naples – poor, proud, improvident and sloppy ? But she had been lovable and kind to her children and her neighbours.

A half moon was sinking in the west and was that pallid copper colour that my German nurse had taught me as a child to call 'bloody war moon'. She heard it was that colour the day Dewey attacked Manila. In its path lay one silent, black ship behind the other. For some reason we talked in whispers on the deck.

Then I went below and practised hanging all my gadgets on my harness: gas mask, spade, first aid kit, canteen full of water, K-rations, knife, two hand-grenades, until I couldn't get through the stateroom door. Without all this bulky stuff they wouldn't let me go over the side. But I couldn't jettison the money in the musette bag. And the weapons – I dared not sacrifice even one of those concrete evidences of security and confidence.

I destroyed my personal letters and all documents except my false officer's identification card. I also destroyed my dog tag (because it said I was a civilian) despite the Adjutant General's having found some obscure phrase in the Geneva Convention allowing 'civilian combatants' if properly uniformed and wearing a blue armband with a red triangle on which is the insignia of the country for which the civilian is fighting.

I preferred to be a phoney Lieutenant Colonel with my home-made AG card! German counter-espionage would be far less curious – and persuasive.

My mind found no solution and took refuge in sleep. I fell on my bunk and slept nearly two hours. The deafening rattle of chains, the landing barges being launched awakened me.

It was 2.30, H-hour less one ... and still no shooting. No action, no flashes, no battle noise but somewhere east of us lay a long white beach and on it were Germans, 16th Panzer and the Hermann Goering Divisions. I felt I knew them already from the agents' reports and the aerial recon photographs which showed, from 32,000 feet, their ant-like activities, assiduously building new strong points, placing their hellish 88's, camouflaging command posts under haycocks, and spreading nets over vehicles.

And manicured officers at Kesselring's headquarters in Naples must have studied our ant-hills at Mostagenem, Oran, Algiers as we loaded hundreds of ships, camouflaged our dumps and moved the divisions step by step towards the boarding ports. Now we were separated by a little night and a quiet peace which neither side cared to break – probably for fear of giving away some secret already known by the other!

In one second all the quiet and peace vanished. The eastern sky was alight with fire. I looked at my watch. It was 03.25 hours. In five minutes the 142nd infantry would hit the beach at Paestum.

The tracers arched up from above. Our planes were at their haycocks and 88 emplacements – if they were on schedule.

A rocket ship let loose her hundreds of rockets. Still seeing the German ants from 32,000 feet above I imagined them scurrying for cover as this infernal new weapon, capable of melting a section of beach into glass, swooshed towards the shore.

03.30 hours. The 142nd infantry was getting it now. They had never seen combat before, those Texas and New Mexico boys and Choctaw Indians and Mexico-Americans.

And 05.00 was for me. The fireworks in the east hadn't let up. Something over Salerno way, something big like an oil storage was on fire and floodlit the white line of the city's waterfront.

Of course, I reassured myself, if the 142nd is thrown back we'll know it. They wouldn't let a boat such as ours land until the front is a mile inland. Or would they ?

04.25, time for the chemical warfare observers and Colonel Smith's HQ. party to be alerted.

The loudspeaker with a Mayfair accent: 'Code 368 stand by at your station for 05.00 loading. 3 – 6 – 8 repeat 3 – 6 – 8, alert stand by for loading. That is all'.

Down below to rehang myself like a fat Christmas tree. Then up and up and up to the boat deck. I was the last to arrive. The chem boys were there, about fifty of them. Our little party nervously chatted and laughed at one another, hung heavy in equipment.

'How's it going ashore ?'

'No news.'

'Is good news.'

'You hope!'

It was light in the east – we could smoke on deck again. Lights began to appear on the other ships. A look over the side revealed no landing barge below – only that squared net falling away in exaggerated perspective and banging against the ship's side with every wave, a thud and then a whiplike snap.

We watched the lines of landing craft make long snakes passing

5

down their mine-free lanes. Big ones, little ones, LSI's, LST's, slow and formal, going towards those murderous fireworks now paling against a cloudless orange dawn. To the west, a vaguely lit sea-haze outlined two destroyers, dashing somewhere with that alert impertinence with which destroyers move at high speeds.

05.00 and no landing craft below.

05.15 and no landing craft below.

'Little off timing, the navy boys,' said the Major.

'You can't call fifteen minutes late – here, with all this – ' Smithy waved his hand towards the shore and the thousands of craft, little and big, fat and lean, motionless or under way, which filled the great two-horned Gulf of Salerno.

A dozen bug-like P38's passed far overhead, golden in the sunlight, their engines drowned in the rumble of the hell ashore and the PT motors roaring nearby.

'Ours' – everybody smiled. The first we had seen.

05.30 – It was quite light but no landing craft below.

Our chatter kept up. No one said what everyone was thinking. Had it gone badly ? Had *Festung Europa* unveiled some new weapon ?

The beaches were a line of white and smoke and flashes of fire nearly six miles away. We couldn't tell – we could only guess, thinking our fears and talking our hopes.

06.00 no landing craft.

06.30 no landing craft.

Our conversation died down. One by one we had unhung our fancy burdens and our helmets and they lay at our feet. The sun was up and hot.

In the sun, the black silhouettes of the ships took on their blue-gray colour. The waves, high for our purposes, sparkled on their crests. We were sleepy and hungry and we were frightened. Each of us was sure something had gone wrong on shore.

07.00 – a little school of landing craft was headed for the *Duchess.*

'Loads 364, 365, 366, 368 and 369 reporting, sir,' cried the senior boatswain to the bridge of the *Duchess.* 'Where shall we stand, sir ?'

Art Blom came running up. 'Good luck, Don, – you lucky bastard. Give 'em hell. Here, have some coffee.' He handed me a paper cup. It looked like coffee. I drank it down. It was Spanish brandy coloured with coffee.

I smiled and could say nothing in thanks because my bad toe and my throat both began to throb and my knees became peculiarly liquid.

If I didn't go first I felt I would never go. The British inspector said, 'OK, sir.'

Just as I got my feet and hands on the prickly manila mesh, I heard a scream. Turning my head I saw a Colonel (who had messed aboard at the next table) in mid-air, head down with his gadgets hanging before him, falling for the steel deck of the next landing barge. I heard the thud.

'Go ahead, get out of the way.' Somebody above was stepping on my hands.

Some kindly mechanism in the human nervous system took possession of me and I climbed down but I do not remember it at all.

The next thing – I was in the landing barge, trying to open my fists which were sealed, clenched tight from squeezing the rope of the nets. My knuckles were bleeding and I wanted to vomit.

In those moments a bomb or a shell had fallen a few yards away. No one knew what it was. I neither heard it nor felt the concussion. I only heard it discussed.

I was standing between Smithy and the Major. We were away.

'I think his back was broken', the Major said, 'he was twisted so funny.'

'Coxswain,' said a chemical colonel, 'why were you so late ?'

'We lost too many craft – there aren't enough. Them 88's near shore are awful accurate, sir.'

We sardined in. Double loaded with standing room only. I lit an illegal cigarette.

An LCI passed close by, going out. Its coxswain, who looked like a grammar school child, stood calmly at the wheel. There was a sailor in whites at the prow. They were both clean and unruffled, but their boat had a rugged round hole as big as a ten-gallon hat just a foot or two above the water line.

They were loaded long narrow bundles covered in olive drab army blankets. Thirty or forty. All of our heads turned slowly with the boat as she passed. Each blanket was rolled round the body of a dead soldier.

The sight gave me back some control of my nerves, so badly shaken by the hours of waiting and the terror of the net and that first minute on the landing boat.

We stopped and drifted. The boat rolled and pitched in the

combers, waiting for the signal to enter the mine-free lane outlined with buoys and tape. The heat was melting. Many were seasick and vomited on themselves and their neighbours.

Somehow I felt cheerful and chatty and tried to make conversation. The sweat, running down my nose and neck, down my spine and soaking my shirt, seemed comfortable and home-like. Sometimes we would look up at a dog-fight above. Then the picket boat gave us the go-ahead. Our prop churned again and we headed straight for the fifth century Temple of Poseidon – in that day's terminology 'Red Beach'.

Traffic was heavy in the lane: Big LST's loaded with trucks, bulldozers, heavy artillery, and human beings. Stubby LSI's, smart roaring PT's, little LCI's like ours, and ridiculous fat Ducks.

The beach was now easy to see. Little coloured flags here and there – one for first aid, another for water, another for the beach command post. Men, tiny as aerial recon ants, trudged heavily in the uncomfortable sand on anonymous errands. A mile or two to the south a fuel dump was burning – some 88 or dive bomber had made a hit. The smoke rose almost perpendicularly in grey and white lazy folds.

Near the spot we were approaching three big LST's were spewing out a line of tanks which bowed and nodded like fat geese as they waddled over the dunes.

The temples were now close enough to see the Doric order of their columns, and the late Corinthian one to the north.

In the water were thousands of life preservers and gas masks tossed away by overburdened combat-troops.

'Attention,' shouted the coxswain, 'when you hit that beach get across it fast and into the brush and dunes. It looks quiet – it looks pretty deserted. It is deserted because it is dangerous and exposed. Run, don't walk, to the nearest dune.'

I ducked, because I saw everybody else duck, and as I went down I heard a screech outlined against a growl. We were being dive bombed. One resentful face after another came up.

'Right out of the sun, the clever bastard. You can't see 'em!'

The boat ground to shore and its prow dropped to bridge us over the waves. We filed off. I wet one foot – the one with the bad toe. Goose flesh (that had nothing to do with dive bombers or the dangerous beach) came up the back of my neck.

Phoenician traders and pre-Greek Aegeans had bartered or raided here. In the ninth or eighth century before Christ the Greeks had come to this same white beach to colonize the fertile plain of Paestum and grow wheat for the ovens of their home city.

But here, as in Sybaris and Syracuse and the rest of Magna Graecia, they had brought something more precious than the seed of wheat. They had brought the coals from the hearth of their civilization and from these were to be kindled fires to burn away savagery and crudity and to offer mankind the warmth of its science, its logic, its humanity, its beauty.

In their greatest moment, these people had built temples to their gods all around the shores of the Mediterranean, the most perfect expression of their beauty, their harmony, and their science. None surpasses the temple of Poseidon at Paestum. Of all it is the most perfectly preserved. It is a temple humble in its materials, the common tufa of the mountains against which I saw it outlined. It has the mystical quality of taking on the colours of the hours of the day, at dawn pink, at noon glaring yellow, at sunset orange or lavender or sometimes that fugitive colour of fine pearls.

The sage elegance and human beauty of Poseidon is an early heritage of the civilization for which every soldier on that beach was fighting, whether he knew it or not, a civilization that has had that same mystical quality of varying its hues with the centuries and the millennia. Its greatness has been that, preserving its foundation of humanity and curiosity, it has been able to reflect the hues and subtle shadings of the widely differing genius of various times and peoples.

Theirs, ours, is not a rigid civilization. It allows man to err and to try again.

But now a man and a nation gone berserk had attacked the very foundations of this temple. To stop him, these Choctaw Indians. Texas farm boys, little Mexican runts, who thought only of life, were dying.

Battle sounds, continuous and metallic, came from the east but we could see nothing in that direction except scrub growth and sand dunes about twice the height of a man. From time to time a German shell whistled over our heads and landed with a thud and a crack on the beach.

The sand dunes where we lay were full of casuals, lost troops, odd observers, British and American alike. A flight of about a dozen of our P38's began making graceful swooping patterns high over our heads. This was our fighter umbrella which we all knew to be vital to our safety and success. Our faces were turned upward. Some waved. Another cupped his hands and called, 'Stick around, boys, we like you.'

A few hundred yards south one of our ack-ack batteries opened up on them with tracers. The double body of the P38 was the one silhouette that every private knew – there was no mistaking it. But now some trigger-happy lieutenant of anti-aircraft had let go at them. Everyone jumped to his feet – the British using their universal adjective, the participle in 'f', the Americans 'goddam-dumb-bastarding' him.

A British Major who knew Smithy rushed over to him with his 45 drawn, 'Come on, Colonel, let's stop that bloody ass before he knocks one of them down.' He and Smithy ran off to the south leaving their packs behind. They disappeared in the scrub.

A hundred of us stood on our feet like tennis fans at a Forest Hills final – heads moving in unison here and there. The tracers came closer – the P38's took evasive action.

Another battery further south, like a jealous hound anxious to be in at the kill, joined in.

Bigger puffs began to appear near the planes. One was so close that we could see the plane jump sideways in the air.

Finally one plane began to smoke, rose up on its tail and fluttered towards the earth leaving a black plume behind it. Silence and hate all around us was broken by something like a mass sob when we saw a parachute blossom.

The ack-ack stopped. Maybe the British major had arrived with Smithy – or somebody at the AA battery had recognized the double fuselage of the P38.

Smithy and the major returned; breaking dispersal rules we all gathered around like a crowd at a street accident.

'It was all over when we got there. Their major and captain had been at Beach HQ and left a nutty kid in command.'

'Why didn't you shoot the punk?'

'He was crying like a baby,' answered the blond Britisher, his face no longer showing hate but pity, 'anybody could have done it. He was new and – hardly out of napkins.'

'That's what they deserve for commissioning some of these cub scouts who'd ought to be sucking their mamas,' from a sergeant.

'Thank Christ the pilot's alive anyway. ... '

'... my pal's a pilot – said he'd rather fly over Berlin than over our AA.'

10

'... you know what happened in Sicily. Twenty big planes and a whole battalion. The goddamned Navy did it. ... '

Someone gave the chemical warfare people orders to disperse. We all obeyed, carrying back to our sand hole new fears and doubts.

CHAPTER TWO

BEACHHEAD II

9 SEPTEMBER 1943

Smithy had decided we should rest another half-hour and eat. Afterwards we would begin our long walk to hunt a spot for the generals.

Somehow I had drunk all my water. A little wooden sign in our sand dune pointed over to the left and said, WATER.

I knew enough to walk in the double tracks of a heavy vehicle to avoid mines. I walked along gingerly and then crawled on all fours where the tank tracks led over the back dune of our declivity, hoping not to make a target of my wide self against the sky.

As I passed over the crest I saw it through some caper shrubs, a huge beach engineers' bulldozer burned out, and still smoking. A few yards away in the shade of another clump of bushes were a couple of dozen jerry-cans painted in white, WATER FOR DRINKING.

Besides myself, the bulldozer, and the water-cans, no one or nothing was in this tiny valley in the sand dunes. The air smelled of gasoline.

Anti-aircraft tracers arched high above and their little puffs floated off like lazy jellyfish in August.

Some place close by a Bofors was giving the hoarse barks of a giant Cerebus.

But in the little cup between the sand dunes there was a local silence. I went on down carefully in the tracks of the bulldozer.

Two sets of foot-prints led round and round the bulldozer. They were at several yards' distance and must have been made when it was too hot to approach.

Close by, a little path led up to the water – a couple of dozen pairs of feet had passed over. I followed this path, opened a can and drank.

I was filling my canteen when I had the sensation that I had seen someone from the corner of my eye, motionless, staring at me. I jerked my head around quickly and fumbled for my pistol as my carbine was lying, where it should not be, out of my reach and in the sand.

13

I saw his head and thought it was a negro sleeping there on the bulldozer – then I remembered it was still hot, and I saw whisps of steam coming from the mouth and nose.

Leaving my carbine and canteen, I went nearer, pointing my pistol at it.

Then I saw there were two. The shell which had made the big hole in the cab had either killed or wounded them, and they had been roasted nearly to charcoal by their own petrol.

The petrol smell became mixed into a stronger one of burned meat and hot fat.

They were completely black except for their teeth which seemed whiter than living ones. The fire had burned away all the lips and cheeks and they grinned at me idiotically – a grin which went from ear to ear. Their eyes had that empty stare which ancient sculptors gave the head of blind Homer. Long pieces of flesh had fallen from the leg bones and hung down and dripped like midnight spigots against the hot steel floor.

I wanted to vomit and wanted to run away. My mouth filled with the water I had just drunk.

Somehow I couldn't go. I touched the crusty chest and neck of the closest one. I felt the marks of his dog-tag chain, which had either melted or sunk into the flesh. I followed it around near to the hole which had been his ear. I found the dog-tag stuck into his neck and pulled it out. It dangled from two short pieces of burned chain.

I still remember his name.

The tag I put back on his chest. Then I looked for the other's tag. It was fused, illegible even when I polished it with a little sand.

The two black faces of war kept on grinning, but I touched them each again under some unaccountably strong compulsion like paying a debt. Finally, I turned away and gathered my carbine and canteen and went back over the dune.

Smithy and the rest were waiting. They had been worried and were about to come for me, as they said I had been gone nearly a half-hour. I was pleased they hadn't, that no one shared my secret of the bulldozer.

Packs were examined for weight. I discarded my rations, my gas mask, and my life-preserver and a few clips of 45 ammunition. First-aid kit, water, carbine, were all too dear to me. The damned money, of course, I had to carry. The fox-hole spade I looked at a long time

14

and decided to keep – and the vast cellophane envelope intended for mustard gas, which I wanted as a shelter from rain.

It was noon and Smithy wanted to report back the next morning with precise information. He gave me the major and one sergeant with half the HQ signs. We were to cover the four miles toward the Sele river and double back on ourselves, meet him before dark at the medieval tower below the town of Paestum.

We outlined our trips on our large-scale maps, planning to visit every wooded spot south of the Sele River between the beach and the railway. My party had seven hours, until dark, to do nearly fourteen miles, much of it in sand.

'There is no use going up to the area of enemy tanks,' said Smithy, 'let's ask the Beach Command here where the front actually is.'

Their answer, when we got there, wasn't helpful; pointing to a map:

'There isn't any front; Kraut tanks were in these tomato fields between the village and the railway station an hour ago. We expect 'em down here tonight. But since ten o'clock the 142nd hasn't seen any Jerry infantry – those 88's are here now.' He laughed formally as one hit a hundred yards south of us and threw sand over the bridge of an LST backing off the beach.

'You sure you got tonight's password ... all of you?'

Everybody snickered. We had it. It had been chosen by the British and no American, especially no Choctaw Indian or cowpunching Mexican, could give it without snickering in self-defence.

The challenge was 'Hearts of Oak'.

The reply, 'Stout fellow'.

Some Ducks waddled up for dispersal orders. The Beach Command was busy; we filed out, feeling like an unnecessary fifth wheel, in contrast to the busy radio operators, officers, and yeomen, efficiently arranged behind their sandbags. They seemed to have some reason for existence, some function in this chaos.

Here we were, ready for a trek in a September sun in the close and even dangerous backwash of a battle. But backwash it was – and our objective, to find a snug spot for generals. We each, I am sure, felt the generals would be better off, more efficient, on the command ship *Ancon*. But the Public Relations Staff had an eye for headlines – GENERAL MARK W. CLARK IS ASHORE WITH HIS TROOPS. SITUATION UNDER CONTROL. VICTORY ASSURED.

The major, the sergeant and I started north, close enough to the dunes to take cover easily when doubtful planes buzzed the beach. The beach was strewn with litter, equipment soldiers had considered too heavy for its value. Here and there were burned-out landing craft, snarls of enemy barbed wire rolled up by 'dozers, bomb craters and the smaller holes left by mines.

There was a good deal of traffic down near the water's edge, which every so often was funnelled-off into the chicken-wire-and-burlap roads the engineers had pushed through the dunes.

There was an occasional dead German lying in the sun, but the American dead and wounded alike lay at the water's edge awaiting transport back to the fleet in the bay.

All afternoon we (and my infected toe) tramped along from copse to woods and woods to copse. Everything looked wrong for the generals.

When we could see there was nothing between us and the Sele River except treeless fields, we turned inland toward a heavy pine wood where the main road runs, between the beach and the railway, from Salerno to Agropoli. There were no British visible in their sector, just north of the river, and no Americans visible on our bank of the Sele. There was no longer any continuous din of battle noises. The fleet had stopped firing. The nearest landing-craft or human being was two miles to the south and at least four to the north.

Grasshoppers and birds and buzzing insects made the only sounds. In a field near the river two water buffalo grazed lazily. We picked ripe plum-shaped tomatoes and sucked their juice as we walked through the fields.

It appeared to us that the whole German army might come down these two deserted banks of the river and cut our landing in two. In fact five days later it did.

We passed a peasant's house – deserted – and we did not go in because of the German speciality of booby-trapping empty houses. Through the door we saw two unmade beds, and a cat slept peacefully on the window-sill under a tomato can of geraniums and another of sweet basil. Sweet basil, the herb, is to tomatoes what the southern Italian peasant is to the southern Italian earth. Basil and tomatoes on a field of poor earth might well be the coat-of-arms of these sweet, miserable people. We passed along our way.

After another half-hour of tomato fields, a few irrigation ditches, wild pigeons, and intense heat, we saw the main highway and

16

decided, for no specific reason, to make for it rather than for the road to the bridge. We stopped to check our maps, and we were worried by the fact that all these last ten minutes with the road in plain view no vehicle had passed in either direction.

The railway was still a good thousand or twelve hundred yards away.

The sergeant spotted him. 'Look, there is somebody on our side of the railway.' He was crouching, facing us, and was making some violent motions with his hands. The major thought they meant 'come here'. We were both sure he was an American.

Since action is always easier than inaction I accepted the major's theory – and, besides, you cannot stay long prone in a tomato field with no cover, it doesn't make much sense. We crawled towards him.

We saw the others as we approached – flat as pancakes against the fill of the road.

We took the hint and did the last hundred yards or so as low as was compatible with reasonable speed, for we now sensed we were dangerously off-base.

'What the hell, excuse me, sir, are you doing out here?' He was a sergeant, and he had with him six men and a machine-gun.

I couldn't say, 'Looking for a camping site for generals'. He would have thought either we or the generals or both were mad.

So I answered with another question.

'What's going on here?'

'We're on recon, sir. My company command post is about two miles back with battalion. A sniper got my lieutenant right through the knee coming up.

'There are Jerries over there at that big house in them pines and on the other side of the highway. Don't they know fuck-all back on that beach letting you guys through?'

'There wasn't anybody back on the beach,' I said, 'it seems to be deserted.'

'Damned if I can figure it out. I know I'm not going to stay here with only six men. Make contact with our outfit on the river? There's no outfit here to make contact with! Damned if I can figure it.'

We filed back, the ten of us, doubled over until the trees and brush on our side of the road became thick enough for cover. Then we straightened-up and moved along at a good clip – toe and sweat forgotten.

In about a half-hour we came to battalion and company in a

17

sort of gravel pit. From close by our 155's began popping at the 88's in the hills and were popped at in return.

By now the afternoon was getting on, and it was obvious that we would not finish our trip before dark. I wrote a note to Smithy saying I would meet him at 09.00 the following morning at the Red Beach CP, where we had landed, and that we had so far seen no place for the 5th Army HQ.

Our sergeant never found Smithy, so he didn't wait for me the following morning. I did not meet him again until 1945 on Lago di Garda, when we were drinking captured champagne that the Germans had stored in the famous 'Last Redout' in the Tyrol.

Alone with the major I began to notice him. He was such a very little fellow with a sad, small, frightened face, and had said so few words since morning that I had begun to think of him as a slightly animated version of the gold maple leaf of his rank – and hardly at all as a person. Majors were like that in our army in this last war. They were neither bright boys of company rank nor graver elders of field rank, they were a sort of loose military flotsam whom nobody took quite seriously. But he proved to be one of those people for whom more than one listener brings on a shyness which makes conversation impossible.

Without the sergeant he began to talk, not of the battle to our left nor of the lines of supply we crossed, with their heavy traffic of trucks and Ducks from the beach going in, and the wounded, and empty vehicles going out, nor even of the fantastic armada which filled the sea to our right – he talked about himself and his family and the little New England town where they lived.

Every so often he was diverted from the stream of his story by the war – our mission for the generals. At some enemy planes we rolled our eyes up like converts in a revival tent. The only smoke came from some buildings burning over towards Battipaglia, and ever since our meeting with the patrol in that peaceful no-man's land, the battle had apparently, like the Red Sea, rolled back for us to pass through, to inspect camping sites for the generals, and to walk, however uncomfortably overladen with military bric-a-brac, pleasantly in the hot September sun.

We decided to go down to the beach for news, and to cut back into the fields to inspect the next copse – which would be about all that the remaining daylight would permit. The rest we would have to leave till morning.

18

As we started over the last dune towards the beach-crew, which was arranging dumps and moving supplies, a couple of batteries in the hills opened fire. This concentration of supplies had been spotted.

The first shell fell behind us – God knows if there were three or thirty. You never remember going to earth – it is as instinctive for man as it is for a rabbit or a fox.

Down we were – faces pressing into the sand – helmets pushed back over our necks. Feeling whole, I began to dig with hands and hips and feet. So did the major. His sand came on my face and eyes and down my sweaty collar to my sweaty back.

The smell of cordite, like a concentrate of volcanic wines, choked us. The beach crew were digging too, like crazy creatures trying to swim in the sand.

I don't know whether I heard the second salvo or sensed it, but I pushed hard against the sand and they came. One at least fell between us and the stuff on the beach. It crashed and hissed at the same time and its fragments whistled. It was close.

Both the major and I got on our knees and paddled hard with our spades. We were down again a full half-minute before the next ones arrived – and reasonably deep – a foot for the head and back, not the standard three feet, but it felt good.

The same hiss, crack, and whistles. But this one sifted some fine sand on my back; against my helmet it sounded like rain on a tin roof.

'After the next one let's run for it, it isn't a hundred yards wide,' said the major between spades of sand.

'OK – down.'

The third salvo hit some petrol.

We ran – I am fat but I ran – money, guns, and jangling junk hanging and bumping along. We made it and were flat when the next volley arrived. Not so close, not so loud, and far less personal. We sat up and peered over a dune at the fire – its black smoke rolled away heavily while the pale cordite smoke floated gently upwards.

Some of the beach crew had stuck it out, dug-in. A few were running between volleys. One was being carried away....

The cruiser *Boise* and a British companion had been told off to silence the 88's. Their red flashes were vivid even against the setting sun, and in the first rise of hills we could see their bursts.

Sand was in my eyes, my hair, my ears, down my neck, between my legs, and packed in the shoe with the hole to accommodate the bad toe. There was the Gulf of Salerno, royal blue, touched by a geranium sunset, and the white spots where the choppy little waves spilled over before reaching the beach.

'A swim?'

'Shall we go?'

'Sure.'

Gobs of lumpy sand came out of shirt, undershirt, shorts, socks spread on a bush.

'We'd better take our guns and helmets – somebody might hook 'em.'

So, dressed in a pistol belt with holster and 45 banging against our bare thighs, carrying carbines and with our helmets on our heads, but otherwise as bare as two plucked turkeys, we stepped from vehicle track to vehicle track down to the water's edge.

The major, sunburned by swimming through the African summer, small though he was, had that perfection of muscle, lithe and flowing in every curve, which reminded me of Cellini's 'Perseus', far north in Florence, probably even now being admired by German officers on leave, with their polished high boots, Baedekers, and heavy, soft platitudes about 'Kunst'.

The red sunset tinted the major's almost hairless body all the shades from deep pink to copper, and as he walked the colours played on the rippling of his muscles.

I must have stared because he said, 'What's the matter?'

'Thought I saw some MP's coming up the beach.' He stared south but didn't answer.

We piled our loads at the wave's edge and ran in. While we splashed about the colours faded quickly in the west to jade green, which shaded up to that infinite, deep blue of Italian dusk. We ran up and down to dry ourselves in the still hot sand.

It was night and we faced the problems of night, a secure place to sleep and company to dilute fears. Just south of us a new negro beach unit had landed, and now and then we heard their voices and laughter. Dressed and loaded, we walked down towards where they were digging into the sand for the night.

'Hearts of Oak?' they had challenged us.

'Stout fellow.'

Yes, of course, we could spend the night, and yes, they had some rations and water. So we dug our holes amid our hosts' laughter and their humming of blues tunes.

As we were about to eat some cold rations, a beach-security patrol came along. It was the first bit of organization evident outside the two command posts we had visited, the first in the morning on the beach, and the second after our stroll in no-man's land near the Sele River.

Its officer was curious as to who we were, but my crazy pass with photograph, made on a piece of file-folder and signed by Colonel Howard, quieted him and suppressed his curiosity.

Donald C. Downes, the holder of this pass, whose photo and signature are hereupon, has the right to circulate at all times in all territories occupied by this Army as he is on special mission for G2, HQ *5th Army.* DO NOT QUESTION EITHER THE HOLDER OF THIS PASS OR PERSONS FOR WHOM HE VOUCHES.

Sept. 1 1943   *Howard, Colonel, USA*
                                                                    G2 – 5th Army.

'Tonight,' the security officer said to the captain of the negro company, 'post sentries – and frequently – at 100 and 300 yards. We'll patrol beyond that. We have no phones in here yet to hook you up, but two reds and a green is our Veɪy signal that there are Germans or tanks this side of the highway.

'They'll certainly try to break in tonight and patrols will undoubtedly get through. Look out that your sleeping men don't get run over by vehicles, especially if our tanks have to manoeuvre back this far.

'You should keep one-third of your men awake and you should check your sentries frequently. You'd better give them grenades to signal you with. Good night.'

The captain gave his orders as we piled into our holes encased in our gas envelopes against the sand.

A mile or two down over Red and Green beaches the Navy was sending up a magnificent display of ack-ack tracers. A part of Salerno was burning like a red-hot toadstool on the horizon. Fitful explosions in the Gulf of Naples, sixty miles to the north, outlined the mountains on the Sorrentine Peninsula which divides the two gulfs.

I laughed at the negro's joke about our spoiling their natural camouflage and fell asleep.

The sky was already light over the mountains of Lucania when I awoke. The anti-aircraft fireworks were after something invisible among those paling stars overhead.

I stood up and looked out to sea over the dune. The moon had set. The fleet lay silent and countless to the horizon. But down on the beach LST's were disgorging vehicles which waddled and purred away in the sickly green, pre-dawn light.

A couple of the negro boys were awake and talking. The major rolled over, opened his eyes, and said rather formally, 'Good morning. Shall we pack and get going?'

To the east was one of our last copses. We came up over the dune and started for it. It was an unusually high dune, and a mile or two to the south we could see the three temples, pink in their green fields. We came to a road, parallel to the beach, made overnight by beach engineers with bulldozers and miles of chicken wire covered in burlap as a surface.

We stopped to discuss the copse and whether to keep on the road or cross the fields. The road, being mine-proof, won out. Jeeps and Ducks and trucks hurried back and forth. At each junction stood an MP, white helmet, white leggings, and white belt, directing traffic with the smartness of 5th Avenue and 57th Street.

Whilst we slept chaos had begun to organize itself.

By the third MP were a lot of jerry-cans over fires, full of boiling water. There was soluble coffee, canned milk, sugar, and 'K' ration biscuits.

'Sure,' said the MP's, 'help yourselves. It belongs to Uncle Sam, don't it?'

So the major and I sat on the edge of a ditch as the sun rose warm and friendly out of those 88 bearing mountains.

'You were saying yesterday, that those temples were BC. Doesn't seem possible, does it? Greek? Tell me about them, will you?'

It was a long breakfast with a good many coffee refills because it was a long lecture that the school teacher gave the electrical engineer. Greek history never seemed clearer to me than in that clear dawn in Paestum. What might have been, had there been no Peleponnesian Wars – had the light and democracy of Athens survived to develop.

We might again construct a civilization worthy of the Temple of Poseidon, but more human and older and more tolerant and kindly than that of Greece.

I knew I didn't really believe all this, not after Africa, not after Darlan, Giraud, and expediency.

Just then I heard myself hailed from a jeep. 'Hey, Downes, you look too goddam comfortable. Got some coffee for us?' It was Major Fordham of MP's who was now hunting a good spot to put his prisoner-of-war cage.

'They tell me you're an expert on this geography,' he said, spreading his map on the jeep's hood. We all four gathered around.

I don't remember it happening. I was under the jeep picking gravel out of my face – pressed into the skin without breaking it.

Four bombs, a stick from a Junkers coming out of the sun, with motors cut, had hit the cross-roads squarely.

Fordham and his lieutenant and I were looking at a big ragged hole in the jeep's bonnet where the map had been, before we missed the little major. It took us a minute or two to find him.

He was in the ditch where we had coffee, lying on his face with a hole between his shoulder blades as big as your fist and another, smaller, just at the base of the skull.

His uniform around the bigger hole was smouldering and smoke curled up from it.

I couldn't move, I could only stare at those holes and the little wisps of smoke.

Fordham called some MP's to get stretcher bearers. I could hear his voice, almost expressionless, droning in yesterday's tomato field. I remember his naked muscles in the sunset, his face. My lower lip kept beating an involuntary tattoo against the upper one.

When the stretcher-crew came I had to turn away. I made conversation with Fordham. Yes, he would take me in his jeep down to the Command Post, where I was to meet Smithy.

23

CHAPTER THREE

SCHOOLMASTER'S ODYSSEY I

WINTER 1939 TO SUMMER 1940

I suppose it was Edmond Taylor who led me into my five years' career of paralegal crime. In 1939 he had published *The Strategy of Terror*, which described how Hitler was deploying a fifth column through all the democratic world and by it paralysing the will to resist. I read the book over and over; it explained all the things I had seen on my recent trips to Europe.

It seemed, too, teaching school on Cape Cod through that bleak winter of 1939–40, that democracy should undertake a counter-offensive, an anti fifth column. Such an undertaking, I felt, must devolve upon the United States. We must organize and entrench democratic men and organizations of every nationality in the danger areas throughout the world. And if this were too late to prevent the Nazis taking over some countries by guile or force, at least there would be left behind the hard nucleus of a resistance, forearmed with the knowledge that they had friends, actively struggling for their liberation, in the free world outside. These resistance movements should be supplied, before the coming of the Germans, with means of communications and, if possible, with the arms essential to the guerrilla warfare and sabotage they would conduct.

The school I taught in was folding up due to lack of funds and the headmaster's thirst. In April I packed up and with a few hundred dollars in my pockets and an insistent idea in my head set out for Washington.

I had a letter to an office of Military Intelligence (G2) in the old War Department building. There I was treated with that mixture of politeness and vagueness which government agencies reserve for crackpots who annoy them, but who just might know an influential congressman. By luck one of my brothers was in a high position in the Navy Department working on the designs of new ships and trying to make good some of President Roosevelt's promises of naval craft to Britain. His old friend Captain Sam Moore was acting Chief of Naval Intelligence (ONI). My brother took me to him.

Sam Moore was an officer, young for his grade and job, completely inexperienced in the paralysing cautions of secret intelligence work but, oddly enough for a professional military man, endowed with imagination.

I outlined what I had in mind: the cataloguing of our friends everywhere in the world with priority to the immediate danger points. This vast cross-indexed file would be a basis for the building of information chains, sabotage units, 'black propaganda' cells, economic warfare, and espionage units at the service of the free countries.

The first move, I suggested to Sam Moore, should be the deploying of a few hundred Americans to begin to make the necessary contacts where the danger of Nazi or Japanese attack was greatest. I believed that big American business houses should be solicited quietly to give cover, including salaries if possible, to these pioneers to be sent out immediately.

While I was having these talks with Sam Moore, Norway was invaded.

Time was even shorter than we thought.

Then came the great disappointment. Captain Moore had listened with what seemed to me enthusiasm for half a dozen hour-long conversations. He had called in colleagues. But the answer was no. The Navy had almost no secret funds to spend. Congress was policing expenditures carefully. All extra funds were going to supply England.

'I have talked to Mr B' (a great name in British chemical industry – born in America), said Moore, 'and they have no cash available. Besides, he thinks it is too late.'

Perhaps I looked so forlorn that Captain Moore did what he did out of pity.

'The only way I can help is this: give you a reserve commission and a letter to our attaché in Istanbul. He can introduce you to the proper British out there. Mr B. says they could use you with an American passport in the Balkans or the Middle East. But I cannot even pay your way out there, much less give you any salary.

'And you'll have trouble getting a passport. The Neutrality Act makes it illegal for you to travel in those zones. And, too, it's illegal to be an agent for a foreign power. You can go to prison for it. But try it out, fellow, with all my unofficial good wishes, and whatever official help I can give you, unless and until some Admiral stops me.'

I was determined to go. But I needed someone to give me a cover job which paid a salary. First I tried the oil companies and a couple

26

anks which did business in the Near East. No one saw any good ιναson to give a job to an unemployed school teacher, and I really had to agree.

A few years earlier I had noticed Robert College as I was sight-seeing from a Bosphorus boat. An unemployed schoolmaster should look to a school for employment.

A group of American more-or-less-missionary colleges and schools in the Near East had formed the Near East College Association for fund raising and to act as joint New York office for the ten or more member institutions. Robert College was the oldest of these and it happened that my visit to the Association's New York office coincided with the arrival of a cable from the college to send out new teachers to teach English to Turkish Army and Navy officers pre-paring to come to the United States for advanced studies.

I got the job and was prepared to leave via Gibraltar when Mussolini slammed the Mediterranean shut by declaring war on the corpse of France. But, remembering Columbus's egg, I knew there were four general directions in which one could travel to reach any given place on the globe.

The Association didn't think much of my chances of getting to the Near East by travelling west through the Far East – besides, it was expensive. Then a good friend replenished my personal treasury and drove me to California where he was going for the summer.

On the way west I stopped in Washington to arrange code matters with Captain Moore. We decided to rely largely on 'innocent text' letters. An innocent text code depends on both the coder and the decoder having identical copies of the same dictionary. Using some simple mathematical formula derived from the date on the letter, the receiver knows which words in the letter form the key to the actual message. The message itself is composed of words found in the dictionary in accordance with a guide number again derived from the date. We fixed two 'letter drops', persons to whom I would address the innocent text letters.

My ship out of San Francisco was the fast Dutch freighter *Klip-fontein*. Her ports of call were to be Honolulu, Manila, Souroubaya and Batavia in Java, one port in Sumatra, Singapore, Rangoon and Calcutta. Of these Captain Moore was interested in the Java–Sumatra ports, especially Souroubaya.

'We have asked the Dutch for specific information about these ports. When the Japs attack, the Dutch expect us to defend their

27

Indies but in months of repeated requests we have no information whatsoever!' He outlined to me the facts he wanted: dockside depths, crane capacity, oil storage (especially underground), dockside water supply, and a considerable list of other items.

'We hope to send naval observers, who will get these facts, to our consulates out there but God knows how long it will take to get it organized and the officers actually reporting.'

It seemed strange to me that my first commission for information should require spying on a friendly power. A few years later it would have seemed quite ordinary. Allies are willing to donate both lives and wealth to the common cause; but the exchange, honestly, of truthful information is nearly impossible. I have noticed that intelligence executives become hoarders, so miserly and overcautious that they frequently render useless vital information which has been collected at great cost in money and men.

*   *   *

The Pacific is a wide ocean – wider when our twin screw vessel threw a propeller. *Klipfontein* had to proceed at greatly reduced speed on right rudder to keep the remaining screw from turning her in perpetual circles. The accident happened shortly after Hawaii and the same day she was alerted that a German surface raider had sunk the s.s. *Niagara* to the south of us. As a belligerent vessel she did not turn back for sanctuary and repairs in Hawaii but instead set a far northerly course and ploughed on slowly with Dutch obstinacy toward Manila.

Since childhood I had thought of missionaries as ignorant, sanctimonious, hymn-howling hell-firers, bigoted and avaricious, or else like Maugham's Reverend Davidson in *Rain*, lecherous hypocrites with an eye for the native undressed. There were eighty missionaries aboard *Klipfontein*, returning to their posts in the Far and Middle East. They knocked my childish prejudices overboard into the Pacific.

They were friendly and stimulating shipmates. From them I learned about agriculture, economic geography, and anthropology, oriental folkways, linguistics and history; about Jainism, Brahminism and Buddhism; about the imperial politics of Britain, Holland and Japan. And at sundown, better companions you could not want for Bols gin and herrings. Even the jokes were of a sufficiently spiced flavour.

28

For their children they organized a shipboard school. I was asked to teach French and American history. I discovered that these missionaries' ideas on education were way in advance of the secondary schools, even the best ones, in the States. The children themselves were greatly superior to the American average. They reflected the high standard of education of their parents and the lack of comic-strips, juke-boxes, and soap-operas in the remote posts where their families served.

Among these missionaries I took careful notes of those I believed could be of service to America in case of war in the Orient. The names, addresses, and an estimate of their value I wrote carefully in a big brown address book I had bought in San Francisco: the beginnings of the files I had proposed to Captain Moore. These names, later turned over to the geographic desks in oss, proved of great value, especially in China and Burma.

*   *   *

Manila in September was a kettle of steam. I left the ship for the week of her stop-over and visited business associates of my family. Morale, civilian and military, was frighteningly low among the Americans facing the already expected Japanese attack. No one suggested doing anything but to accept disaster. Local political corruption was the order – and jest – of every day.

Some temporary repairs made, we sailed out of Manila Bay, past Corregidor, and down the Philippine Sea into the Celebes Sea and the Straits of Malacca, past Leyte and Negros heading for Souroubaya in Java. In Souroubaya we were to have final repairs and a new propeller. That meant at least ten days in Java, maybe three weeks, enough time, I hoped, to answer most of Captain Moore's questions about the ports.

Two missionaries bound for India decided to hire a car and see the island. They asked me to make a third to share expenses. We would meet *Klipfontein* again in Batavia. I agreed, with the reservation that we spend a few days in Souroubaya, important on Sam Moore's list as it was the chief Dutch naval base. We invited an officer of our ship, a naval reservist who had been formerly attached to the base, to be our guide in the city. This was my first job of espionage: I posed as a half-baked scientist to cover my excessive curiosity. Each evening with considerable pride I noted down the facts and figures gathered in the day's sightseeing: dockside depths, crane capacities, air strip dimensions and possible extensions, water supply and so on. The fourth day we left to motor slowly the length of the island. Java is a fruitful fairyland; fifty million people support themselves mostly by agriculture in a country smaller than England, Scotland and Wales. Many parts of the world, like the coast of California, are beautiful by nature, but ugly by the touch of man. Java and the coast of Southern Italy are also naturally beautiful, but have been made even more beautiful by what man has done. It is some instinctive art, expressed in even the most utilitarian buildings and the husbandry of the soil. The Oriental and Mediterranean peoples stand apart from Northern Europeans and Americans whose occupancy of the earth so often produces ugliness.

After I had gone through my snooping routine in the third port one of the missionaries began to suspect my purposes.

'Don't answer if you don't want to, but why are you so interested in the details of ports ?'

I have always thought that a man in on a secret is a better security risk than one who suspects a secret.

'I am interested for the United States Government,' I said, 'and that knowledge puts you, I hope, under a strong obligation to keep it to yourself, completely to yourself – and not to ask any more specific questions,' I added with a laugh.

'Could I help in any way ?'

'Probably, in Batavia. Certainly later, next year or the year after, right where your mission is. I already have noted your address to give to *the proper authorities*' (whoever they may be or if they ever are, I thought sadly) 'with a recommendation. You are already *in situ*, you know the Burmese, their language, and, I presume, the geography.'

(In 1942 I gave his name to the OSS Mission leaving for the China-Burma-India theatre. He is said to have done some fine work.)

Sumatra was followed by Singapore. In Singapore it was evident that Mr Churchill, through no error of his and despite his later denials, was indeed destined to preside over the dissolution of the British Empire, at least in the Orient.

'We'll be here,' said a forty-year-old fighter pilot at Ruggles' bar, 'until the first Jap plane knocks us down or until our craft disintegrate with mechanical senility.'

Rangoon a few days and then on to Calcutta, where I left *Klip-*

fontein. Calcutta is (or was) the second city of the British Empire. It is a city so loathsome to western sensibilities that it leaves a sort of scar on the memory tissue.

Sahibs' wives in evening slippers and members of Nehru's and Ghandi's Congress Party alike stepped over naked, rotting beggars lying in the gutters. I learned that Congress Party delegates were expected to wear to meetings cashmere shawls valued then at over a thousand dollars. (Imagine if a congressman from Arkansas had to pay for a thousand dollar suit!) I learned, too, that the extremely rich Hindu manufacturers were the real bosses of the party.

In Bombay I saw the great Ghandi himself come to visit his British dentist in a green Rolls-Royce on which was mounted a sign in five languages saying 'Boycott British Goods'.

I discovered that a Hindu labourer paid roughly twenty-five per cent of his pay each day to a priest to paint his caste-mark on his forehead.

Mohan Lal, my bearer in Calcutta, told me that a third of his earnings went to decorate an idol in his house which, once a year, bedecked in the results of his labour, was thrown into a holy river.

In Calcutta cages with thirteen- and fourteen-year-old girls for sale were hung in the brothel streets. They sat still like dying canaries, eyes down, neck bowed. The price, I was told, was less than ten pounds of rice.

Medical officers said that Hindu priests had defeated a recent campaign against syphilis. They saw the pamphlets designed to inform the Indians how to avoid and cure the disease; one such had a magnified sketch of a spirochaete. 'These little spiral creatures are God's creations, and if you harbour them in your blood, as the English doctors say, you must not kill them.'

India is an upside-down country. It was much more difficult to blame the British, after sampling India, than before. But it was obvious that the British Rajh was dead. India's foreign rulers had already abandoned hope, and the Indians seemed incapable of it.

From Calcutta – where Indians serving in HM Forces and wearing His Majesty's decorations were refused entrance as guests to the sahibs' clubs – I took the Karachi Mail for the West Coast. Electric fans playing on ice made the crossing of the Sind desert bearable. After two days, at Karachi, you enter the West – the West because this city on the Indus river is the extreme point reached by Alexander the Great. Here you begin to sense Greek civilization, however

31

diluted, and feel the kinship with our own diluted version of Hellenism.

On the Persian Gulf leg of my travelling I was fortunate to have a short conversation with H. St John Philby, adviser to the King of Arabia and Ford agent for the Persian Gulf countries. In the first world war Philby and Captain Shakespeare had tried to persuade London, through the India Office, to back Ibn Saud against the Turks.

T. E. Lawrence, as agent of the War Office, wanted to back the Hashemite family, long residents of Constantinople and relatively out of touch with the Arab world. Lawrence, with the backing of the Arab Bureau of SIS in Cairo, and General Allenby, had his way.

In this period of indecision a war was fought between Arabs of the India Office (Ibn Saud) and the Arabs of the War Office (the Hashemites). There were British casualties on both sides. Lawrence shared in Allenby's victory and became a legend – as much for his bitterness against his government as for his Arabian exploits. Philby in defeat became even more embittered, and remained in Saudi Arabia, a convert to Islam.

I was anxious to know how this thoroughly English scholar and soldier became so estranged from his homeland as to renounce his citizenship and his religion; it was even believed in 1940 that he was conspiring against Britain in her extremity.

But the protocol of my meeting him could allow no such question. However, I remembered how Philby's enemy, Lawrence, refused his country's decorations, and later even a commission in the RAF, and enlisted as a simple airman.

In 1940 this seemed irresponsible and hysterical to me. But by 1945 I had seen a score or more of British and Americans on the verge of treason through similar bitterness.

It is in the nature of secret intelligence work that promises are made and loyalties joined which would never be done in the light of publicity. The military need the help of some national minority or political or social group. The man chosen to make the contact is always a specialist in and an enthusiast for the group to be used. In all good faith he makes bargains and promises, implies even more, especially when the need for help is vital to the military situation.

In the cold judgments of peace, the legally constituted civilian authorities of the state do not honour these promises made by their secret agent under pressure. So he is left in the position of having lied to, betrayed, and swindled the leaders of a cause for which he has great sympathy. The agent turns with anger and shame against his own government. By 1945 I grew to understand the Philby–Lawrence reaction and to consider such men, and their honour, as casualties of war – for war cares no more for honour, or for decency and honesty, than it does for life.

CHAPTER FOUR

SCHOOLMASTER'S ODYSSEY II

WINTER 1940 TO 1941

For two hellishly hot weeks I sailed up the Persian Gulf to Busrah in Iraq. It did not seem possible that the war I was going towards could have anything to do with this fantastic world of Sindbad's Moscat with its pearl catch spread out on Persian carpets in the Sultan's palace, its great lolling multi-coloured water-snakes, its slave market, its other-side-of-the-moon qualities.

But it did – and it does. The whole Persian Gulf, with its oil deposits, is a highway from Europe to Western Asia, the highway of Alexander the Great to India. So down went the names, addresses and estimates of the men and women who could be counted upon as an 'anti-fifth' column. As many as possible were sounded out, with reasonable vagueness as to the font of my authority to speak.

From Busrah a narrow gauge railway runs through the desert, past the point where the Chat-al-Arab is formed by the Tigris and Euphrates joining waters, through the scene of Britain's disastrous Mesopotamian campaign of the first world war, north to Baghdad.

Baghdad was already full of the conspiracies and counter-conspiracies which were to come to a head the following spring in the Axis-aided and Axis-inspired Raschid Ali revolution. America had two young diplomats in Baghdad who were compounding the felonies of their British colleagues in every cloak-and-dagger way – possible only because of the long absences and advanced age of our Minister in Iraq.

Through these all too untypical State Department representatives, I met the British Intelligence men who were working against Raschid Ali. The Axis was already in French Syria and Lebanon as the Italian Armistice Commission, subservient to one of Germany's ace intelligence operators of the first world war, Otto Hentig, and to Germany's great Arab expert old Baron Oppenheim (a Jew who served his Nazi masters faithfully!).

If the Germans could pull off the defection of Iraq from Britain's side they might deny her the oil of Mosul and Abadan, and be able to threaten India and the whole British Imperial position in the Middle and Far East and could have outflanked Russia before invading her. Defeat in this microscopic war might well have meant a general German victory before Russia or America could take their place beside lone and groggy Britain.

Just how far things had gone was known to these Englishmen, Pete and Archie, who had successfully broken into the Italian ambassador's safe and had his decoded correspondence.

The German ambassador, wily Dr Fritz Grobba, had been sent packing some time before and his scheming was being done by the Italian legation under Minister Luigi Gabrielli. The route of communications for Raschid Ali, Berlin's man in Baghdad, with his German bosses and with the Grand Mufti of Jerusalem, already in Berlin, was by way of the Italian legation.

Two gayer thieves than Peter and Archie never set about their work; living up to the tradition of Philby, Shakespeare and Lawrence. The conspirators met for the most gourmet of dinners at Archie's, whose cellar of French wines would have been extraordinary in pre-war London. His crystal and silver were precious family heirlooms.

Archie himself was a sort of precious heirloom. His clothes were slightly too luscious for his impeccable, if infuriating, Oxford-out-of-Bond-Street accent – and he was not long down from Oxford. Pete spoke near perfect Iraq Arabic and the Arab gang which did odd intelligence jobs was recruited and controlled by him. But the *éminence rosée*, behind the blond curls and baby face of Archie, had rented the villa which was garden-to-garden to the Italian legation. The whole thing had that air of gaiety expected of two undergraduates who are planning to paint the Dean's toilet seat with glue.

Iraq broke off diplomatic relations with Italy only in June 1941, after the Raschid Ali uprising had been defeated and Mosul and Abadan saved. That Britain succeeded was in no small part due to the fact that these likeable rogues knew a great many things were going to happen before they did, by the old and venerable methods of artful-dodgers, skittle-sharpers and cat-burglars. I viewed them and their work with considerable awe.

Through the unorthodox helpfulness of our embassy staff in Baghdad, I sent off a long uncoded report to Sam Moore in the diplomatic pouch – a dangerous procedure, as I was to find out later when I opened for my own government other nations' pouches in the furnace room of the Park Central Hotel in New York.

*   *   *

At the Istanbul slip on the Golden Horn I was met by some faculty members of Robert College. It was sunset, and the minarets on the Stamboul side of the Horn were violet and rose. We boarded another ferryboat and laboured up the Bosphorus against its swirling current towards Bebek, the little town half way to the Black Sea, with Robert College on a hill-top looking toward Asia.

I presented my letter from Captain Sam Moore to our naval attaché, requesting what help and encouragement a naval attaché can give within the restrictions of his budget and the protocol and niceties of an embassy. His function, in my scheme of things, was to present me to the proper Englishmen, and from time to time grant me communications, when it could be done without exposing my activities to the diplomatic personnel of the embassy.

Among the first people I met was Commander Matsuhara, the Japanese naval attaché. My suggestion to our naval attaché that the good commander's appetite for white girls might make it possible for us to procure information or documents was turned down rather flatly; in fact, it shocked him.

However, I felt Matsuhara would be good camouflage for future activities, and besides he made delicious 'sukiyaki' on his living-room floor – so I cultivated him. Our usual conversation was on the coming war in the Pacific. He felt confident Japan would win, despite superior American equipment and numbers.

'It will be a war for existence of a disciplined nation against an undisciplined, luxury-softened America for which the war will be a side-issue.'

In his western moods, Matsuhara regretted war and he even had moments in which he conceived the possibility of defeat. In one of these he said to me, 'If you should defeat us, it is the end of Japan, afterwards we would become merely Oriental Americans. We should want, it is in character, to imitate anyone who can defeat us'. And he looked wistfully at the great glass-covered family Shinto shrine, occupying one third of the room, which he had brought from Japan with him.

I liked Matsuhara, and I hope he survived those naval massacres of the last year of the war to see one of his predictions come so

37

nicely true; that is, I hope he survived – if he wanted to. He loved his Shinto shrine.

My first British contact was with Commander Brass (*sic*). He was chief of a group of his fellow-countrymen in Rumania under various covers, planning to sabotage the Danube gates *when* (no one said *if*) the Germans took over Rumania.

He had come down from Rumania to talk with two American oil men from Ploesti who had theories, which they were willing to help put into practice, about sabotaging the oil fields at the moment of German entry. But they received such cool support, so many excuses and postponements from the British, that they believed, perhaps erroneously, that Whitehall did not wish to sabotage investments in Ploesti. I could see Brass was embarrassed, and I think that he had some doubts himself as to why London dilly-dallied and refused him the clear authority to go ahead with the plans of the American engineers. Three years later the Allies were to pay heavily in aircraft and trained men to plug these wells by bombing – done by American crews at suicidal chimney-pot level in daytime.

Before we heard the final negative orders from London on the oil project, I had offered to run courier for Brass even if it meant giving up my cover job at Robert College, provided somehow the project would find me another disguise. But as an untrained neophyte I doubted that the British would use me. This doubt was confirmed by my reception in Istanbul by the upper crust of the English intelligence and sabotage organization in Turkey and by my own country's naval attaché. I was an intruder, an upstart outsider, an uninvited amateur forcing his way into the holy-of-holies of the hocus-pocus of secret services. Often I felt like a mere person in trade daring to enter a hoary and aristocratic club – the members lowered their copies of *Punch* and glared at me vacantly over their bifocals. (I learned before the end of the war that the British had no corner in this occupational snobbery!)

But Americans were scarce at that point in time and geography, and it was important that the Balkan work be largely American-staffed. It was daily becoming obvious that the Germans were planning to move openly and in uniform into Rumania, then controlled by only a few thousand German 'military instructors to the Rumanian Army' and Gestapo 'tourists'. But their real military nature was known to everyone. When the Germans officially moved in the British would have to move out, and an American passport would become invaluable for the communications between head-quarters in Istanbul and the group left in Ploesti and Bucharest.

The only American I took into my confidence and my personal security in Istanbul was young and spry old Tom Whittemore, the nearly eighty years old archaeologist, who had secured permission from Ataturk in the twenties to restore Santa Sofia to its Byzantine glory. Tom was a born eccentric and a great scholar. He was disliked by the provincial and narrow-minded Americans in our Istanbul colony – if for no other reason than that he went around the city in the ragged overcoat of a private in the Turkish Army and was endowed with wit, taste and a brain.

Tom Whittemore was a great help to me. He knew the Turks well and had friends high in their secret police. On at least one occasion, he was able to save me from an expulsion order issued because of my strange behaviour and too frequent trips into the German controlled Balkans.

The last three times I saw Tom are characteristic of his eccentricities: on Ascension Island in the South Pacific in 1942 dressed as a Kurd peasant in quilted clothes and a goatskin coat, casually changing planes; alone one summer midnight in 1944 throwing stones at a desert fox on the hillside behind the Sphinx in Egypt; and the last time at a reception given by Umberto in the great hall of the Quirinal Palace in Rome to the new cardinals created by the Consistory of 1946; the huge doors opened and Umberto entered, not with his royal wife on his royal arm – but with Tom! When I asked him how he came to be substituting for Her Royal Highness he screwed up his nose and winked, 'I'm just an old friend of the family.'

Tom died in 1950. You couldn't ignore him. You could hate him or love him. I loved him.

'Let me go up there to Rumania,' he had said. 'Ask your British friends. The Germans would think I am too old to be dangerous. They probably do counter-intelligence as they write history, on the mistaken, ridiculous, asinine conviction it's a science, an absolute science. They'd never catch up with me!'

Tom it was, with information from God knows where, who told me nearly two weeks before the Italians invaded Greece to expect just that. Perhaps he heard it as 'just an old friend of the family!'

*   *   *

When Greece was invaded early in November the war was brought close to us in Turkey and it became more obvious that, as things began to go wrong for the Italians in Greece, the day was nearer when the Germans would enter the Balkans.

The British were watched every minute they were in Bulgaria by the *Sicherheitsdienst* 'tourists' from Germany and their Bulgarian allies. So they suggested that I try to make a 'free lance' contact with the opposition to the pro-German policy in Bulgaria. And because these people were already wary of British indecision, I was to contact them in the name of the U.S.A. Either the Macedonians or the Agrarian (Peasant's) Movement was available – 'but you mustn't say you are sent by us', added my British adviser.

Orthodox Christmas, Sofia, January, 1941 – it was not a merry Christmas. It was Christmas in the death house with the execution date unfixed but soon. In the corridor of the miniature luxury hotel *Grande Bulgarie* stood the black officers' boots of the 'civilian' visitors from the north.

My first assignment was to contact the Imro, *The International Macedonian Revolutionary Organization*. Macedonia was split up between Serbia (Yugoslavia), Greece and Bulgaria. In the cause of their independence, the Macedonians have served some odd masters – revolutionary and reactionary alike. The Imro, like the Stern gang and the Mafia, was world wide – wherever there were two or three Macedonians, be it in Chicago, Marseilles, or Montevideo, you would find a 'chapter' of Imro. It always specialized in terror and assassination, and real epicures of these arts give undisputed first place to Imro. Traditionally the leaders have been pastry cooks, patriots, poets and wanderers. A good pastry cook can always get a good cover-job in whatever part of the world his task of terrorism may take him.

Three oddly diverse groups have long traditions of the techniques of secret intelligence and operations: the Chinese, the Russians and Imro. Chinese say that in their country for centuries there have never been fewer than half a dozen resistance movements against concentrations of power. Russia's ability, too, is an inheritance – from the Tzarist secret police. Imro's is the result of long foreign occupations and repressions, Byzantine, Turk, Bulgar, Serb and Greek.

In my negotiations with Imro I came to know five members of the organization. Both Nazis and Communists have had a price on all their heads, and as I am not sure which are living and which are dead, I shall use false names, except for Smile Voidonov. Voidonov I know was executed by the Nazis.

40

I had, from an Albanian nationalist in Istanbul, the name of a university student in Sofia – here I shall call him Kimon. Kimon was not hard to find. I gave him the greetings of his Albanian friend and told him I was from Robert College in Istanbul.

'Democratic nationalism has always been sired in your colleges, sir. Robert College educated the founders of our free Bulgaria. Now I hear that your university in Beirut is the centre of Arab nationalism. Where will you shelter us Macedonians ? – why not in your college in Bulgaria ? or Athens ? For as Byron said of Greece – one day Macedonia shall be free.'

He put his nervous hands on my shoulders, stared wild-eyed into my face, and after a full stop of six counts he began:

> *The mountains look on Marathon –*
> *And Marathon looks on the sea ...*

He drew himself back to strike a nobler pose and looking dreamily over my head went on to the end:

> *... I could not deem myself a slave.*

Again the full stop, six counts – and then:

'Sir, *I* do not deem *myself* a slave. You! America! shall free Macedonia.

'First you must get in touch with Y, he is no longer in Bulgaria. We do not know exactly where he is. But there is a good chance he is in America as he went to raise money among our exiles. There you will find him easily through any Macedonian. He is certainly supporting himself as a pastry chef – an exquisite pastry chef he is. His puff-paste is famous throughout our world.

'Second, you must see Smile Voidonov. He is here in Sofia. He is constantly watched not only by the dogs of our traitorous Bulgarian government but also the German swine of the Gestapo who swarm in Bulgaria like maggots in the belly of a dead rat.

'But you shall see him, safely, with no one following. For if Smile is seen making a contact with an American, it would be most dangerous for him. If you are seen talking to Smile, wsssst – you will be escorted across the border within the day.

'Smile is a kind, gentle man. He, too, is a great pastry cook and one of the great poets of Macedon. Because he has killed many men for our cause, these ignorant, Balkan bourgeois consider him a murderer – albeit they cannot prove anything. He loves dogs and children and our mountains in the spring. He loves to make a big complicated dessert or compose verse about when Macedon crossed the Indus river with our Great Alexander on his white stallion. He is kind and gentle; but, before God, he is a magnificent shot, with the nerves of a baby and contempt for his own safety.'

The next day I met Smile, after a hide-and-seek around Sofia to throw off any shadowers. Kimon was my guide. We arrived at a tiny wine shop in an industrial quarter. From its kitchen a stairs led up to a small room. There, with a hunting dog and a shot-gun, sat Smile. Fattish, pink-cheeked, grey-haired, and benign – sort of a cross between King Cole, Humpty-Dumpty and the Santa Claus of *The Night Before Christmas* – especially the 'nose like a cherry.'

Any interview through an interpreter is difficult. But the point of my conversation with Voidonov was also being constantly lost among pastries, past assassinations and poetry. He wanted Kimon to translate some poetry. I started again on organizing an informa-tion chain. This time he excused himself and dashed down the stairs to bring me up a creation in *mille feuilles*, honey, nuts, raisins, and prune brandy, certainly the best piece of Balkan pastry I have ever eaten. It was discussed at some length.

I returned to the conversation about an information network. He waved it aside as a measure already agreed on. We could discuss details at our leisure. Besides, things like radios were better left to technicians; he gestured toward the empty chairs as if they were filled with Marconis and de Forests ready to do our bidding.

'He wishes to take you to the street where some years ago he assassinated three enemies of Macedon at once. He wishes you to know he was disguised as a hunter with a double barrelled shot-gun and two dogs. In fact, he says, one of the dogs was the mother-dog of this one now at his feet. He says it was difficult because he had to reload and fire three times, and then escape with the dogs – as he was too fond of his dogs to leave them.'

I protested it was too dangerous for us to be seen together on the street. Voidonov agreed and added boastfully that he was even now sought by the police, 'as usual for something I did *not* do.' We compromised on a map of Sofia which I had and on which he reacted the killings, grabbing up his gun at the appropriate moment and saying 'bang' four times.

Finally, I succeeded in bringing him down to a concrete plan. He would put Macedonians in a dozen principal railway towns to report. He would find what sympathizers his branch of the Imro had in various ministries, in the transportation system, and in communications. We fixed a date in Sofia for May, and an identification word in case another person came. Most important, he armed me with the names of his friends in Istanbul and Athens.

After some more prune brandy and another and different pastry we parted. Kimon kept urging me not to discount Voidonov and his followers because of his eccentricities and his simplicities – he and his followers were capable and honest. Frontiers they laughed at. They were experts at making fools of the police of the Balkan countries. 'They will never double-cross you.'

After the war I discovered that no real use had been made of Imro by the British. When Packy McFarlane and the oss teams reached Istanbul in 1943 it was already too late. Without outside support the forces of Voidonov had been dispersed in other activities – that is, the survivors.

That night Kimon and I went to the little Opera House, a doll's house theatre in the snow. The sleighbells were gay and the people were grim. This was the coming of the end for Bulgarians. No one, the caviar vendor in the market, the toy hawker in the square, the barman at the opera, doubted that the Germans would soon be there.

The next day Kimon wanted me to meet Kimon Georgiev and Nikola Petkov. Georgiev, an ex-prime minister and New Dealish politician, offered to work with us, but only when Bulgaria was in fact under military occupation. Petkov was leader of the peasant party – a sort of radical agrarian movement – and a charming man. He expressed his open disillusion with the British. He felt that their love for monarchy, any monarchy, anywhere, sometimes blinded them to the political merits of a question and that they had a long record of broken promises in the Balkans. But with America, 'the mother of my country's independence and the father of our democratic movements,' he was willing to conspire. He warned me that the American Legation considered him effectively a Communist. 'I have in the past co-operated with the Communists and I shall probably again, when they are in the right or when we have a common enemy. Just now they are Hitler's puppets here in our part of the world. Some day the Communists will betray him or he them. That we must be prepared to profit by.' One day too, they would betray Petkov and give him a farcical trial and hang him as a reactionary! Of all the leaders only Kimon Georgiev survived to escape from the Communists and lead an exiles' movement in Washington where he is now *persona gratissima* to the State Department.

*   *   *

At the end of March I received an innocent text message from Captain Moore – coded in a letter from Washington describing a football game – with the prearranged signal to 'come home; war close; you will be of more service here.' So I prepared to go.

As I was packing to take the train from Hydarpasha to Syria I was asked to take some sealed reports to an address in Jerusalem. I was told the papers were compromising and that I should destroy them rather than let them fall into the hands of the Germans and Italians controlling Syria.

Until the train had rolled out of Hydarpasha, I had no organized plan for getting the papers through the Syrian frontier twice – once to enter and once going out to Palestine. Then I saw the Countess!

I had met the Countess in Istanbul at the dinner party of an American attaché. Later she had invited me to dine with her at the Park Hotel. Just that one glance of her boarding the *Wagon Lit* in Hydarpasha jelled my plans. I had only to carry them out.

The Countess was hysterical, selfish, overdressed and overjewelled. As a bride, she had bolstered up the finances of a noble Hungarian family by bringing with her a great American middle-western fortune.

Tom Whittemore had thought the lady protested her anti-Nazism too much. She had, she said at the attaché's dinner, over a half million dollars in jewels with her, and the Turkish customs 'are such barbarians. They made such a fuss over my jewellery. Would you believe it, they insisted on seeing every piece and sealing it up and said I cannot break the seals until I leave Turkey. So tiresome. And really I should have diplomatic immunity, you know. I have an Hungarian diplomatic passport as well as my American one. They're really savages, the Turks, don't you think?' She had emphasised the word 'savages' by slashing at a large glob of whipped cream with her fork.

'I had a crisis of nerves there at the custom house. The American Embassy wouldn't help me at all. And I with a weak heart. I am so afraid of the trip to India. I suppose at every frontier the same fuss … and they may steal them. Travelling is so bad for my heart. So is heat. They say India is a frightful inferno of heat. I am afraid I shall never reach America. I shall break the trip in Palestine.'

I remembered it all in that second in the Hydarpasha station. Aha! I thought, she will take my papers into Syria – and out again to Palestine!

As I went by her compartment, I saw the porters stowing her jewel chest in the rack. It was just as she had described it. An oblong box in pigskin, bound and studded with brass – and covered with the red seals of the Turkish customs. I went on into my own compartment and made myself comfortable for the two nights and one day trip to the Syrian frontier.

Ten minutes out, I knocked on the Countess's door – she had it double barred – and she answered nervously in French: '*Qui est la?*' and '*Qu'est-ce que vous voulez?*' Before I could announce myself, she let me in.

'Oh, I'm so glad you are on this train. I am so afraid of these jewels in this country.' I didn't want to disillusion her by telling her the truth – that the Turks are proverbially honest and that her jewels were safer than in Budapest or on the Twentieth Century Limited bound for Chicago.

I invited her to dine with me but she protested she could not leave the jewels. 'You are quite right. It *is* terribly dangerous for a woman to be travelling alone, especially in *this* country, with such valuable jewels – but couldn't we dine here?' I bowed and I rang for the guard. 'Madame is not well. Make it possible for us to dine here and bring us two whiskies and seltzer.' I tipped him heavily.

All through dinner I told stories of Turkish dishonesty, of the thieves in the Syrian customs, of the bad reputation of this particular train. She must be extremely careful. 'Never leave that box a moment. When you go to the toilet take it with you – or better still call me.'

After dinner we talked a few minutes. As I left I leaned towards her ear and whispered, 'You'd better not carry that box to the toilet. It is next to the door. Nothing easier than to grab it and push you off the train.' Her nervousness was pleasantly increasing. She caught the whisper – 'Oh, Christ, I never thought of that! If you don't mind I *shall* call on you.' She did call me, once during the night, and again before dressing in the morning. Her frowzy, blonded hair and unmade-up face over her pink moiré dressing gown, with its count's coronet on the pocket, gave her an air of decomposition.

45

We lunched and dined together again. I pointed out several suspicious characters who passed the compartment. My last advice was, 'Going out of Turkey at the customs and when the French come aboard don't take your eyes off that box a minute. They may want to take it off and count the jewels – but, I have it, you play ill tomorrow morning. Be awakened a half hour early. But don't dress. Send for ice – for hot water – make a fuss. Then they won't bother you so much.'

Like all of her hysterical breed she was a superb actress. At 6.30 the guard called her. She sent for ice, for water, for a hot bottle for her bed and for me. I slipped my contraband papers into my dressing gown pocket and went to her.

When I arrived she winked at me, 'I'm going to the ladies' department, so you watch the box. When I come back I shall be much more ill – am I doing it well ?'

'Marvellously,' I replied.

She went out holding a hand to her head in case the guard should see her. I slipped my papers between the mattress and the bottom sheet below the pillows and patted up the pillows and straightened the sheets.

'Oh, you are so kind. And it was so clever of you to think of this being ill.' Then the guard returned with the ice and hot bottle.

'It is your dining car, guard, I was poisoned – ptomaine – please see if there is a doctor on the train,' and she doubled up with her imitation cramps.

The Turkish customs were easily in the bag. They glanced at the document about the jewels, looked carelessly at the red seals, and were profuse in their sympathy for the poor, ill gentlewoman with the American passport. A minute later and the Turkish border police only saluted on seeing her Hungarian diplomatic passport and bowed themselves out.

Two miles later the Axis came aboard – Vichy officers and a pompous looking Italian with an interpreter. Despite her Hungarian diplomatic document (she didn't show the American one) they asked many questions. She was going to Lebanon for her health and, if it did not improve, to America for an operation. Didn't they see how ill, how weak she was ?

To me they gave the works. Bags were tapped for false bottoms, socks unrolled, letters read, my wallet opened, a book fanned through for papers between the pages. Another American down the car had much the same treatment.

My greatest fear was that the guard would get back to make the Countess's bed before I could recover my papers. But he didn't. When she, her health suddenly restored, went to the lavatory I retrieved my papers while guarding the jewels. Her box had been resealed by the Syrians and I was now comparatively safe.

We spent the night in Beirut ... and the papers spent the night behind the water tank of the public toilet on the second floor of the Hotel Saint Georges, lest the Vichy *Deuxième Bureau* pay me a midnight visit.

Yes, the Countess would be delighted to share a hired car to Palestine with me. She was full of thanks for my helping her through the customs 'so neatly and so cleverly, my dear.'

During the drive to the Palestine border we kept the jewels under our feet. The papers, my precious papers, were still in my pocket as we discussed her becoming ill again to pass the two frontiers ahead. Her topcoat, where I planned to put the papers, was still on her lap. So I suggested we stop for a drink – chivalrously I carried the coat and transferred the papers.

Due to Madame's unfortunate illness the French respected the seals on her jewels, but again searched me – clothes, bags, wallet and all. In the few yards between the two customs I openly took back my papers and held them in my hand. She took no notice of having her pocket picked.

An NCO of the British security control came first. I asked him if I could see him in his office for a minute. He said yes. In we went. I explained that I had some secret documents for Major T in Jerusalem – and I showed them to him.

'I am sorry I shall have to open them,' he said.

'I am equally sorry but you must not. Call Major T on the telephone if you want to, but don't open these papers.'

'That might hold you up several hours.'

Just then a lieutenant came into his office to say good-bye – and asked: 'Do you know anyone going to Jerusalem ?'

'Yes,' I replied for the security officer, 'I am,' and to the other, 'Let him carry the papers with me to Major T.'

So my papers arrived in 'T's' office unopened save for my own undisciplined peek at one of them in Beirut. That peek rather more than half convinced me that the 'great secret documents' were in effect a plant to test my discretion and ingenuity without endangering my liberty or my life.

47

Maybe that test had something to do with the flattering confidence later put in me by John Pepper and the British Intelligence Organization in New York. For they almost certainly checked with Istanbul as well as London before entrusting me with large sums of money and, even more so, with a delicate operation at the time when the FBI was being especially obstructionist to British Intelligence's efforts ... or maybe the papers *were* important!

In any case, my thanks to the Countess!

*   *   *

Unable to get passage to New York for six weeks, I decided to return to Beirut where, among the anti-Vichy French and American missionaries, pickings seemed good for my Brown Book. Back I went to the Hotel Saint Georges, on its blue bay with the snow mountains in the distance. Hunting was excellent among the French officers, especially those commanding Arab troops. '*Je ferai tout mon possible contre les Boches – quand ça peut aider*' – it was almost a chorus. 'If your country would only enter the war we would all come over to you, *malgré ces salauds Dentz, Darlan, Laval et Cie, qui se sont vendus aux Boches.*'

On my third day in Beirut a French medical officer with whom I had had a long talk at the bar of the Saint Georges asked me to go swimming with him. We went in from the rocks on which the hotel is built. Some distance out he began to tread water.

'I want to talk to you. You said you are a journalist, did you not ?'

'Yes, I am.' I was travelling with credentials as roving correspondent of *The Nation*.

'I am on leave from my hospital at Aleppo – up north. I advise you to go there if you can. They may not let you. Still, they may not catch you if you go by car. It is *very* interesting.'

'What's so exciting in Aleppo ? I just came through on the train and it seemed quiet enough. What is it ?'

'The airport.'

'What at the airport ?'

'The Boche, my friend, many, and planes.'

He turned towards shore and began to swim back. Over his shoulder he added:

'You stay there. I'd better not see you again. Good-bye and good luck.'

'Good-bye, and thanks. I guess I'll go to Aleppo tomorrow.'

48

Up in my hotel room it was obvious that someone had given my two bags a going over. Vichy's *Deuxième Bureau* or the German-Italian Armistice Commission ? A useless distinction, I was soon to learn. But on the strength of the search, I was afraid that if I rented a car the next day it might be questioned – or followed.

I had a letter in my pocket from Makmud Sheikali in Hollywood to a friend. 'So pro-American it hurts. He'll give you his house if you ask. And my oldest friend in Beirut,' had said Makmud. So I invited him to dinner and afterwards I came to the point.

'Can you get me a car for tomorrow, cheap ? Those through the hotel cost too much. We'll go for a two-day drive, you and I, if you can be free. You shall be my guide and show me your beautiful country. But not a word to anyone – I'm supposed to have some silly permit from our Consulate before I can travel in these troubled times.'

'Ah, yes, with great pleasure, I'll come for you at the hotel. What time ?'

'No, I prefer to come to you first. I may want to leave some bags at your home, if you permit. And I don't know just what time I can leave. But certainly not before nine.'

The next morning I left my hotel with no baggage and idled down towards the centre of town, looking into shops, buying papers and having coffee. When I was sure I was not being followed, I hurried to the house of Makmud's friend. There was an old Nash standing in front with an Arab chauffeur sleeping at the wheel. I explained to my guide I had decided to come with only my toothbrush which I fished out of my pocket.

'You Americans are wonderful ... So casual. So *sportif.* Have you decided what you would like to see ? The Cedars ? Tyre and Sidon ?'

'No. Not even the Cedars. I'd like to go to Tripoli – up the coast – on to Latakia.'

'OK. That's the ticket.' He awakened the chauffeur and jabbered with him. 'Get in. We're off. We can lunch in Tripoli. Away we go !'

'I'd rather buy something and eat along the road,' I said – there was also a *Deuxième Bureau* in Tripoli where the trains stopped.

We had a beautiful drive and spent the night with friends of my guide and of Makmud's. I slept well, not only because I could hear the sea and was full of good food but also because we had not encountered a single road block of the Vichy military.

At our coffee the next morning I suggested going on to Aleppo.

'Then we can take the short cut back by Homs and Hama.' My guide thought it a fine idea. We made all the polite Islamic farewells and drove off.

'Listen, my friend. I speak very bad French. If we are stopped by a French road block you tell them I speak neither French nor Arabic, that I am a missionary on his way back to Turkey and must catch the Baghdad train for Istanbul at Muslimiya north of Aleppo. Your suitcase is mine. See, here in my passport it says *teacher*, and here is my Turkish permit as a teacher to circulate freely in Turkey, and a Turkish visa. If they suspect I am a newspaper man, they won't let me enter Aleppo, I am sure of that.'

'Why ?'

'Because,' I said looking him in the eyes, 'there are Germans in Aleppo – Germans in Nazi uniforms.'

He swore in Arabic by quite a few of the names of God.

'As an American journalist I must let my countrymen know. That is my duty. Makmud says you love America as he does. I know you will help me.' – all as ham-dramatically as I could.

'Yes,' he took my hand and squeezed it equally dramatically, 'yes. Even if I end in a dirty jail of the dirty French dogs! Son of beeches, son of beeches, the French. First we have a butcher Weygand who killed us like sheep. Now a butcher Dentz who sells us like goats to the Germans. We of my family do not agree with the Grand Mufti el Hussein. We believe he is wrong. It is not wise to trade French oppression for German. They consider us no better than they do the Jews.'

We drove on towards Aleppo. The road block was at the little town of Talib where a left fork leads into Turkey, only a few kilometres away. There was no officer present: a French NCO and four or five Arab soldiers.

'I regret but no foreigner may enter Aleppo without a special *laisser-passer* from Beirut or Damascus. It is quite impossible.'

Then my Arab friend began his speech. It was in elegant and elaborate French: 'This poor missionary, this teacher, his family are on the train from Baghdad ... he was told in Beirut he could join the train at Aleppo ... in fact it was the *aide-de-camp* of General Dentz who bade him farewell ... he sent by my friend a message of greeting to General Salbert at Aleppo ... if such a permit is necessary this is the case of the great injustice where it would be wise to waive it. Do you not agree ?'

The NCO was doubtful. He examined all my documents again.

'I can at the most offer the compromise to send your friend to the headquarters of General Salbert under escort. If, as you say, everything is all right, someone will return the escort and give your friend permission to enter Aleppo. If not ... that will expiate my responsibility.'

An Arab soldier, our escort, entered the car. We thanked the NCO, gave him a package of English cigarettes and drove on.

'We are not much better off,' I said, 'What the hell will I tell Salbert's headquarters ?'

'You shall not go there. It will not equal more than five dollars in your money. The soldier will be happy and so shall we.'

He talked low and rapidly in Arabic with the soldier. In two minutes everything was agreed – some bills changed hands. At the first sign of town the car stopped and the soldier left us.

'Let's not be seen in town before we go to the airport. I'd hate to be picked up now.' The driver asked the way of a couple of townsfolk and we drew up in an olive grove off a dirt road outside the town. After five minutes' walk to the top of a little hill, we found ourselves in another olive grove behind a prickly-pear hedge over which there was an excellent view of the airport.

And there they were. We counted seventeen Junkers transports outside the hangars. Heavy cases were being unloaded. While we watched, six more came in, droned lazily over our heads, and one by one they landed, giving us a fine view of their black-cross insignia.

We sat behind the cactus hedge and ate a chocolate bar. '*Le Général Salbert est un salaud*,' said Makmud's friend. We jumped to our feet at a loud calling of orders below us on the airport. There before a hangar were at least a company of Germans, apparently parachutists, forming in ranks. An officer harangued them for a few minutes and they filed back into the hangar. Again my friend said, '*Salbert est un salaud et Dentz est encore plus salaud que lui.*"

We left in mid-afternoon and drove back to Beirut via Hama and Homs. Going away from Aleppo the road blocks did not bother us and the route avoided our NCO of the earlier encounter. It was night when we arrived in Beirut and I thanked my guide profusely, 'I am so thankful for your help, not only on my own behalf but on the behalf of our dear friend Makmud of Hollywood, and for the America we all love. America shall know how false are the Vichy pigs, thanks to you.' He blushed and bowed.

At the hotel the concierge told me that 'two French gentlemen' had been to see me; holding up two fingers he added in a whisper '*Deuxième Bureau.*' So I slept fitfully with that sword of Damocles feeling that you have when there is unconcluded business with some secret police hanging over your head. It is a cross between indigestion and loneliness. It makes the hearing extremely acute and the imagination both active and pessimistic – especially when you have a guilty conscience.

In the morning I awoke with a plan: Go to see the British Consul. This poor gentleman, accredited to a theoretically independent country, Lebanon (over which France had a mandate from the defunct League of Nations), had not gone away when the Vichy régime received the German-Italian Armistice Commission. He was under a sort of siege. As long as he stayed in the Consulate no one bothered him – much. But he was told he would be expelled from the country if he ventured forth.

To this prisoner I hurried even before breakfast. Yes, he had heard the Germans were in Aleppo but he was glad to have an eye-witness and I gave him the particulars as I had observed them from among the prickly-pears.

'I don't know how soon I can get a message out. Could you, Mr Downes, go to Palestine? I could probably send word by the next Nairn bus to Baghdad, if they are allowed to continue under these conditions, which I doubt. The Nairn boys don't dare to visit me just now. Perhaps you could tell Mr McEwan, the archaeologist, and he would go to Jerusalem. I am sure he is to be trusted.'

'I'll go myself. But I thought you ought to know.' We talked a while; he seemed really grateful for a visitor and offered me some tea. Finally I left, with the idea of going to Palestine at once.

That 'at once' idea was conceived without the knowledge of the two 'French gentlemen' waiting on the sidewalk just outside the Consulate gates. As I saw them I patted my pocket to be sure I had my passport and papers.

'Excuse me, you are Monsieur Downes of the Hotel Saint Georges?'
'Yes.'
'Your documents, if you please, a mere formality.'
'I am sorry, Messieurs, but I cannot show my documents to any casual person who may demand them on the street. I have no doubts as to your authenticity but I must see your documents first, a mere formality.'

They conferred in whispers. Finally one of them produced a document of the *Sécurité Militaire*. 'Thank you. Now if you care to come to my hotel I shall show you mine.'

'That will not do, Monsieur, you must show them here.'

'Under those circumstances, I regret but I must refuse. You may of course arrest me. But that would have certain consequences at the American Consulate, which I am sure would be regrettable to all concerned. In any event, unless prevented by force, I intend to go from here to Mr Engert's office at the Consulate and inform him that I am being molested by the *Sécurité Militaire*. Then I shall go directly to the Hotel Saint Georges where I shall be at your disposition.'

'Would Monsieur care to say why he, an American, was visiting the British Consul ?'

'I am the citizen of a neutral country, friendly to France for a hundred and fifty years, and I am not convinced that I have to respond to the French military authorities every time I make a social visit.'

'Then you must accompany us to the Police Bureau.'

'If you take me by force and assault an American citizen in so doing, I shall go. Otherwise, I shall proceed to the office of Consul-General Engert.'

Anything, I thought, not to go to police headquarters before the American Consulate knew where I was going and who was taking me. I wanted to get to Palestine before my news was stale. Perhaps, *Sécurité Militaire* knew I had been to Aleppo; perhaps by holding me 'regrettably and in error' for a few days they could neutralize my knowledge – at least keep me from telling the British that Germans and German airplanes were in Aleppo. I was not afraid of being expelled, but of being held.

'But, Monsieur, you *must* come ... our orders.'

'Oh,' I compromised, 'will you accompany me to the American Consulate. From there, I shall go with you to your office.' More conference.

'Monsieur, we have our orders.'

'And I, certain regrets. Good day, Messieurs.' I started towards the Consulate with my heart pounding in my throat. But the bluff worked. They fell in behind like two dogs well trained to heel and did not touch me.

At the Consulate I saw a Vice-Consul. 'For some crazy reason the French *Deuxième Bureau* is making it tough for me. I want to go to Jerusalem. Can you help me ? '

'By chance I have a car going in a couple of hours to Haifa. Come back here and we'll give you a lift.'

'And if I don't come back,' I said, 'look for me in the Bastille. Thanks a lot. I'll be back – I hope!'

And on the street my heelers were awaiting me. I explained that Mr Engert personally expected me back in an hour. In the meantime I would gladly answer all questions and show my documents.

'Monsieur is more reasonable. Simply, why did you go to see the British Consul ?'

'That is all that interests you ? Well, it is simple,' I said, taking out my *Nation* credentials. 'I am a journalist as well as a teacher. It is an interesting story that a Consul, practically a prisoner, should remain here under the present régime of France and in Lebanon with a German-Italian Armistice Commission. I give you my word that before I send the story I shall submit it for censorship.

'And besides,' I smiled, 'in truth I shall have to report that the Consul is well treated and that you French have handled the situation with much diplomacy.'

'Thank you, Monsieur, here is your passport and your documents. If *Monsieur le Chef* wishes to know more we will come to the Saint Georges this evening.'

'No,' I lied, 'come to Mr Engert's house. I shall be his guest. *Au revoir.*' We shook hands.

I taxied to the hotel. In a half-hour I was back in the Vice-Consul's office reading an old issue of the *New York Times*. 'You are early,' said the Vice-Consul.

'It's comfortable here. I'll wait, if you don't mind.'

'No, indeed, make yourself at home.'

I ate a late lunch in Haifa and hired a car for Jerusalem. By six o'clock I was with Major T in Jerusalem eating marmalade with the tea and telling my Aleppo story.

Two years later in Morocco I was again having tea – this time strong, mint flavoured, green China tea – with Captain André Bourgoin of the *Deuxième Bureau*.

'You must report to 5th Army G2,' said Bourgoin, 'that sooner or later there will be trouble here in Fez. General Mark Clark has permitted the French General now commanding in Fez to reconstitute two battalions of parachutists. They are decent French boys, but he is indoctrinating them with *la merde fasciste de Vichy*. Every morning before breakfast they must sing, *Maréchal, nous voici,* the song of the Vichy Youth Movement. They are being forced to take an oath to that ancient pig, Pétain. Either they will constitute a menace to your army if the indoctrination is successful or they will mutiny. ..." Lamidu the Jackal brought us more sweet tea.

'Who is this General ?'

'*Général Salbert*; *c'est un salaud.*'

My mind went back to Makmud's friend behind the cactus hedge. '*Salbert est un salaud.*'

'I do not have the honour of knowing him,' I said, 'but I once saw his guests, Nazi soldiers, arrive in twenty-three airplanes on the airport of Aleppo when it was commanded by *salaud Salbert le sâle.* And afterwards Dentz swore on his military honour there were neither German soldiers nor planes.'

Our report to G2 5th Army was soft-pedalled. The French parachutists were a pet project of the Commanding General and his housekeeper, Colonel Saltzman. *Rien à faire.*

But on 14 July 1943, Bastille day, it happened: these parachutists mutinied in Fez. It began by their singing the *Marseillaise*, banned by the Vichy régime, instead of *Maréchal nous voici.* The mutineers arrested their Vichy officers, barricaded themselves in their barracks, and defied Salbert's orders.

They sent out, under white flags, a list of demands – one was that their General be removed, and another that those cadets who wished to should be allowed to join de Gaulle, already established in Algiers.

General Salbert asked General Clark for artillery to put down the mutiny. Fifth Army headquarters in Oujda was about to comply. It began to look like a repetition of the case of the nineteen 'mutineers' of Mers-el-Kebir.*

---

* These 19 heard Roosevelt's recorded voice from the battleship *Texas* on North African D-day. He begged all Frenchmen to help us land as we were coming only to liberate France. The nineteen complied: they cut the wires to their officers' quarters; they dismantled the breach-bolts of their big guns and tossed them over the cliff. Those guns, at least, killed no Americans. The French Vichy military régime which we backed in Oran court-martialled the nineteen for treason, and they received long prison sentences, necessarily ok'd by the American general commanding. This same general, to complete the Alice Through the Diplomatic Looking Glass atmosphere, decorated the leader of the Vichy opposition to our landing – a civilian! Later when oss tried to persuade General Patton

Bourgoin and myself felt that certainly American artillery should not be used to coerce the Fez parachutists. Art Blom, the G2 counterintelligence officer, was on our side. He scraped up our reports on the Fez situation and sent them to General Clark.

That afternoon, General Clark summoned me 'to ask where there was good trout fishing in the south of Morocco for some guests of headquarters.' I went around with the artillery map co-ordinates of a number of good trout streams. After we were through with the trout talk, the General said, 'What's all this about Salbert ? Is he really a bad egg ?''

'A rotten egg, sir!'

'You saw this Aleppo stuff with your own eyes ?'

'I did, sir.'

That night Clark telephoned Nogues,† the still-tolerated Vichy Resident (Governor) of Morocco, and Salbert was transferred to the Sahara. The parachutists affair was easily settled.

* * *

Back in Palestine – the sailing date of my ship *President Grant* from India was close. However many jobs were developing everywhere in the Middle East, Captain Moore's message had said *come home*. So I left by bus for Baghdad and on by bomber with the RAF for Bombay.

to intercede for them he waved us aside with, 'They got what they deserved; it *was* treason, wasn't it?'

De Gaulle set it right when he took over the Government of French Africa: 19 pardons, 19 promotions, and 19 decorations.

† Nogues later absconded like an ordinary thief to Portugal with the gold of the Bank of Morocco. He was one of Murphy's and the State Department's choices to govern Africa!

CHAPTER FIVE

PRESIDENT GRANT TO AMERICA FIRST

SPRING 1941

All the *President Grant* (which we soon came to call her) lacked was Noah. For she had aboard one or two each of the stranger political animals. There was Mr W. Y. Evans-Wentz who said he was a Lama from Tibet on his way home 'to visit the folks' in San Diego. There was Sir Yeshwant Rao Holkar (the Maharajah of Indore) and his American wife, Marguerite, who were both too reformist for the other princes and for the British in India. There was Major W. L. Kirby, retired, of the Indian Police, going to Canada to enjoy his pension. Politically, he was still fighting the war against Kaiser Bill – 'Let's be beastly to the Hun.' There was Martin van Niekerk, a Boer, a friend of Marshal Smuts, a veteran of the war against England. He was, along with the Maharajah, one of the strongest anti-Axis liberals on the *Grunt*.

The pro-Axis group was led by the ship's master, Gregory Cullen, USNR. In his office-cabin was a large autographed photograph of General Franco, dedicated 'to my friend, Gregory Cullen'. The ship's crew followed the current Communist Party line. The Ribbentrop-Molotov agreement had another month of life before Hitler and Russia were to be at war. So the crew believed England 'the aggressor in an imperialist war'.

The war on the *President Grant* was set off by the sinking of the *Hood* by the *Bismarck*. It gave the Axis side some strange allies, a half-dozen of the German Jewish refugees. They were unable to conceal their delight in the success of *unsere Marine*. That night the crew gave a party to celebrate the great 'anti-imperialist naval victory'. We protested to the captain, who told us the crew were free to celebrate what they liked. His own pleasure in the sinking was obvious.

A few days later the *Bismarck* was sunk by the Royal Navy and we, for our part, planned our own celebration. We would have champagne (California) and caviar (salmon), the best the steward's department of the *Grunt* offered.

57

The chief steward came to us at about 4 o'clock in the afternoon: 'Captain's orders, sir, there will be no celebration tonight.' We went again to Commander Cullen's cabin, where Franco frowned down on us from his frame, to protest. The captain was adamant.

'The crew have protested. Their delegate pointed out that over a thousand sailors died for their country when the *Bismarck* was sunk. They refuse to bring up the drinks. They demand that I prevent the celebration. They are in an ugly mood about it. For the sake of harmony I must forbid the celebration."

Our reply was that we would celebrate if it had to be with soda crackers and water. We were, we pointed out, passengers who had paid our passage. If the crew had been allowed to celebrate the sinking of the *Hood*, we, the paying passengers, would insist on our right to celebrate the sinking of the *Bismarck*.

The captain warned us there would be trouble with the crew and, if there were, he would hold us responsible. 'You know I have the right to hold you in irons until we reach port, if you disobey me.'

We allowed that it would be a pleasure to be put in irons for this reason; that we had no doubt who would be in trouble in an English or American port should he, in fact, put any of us in irons. I asked the captain if he would refuse me the use of the ship's radio at regular commercial rates to send the story to my paper in America. He replied that he would have to think it over.

We held our celebration, with champagne (California) and caviar (salmon), and sang the British songs of both wars. It ended with Major Kirby's toast to His Majesty's Navy, and our singing of *God Save the King*, while the crew, just below on their liberty deck, tried to drown us out with the *Internationale*.

If the sinking had occurred a month later the crew would have been our allies in the war of the *President Grunt*, such are the marvels of the dialectic.

For the rest of the trip to New York, nearly three more weeks, half the ship's company didn't speak to the other half. But, somehow, the cruise of the *President Grant* prepared me for what I found in the United States – the Isolationists apparently winning their battle to keep us neutral, while Hitler conquered the rest of the world. They had a hodge-podge of collaborators: domestic fascists, the German Bund and, I suspected, the *Auslands Dienst*, the S.D.*

---

* *Sicherheitsdienst*, Himmler's private intelligence organization.

58

and the *Abwehr*, Hitler's organizations for secret operations abroad.

In the Balkans and in the Middle East I had developed a bit of a nose for the Nazi organizations. I went to a couple of *America First* rallies – and detected the unmistakable odour of National Socialism, German exported.

*　　*　　*

I gave my time and effort to the various interventionist organizations and to the *Free World Association*.* The European exiles I met in this work were to be of great value to me later when I was recruiting for oss.

In New York I made contact with British Intelligence. I was to meet a Mr 'Howard' in a little chop-house near the skating rink in Rockefeller Plaza. Mr 'Howard' came quickly to the point. 'You are not unknown to us. We had thought of sending you to French Africa. But instead I would like to suggest a work for you which is far more important to us.

'Our primary directive from the PM' (Mr Churchill) 'is that American participation in the war is the most important single objective for Britain. It is the only way, he feels, to victory over Nazism.

'Our best information is that the forces of isolationism, a front here for Nazism and Fascism, is gaining, not losing ground. How do you personally feel about these forces, for example, the *America First* movement?'

'I couldn't feel stronger. I can say further that I am quite honestly ashamed that my country is not a full-fledged, belligerent ally of Britain's.'

---

* The FWA was an organization of statesmen exiled from the various countries occupied by the Axis or actual refugees from axis countries: Count Carlo Sforza from Italy; Pierre Cot of France; Julio Alvarez del Vayo of Spain, General Deutsch of Austria, and so on. Their purpose was to organize their fellow exiles for propaganda, for political preparation against the day of liberation, and to publish a magazine, *The Free World*. The Association had well-organized offices in New York, and was in contact with hundreds of thousands of other refugees. Further, FWA controlled excellent sources of intelligence which led back to their several countries.

'Do you feel strongly enough on these matters to work for us in your own country? To spy on your own fellow Americans and report to us? For we feel there is German money and German direction behind the *America First* movement, though many of its followers may not know it and would in fact be shocked to know it. If we can pin a Nazi contact or Nazi money on the isolationists, they will lose many of their followers. It might be the deciding factor in America's entry in the war, if the American public knew the truth.

'But be careful of the F B I, and the Neutrality Act can land you in prison, for in this work you could not register as the agent of a foreign power as the law requires. It would give the whole show away.'

'If the President,' I replied, 'can risk impeachment by breaking the Neutrality Law wholesale to aid Britain, who am I to refuse?'

'And if you are caught,' he added, 'we have never heard of you! – you understand that?'

'Perfectly, but I make a few conditions. One is that I am free to give any of the information I may turn up to any American government agency to which I think it would be interesting. Another is that on a personal, unofficial basis, I am free to inform a friend in Naval Intelligence what I am doing. The third is that I take no pay above expenses, which will include my living expenses."

'Agreed.'

'I shall keep my contacts in *The Free World* and in the anti-isolationist organizations for which I'm now doing some voluntary work. It will serve as cover. Don't you think that's wise?'

'Yes,' agreed Mr' Howard'. 'When can you start?'

'This afternoon.'

We arranged cut-outs (means of communicating through two other people), where to deliver my reports, and other details. During the next four months I built myself an organization of some size. We were interested in the German Consulates, the attachés of the German Embassy in Washington, especially a certain Herr von Geinant, and whom they saw and why.

Charles Payson, Seward Collins, Senator Nye, Senator Wheeler; an obscure Republican county chairman in Ohio; Charles Lindberg; a country town in Wisconsin where *Scribner's Commentator* was published; the Bund headquarters in Yorkville; a German-born instructor in biology at Amherst; an ex-officer of the Czarist secret police named Boris; a bakery shop on Upper Madison

Avenue too frequently visited by Geinant's secretary with a fat brief case; the German Consulates in Boston and Cleveland; the Italian consulate-general in New York; the *Chicago Tribune*; a retired general of the United States Army; two officials of the export division of General Motors – these and others were the raw material of the investigation.

I thanked God Germany had attacked Russia in June, and the Communists no longer helped the Nazis and no longer decried Britain's 'Imperialist War', and were no part of my job. There were other allies I could have more trustworthy than the Communists – the Jewish *Anti-defamation League*, the Political Action Committee of the CIO, the *Friends of Democracy* and, especially, *The Committee to Defend America by Aiding the Allies* –all believing my work was for the *Free World Association*. My best ally was Colonel Eugene Prince and his Army Counter-Intelligence Corps office at 17 East 42nd Street in New York. I told Eugene Prince the truth, that I was working for the British, and he and his assistants kept my secret well. Moreover, they gave me pertinent information from their own files; allowed me to see the papers taken in some of their raids; and gave me invaluable tips on subjects not in their field, but definitely in mine.

Prince understood my difficulties and fear of the FBI and would often steer me off a certain investigation saying, 'I think J.Edgar's boys are around there now and they're awful sensitive to competition. I'd wait a while if I were you.'

My reports, about October, began to have meat in them. But since most of the individuals concerned turned a complete about face after Pearl Harbour, I do not want to recall the findings in detail. In general, I did find most of the leaders of the *America First* organization to be ignorant of the Axis contacts of their fellow members.

New York, Washington, Chicago, San Francisco, Cleveland, and Boston were the chief centres of contact with the Nazis. In the last two we traced actual transfers of funds from the Nazis to America Firsters, and we strongly suspected it in New York. But New York funds came directly from Washington, as the Nazis did not trust the personnel of their own New York consulate. *

One Sunday morning my report was done. Mr 'Howard' paid me

---

* Otto Kiep was Consul-General. See page 73.

the exciting compliment of saying that a copy for the PM would leave by bomber-ferry route on Monday.

At about 1.30 p.m. I turned on the radio. The Japanese had bombed Pearl Harbour and my report became an unnecessary package of paper, to end in some file or 'top secret' incinerator. America was at last where she belonged, in the war against the Axis.

Even the *President Grant* and her officers and crew served with credit in the war.

CHAPTER SIX

THE ENTHUSIASTIC AMATEURS

WINTER 1941 TO 1942

In the weeks after Pearl Harbour I kept begging John Pepper, my British boss in New York, to make contact with someone in Donovan's organization,* just then being established. Now that America had been bombed into the war, I wished to transfer my activities to my own government.

My first contact was with Allen Dulles and a group of aides whom Donovan had sent to establish a New York office. I was asked for references and for my life story and, a week later was invited to Allen Dulles' new office, in a confusion of builders and painters. It was in Rockefeller Plaza, just a floor over the British secret office which was called, comically enough, 'Rough Diamonds, Ltd.'

Donovan's outfit agreed that I should continue my work along counter-espionage lines: to try to dig out whatever disloyal American agents the Axis embassies and consulates had left behind to work for them. I was also to continue my interest in the *Free World Association*, to stay in contact with the flow of refugees for the purpose of recommending recruits for their immediate information value, or for actual espionage missions in their home countries.

At first Dulles and his aides were, quite justifiably, afraid of me – I had been an agent of a foreign power when that was prohibited by the Neutrality Act. So I was to work out of my own office in another part of New York, come as little as possible to Radio City, consider myself an 'agent' and not a 'staff member' of the new OSS. In short, I was outside security – that mystical and theoretical veil (full of holes) which divides the 'insiders' from the 'outsiders'. The arrangement pleased me as it allowed wide scope and freedom from the nervous supervision of certain ex-diplomats and old scaredy-cats who infested OSS in its early days.

Frederic Ullman, jr (President of Pathé newsreel), gave me an

---

* The Office of Strategic Services (OSS).

office inside his own, which never closed day or night. It thus provided maximum security against a search by FBI, or, worse, some enemy organization. Freddy Ullman, a friend since college days, knew only that 'it's important secret work for the government and you mustn't mention my presence to anyone'. He never did.

The weak spot in all security is a man's secretary. How well I knew that from my investigations behind *America First* and other isolationist and pro-Axis groups! The German diplomat, L.C. Moyzisch, can give sad testimony to this fact – he had established the most brilliant espionage coup of the war whereby a certain 'Cicero', apparently a *valet-de-chambre* to the British ambassador in Ankara, brought him for a period of four months photographs of the most vital and secret allied documents, already decoded. Moyzisch's secretary, Elisabet, spilled the beans to the British – and Cicero disappeared.

I have a niece, Edith Rising, then only twenty-one years old, a sphinx for silence, and one of those rare people with an intuitive sense of security. I decided to have her for my secretary although she was already doing an important job as secretary to the head of a big war-production plant. Allen Dulles wrote to her boss, and he willingly granted her a leave of absence 'for the duration'.

Some valuable results came from my counter-espionage snooping, but far more satisfactory was the recruiting of personnel for OSS staff and for overseas missions. About this time (February 1942) George K. Bowden of Chicago was attached to the New York office. George was a young (forties) successful corporation lawyer who had been a 'wobbly' organizer and a professional football player in his youth. He had had G2 experience in the first war and, despite it, had developed real imagination in intelligence work. Big Bill Donovan had great confidence in George Bowden, and he carried, in the early, unmilitarized days of OSS, more weight than anyone with the big boss.

In George I found an ideal fellow conspirator, willing, even enthusiastic, to present my wildest schemes to the powers-that-were. He it was who urged on Dulles, Bruce and Donovan to take me behind the veil of OSS security and set me up in an office in 'Q' Building, OSS's inner sanctum in Washington.

I wasn't sure that it was a wise thing for me to enter more or less officially inside OSS. I would lose freedom of action, and feared, moreover, the old Washington game of sticking knives in the backs of competitors. I didn't know how to play that survival-of-the-most-ruthless game. I was always hearing that Mr X was out to 'get' Mr Y so he could put his man Z in his place. Or that Economic Warfare was in danger of being 'captured' by The Reconstruction Finance Corporation. No man's official life was entirely safe.

I told this to George Bowden and he only said, 'Let me worry about that. I'll protect your flanks' – and he said it with that look in his eye which has always made me hope he would be on my side in any fight, any time, anywhere – and never my opponent. So I passed the veil of security and moved into 'Q'.

But in the great Washington Civil War of 1942, I was not wounded. This was because I had such strong defenders on my flanks as Donovan, Dulles, Bruce, Rehm, and George Bowden. About March, I got the job procuring the codes from the Washington embassies of certain neutral countries which were flirting with the Axis.* My lucky success in this second-story work increased our influence up in the Kremlin, as Donovan's office was called.

Once inside oss, I found top-executives easy to deal with and willing to try any idea which might hurt the Axis or supply the armed forces with information: David Bruce in Washington as head of intelligence; Allen Dulles as head of the New York office; Lane Rehm, finance officer; and George Bowden as head of *Special Activities*, of which I was part. But above all Donovan, easily accessible, kindly, and always willing to rule against the conservatives if we 'actionists' in our enthusiasm demonstrated a real chance of success for our long-shot projects.

Inside *Special Activities* George had brought his friend, Arthur Goldberg. He was a labour lawyer from Chicago, then almost unknown, but now chief counsel of cio and a leader of its fighting anti-Communist wing. We were a fortunate combination, able to work together at high speed without friction. Our ideas, our plans, our points of view almost perfectly meshed; our abilities were peculiarly supplementary; our work so mutually understood and developed that each was able at any time to carry on or make a decision for the others.

Arthur, George and myself conceived the idea of a Labour Desk in oss. The theory was that the suppressed labour organizations in the Nazi, Fascist and occupied countries must exist in some hidden

* As told in Chapter Eight.

and skeleton form anxious to help if contacted by other labour men.

I had already completed one project in this field, supplying Leon Jouhaux, the French labour leader, with a large sum of money for clandestine work in France. This had been made possible by certain exiles in the *Free World Association,* and the money was sent to him through Switzerland.

Art Goldberg surrounded himself with a group of hard fighters. The contacts we made for them, with such suppressed organizations as the *International Transport Workers Federation,* supplied the armed forces with some of the best target information for strategic bombing to come out of the war. Transport workers reported in detail on railroad and barge loadings inside Germany, giving us the location of hidden factories and prime military targets of all sorts.

A Belgian, named Omar Becu, made possible the dozen projects founded on the International Transport Workers Federation.* An officer in the Belgian Army in the calamity of 1940, Becu had previously been an official in the International Transport Workers Federation. He had started life as marconist on a merchant ship and had come up in his union through the radio operators. Under Prohibition he had known most of the radio operators on America's Rum Row. During the phoney war, Becu had recruited several German radio operators used by British Intelligence.

In the spring of 1942, Becu came from England to a labour conference in New York, as secretary of the ITF. George Bowden met him and heard his story of the existing cells of ITF still holding out in Axis and occupied countries. To George he seemed perfect raw material for the new Labour Desk. He was provided with funds and told that OSS London would contact him.

Unfortunately, there was, as yet, no Labour Desk representative attached to OSS London. Before the arrival of David Bruce, as chief of the London mission, the personnel on the spot had no idea of the value of labour contacts, and the matter, for a few critical weeks, was allowed to slide along.

In May 1942 a congress was held in London of as many ITF representatives as could get out of Hitler's Europe. Becu had promised George Bowden to recruit radio operators, organizers, and general

---

* The ITF was a large international labour union open to all types of workers in transport – land, sea and air – including, as well as the usual workers, radio operators, signal men, air crews, goods clerks, etc.

personnel for oss, to be trained in the specialities of espionage. Donovan and his Chief of Secret Intelligence, David Bruce, were enthusiastic about this coup. George and Art, overcoming jungles of red tape and prejudice, were able to establish a Labour Desk of oss London quickly enough not to lose the harvest of Omar Becu's offer. itf produced an abundance of recruits and contacts on the Continent, all of prime excellence.*

In the next three years these men were:

1) To locate a great many of the secret synthetic oil and rubber plants and ball-bearing factories in Axis territory.

2) To locate through train loadings the principal supply points and the direction (i.e. to what point) supplies were flowing in greatest quantity – a dead give-away of a coming offensive.

3) To supply the only effective radio teams to be dropped behind German lines in the Reich itself after the landings in 1944.

It was because of America's failure immediately after the war to aid and subsidize these organizations, as Art Goldberg had done, that the overwhelming majority of Continental European labour fell, *faute de mieux* and uncontested, into the basket of the Communists.

During the months from February to December 1942, *Special Activities* and the *Labour Desk* worked as a team, without internal secrets or jealousies. Our day began in old, temporary, ramshackle 'Q' Building about 7.30 in the morning. Our last conferences ended over a bottle of Scotch in George Bowden's apartment in 'Q' Street– the other end of Washington – at one or two a.m. We ate together, thought together, and together we produced a vast number of recruits and projects.

* * *

I–SCHWARZ-PUTLITZ GERMAN ENCYCLOPEDIA

Dicke means fat in German. Dick Schwarz is fat in the worst sense of that word. His belly hides from him the gravy spots on his trousers, his chins hide his necktie, and his waistcoat just misses his trousers enough in front to let a good, big piece of shirt-tail habitually hang out.

---

* For some strange reason Becu was apparently overlooked when American decorations were distributed after the war, an ungrateful injustice.

Dr Paul Schwarz was German Consul-General in New York in 1933 when Hitler took over Germany. Having had one Jewish grandparent, Dicke was unclean under the Nuremberg laws. Anyway, he had been outspokenly anti-Nazi – and when Dicke speaks out it is so loud everyone hears and the adjectives are ripe and vulgar – from lavatory and brothel – so Dicke knew he was on the skids when Hitler came in.

He resigned with a maximum of protest and applied for American citizenship. It took five years to get. Dicke lay low until he was sworn in as an American in 1938.

Dicke began to spill the German beans – scandals, indiscretions, skeletons. In his forty years in the German foreign service, he had kept elaborate notes and now he began to write for newspapers under the pseudonym of 'Diplomaticus'. The pseudonym was the only thing diplomatic about Dicke's articles. This information he kept in huge filing cases, where there was all the gossip and facts about everyone of importance in German diplomatic and military circles for nearly half a century.

We teamed Dicke up with Baron von und zu Putlitz, former German *Chargé d'Affaires* at the Hague, who had warned Britain that the Germans were about to strike through the Low Countries, and had to flee for his life. If someone in Washington wanted to know, let's say, how General Jodl could best be approached, Schwarz with the help of his files and Putlitz could tell what sort of man he was:

His social position.
Whom he had married and why.
Rich or poor, self-made or inherited.
Weaknesses, gambling or girls or schnapps.
Family connections.
Shady incidents in his past.
Relatives or wife's relatives living abroad.
Prejudices.
Easy to corrupt with money or not.
Close friends in neutral countries.
Present position of influence in Germany.
How he climbed to that position.
Political affiliations before Hitler.
Precise moment he had mounted the Nazi bandwagon.
In fact all there was to know of value.

In the early days before we got the encyclopedia set up on government funds with secretary and office, Dicke liked to give me the information at Luchow's on 14th Street with Bismarck herrings, beer, boiled beef and horseradish sauce, cheesecake and coffee. The menu never varied. There was so much of the great lover in his seventy-year-old make-up that it was hard for him to stick to the scandalous subject of some overripe German diplomat.

'That lovely girl in the subway. Not over eighteen, I'm sure. Pretty, and such legs and eyes. I almost didn't get off at 42nd Street. She wanted me to come home with her. Of course I couldn't. I knew you would be here and, besides, I am a married man, but I almost....'

Then between bites of cheese-cake I would hear of the dishonesty, perversion, or anti-Nazism of General von Sauerkraut who could be bought or blackmailed or both. Schwarz's information, detailed as it was, never proved unreliable.

One thing he liked better than cheese-cake or memories of Constantinople in the First World War, or even pretty girls, was the U.S.A. In Schwarz's mind existed an America too perfect to be true.

'I have visited all forty-eight states and I'll do it again before I die. Why wasn't I born here?'

II–TREVIRANUS-KELLER PROJECT

One day Colonel Eugene Prince of the Army Counter Intelligence Corps in New York called me in to meet a German, Count Keller, a huge, jolly ham of a man who had been arrested by CIC as an enemy alien too close to an army camp on Long Island. Keller had married an American after escaping from a Nazi concentration camp. He was frankly a German nationalist of the old stamp. In 1919 and 1920 he had been a member of the *Freikorps* terror organization, a sort of partisan movement, which opposed the annexation of East Prussia to Poland and the Saar to France. Keller was physically a giant, tough – a younger edition of Count Luckner. Colonel Prince thought he might be useful to us.

When OSS is accused of using the extreme left, let it be said that it also used the extreme right. Our theory was that we would use the devil himself if he could help defeat Hitler. Keller recommended that we invite Gottfried Reinhold Treviranus to the United States from Canada.

'Skipper' Treviranus had been a submarine commander in the 1914–18 war, and immediately afterwards had entered the Reichstag, as the protégé of Grand Admiral von Tirpitz. Once or twice he had been a minister in the German Weimar Republic. Later he joined the German Nationalist Party, but had been unable to stomach its union with the National Socialists in 1934. He was marked for purge. The Gestapo came for him while he was playing tennis. He climbed the wall which served as a backstop and fled. He became a gentleman farmer in Canada.

The plan to bring Treviranus to the U.S. was presented to Donovan and he approved. Treviranus was given an American visa. We rented a big house on East 63rd Street in New York to be his home and the headquarters of *Project Skipper.*

Treviranus, using our communications, was to make contact with certain Germans still *personae gratae* to Nazism, but of whose fundamental anti-Nazism Treviranus was sure. Some of these individuals were in German military, business, and diplomatic posts in the 'border-countries' – Portugal, Spain, Sweden, Switzerland, and Turkey. With these he was to build up chains of information into the War Office, the Foreign Office, and high industrial circles in Germany. What we wanted was the information. But in compensation we were to allow Treviranus to use the same route to reconstruct a political opposition to Hitler from the right. In fact, many of his friends became involved in the attempt on Hitler's life in July 1944.

At such a time as Treviranus should need an agent of his own, we were to parachute or otherwise introduce Count Keller into Germany. Keller's part of the project was to organize cellular types of terror teams modelled on the *Freikorps.* They were to exploit the schisms within the Nazi Party.

The plan was based on a series of assassinations, which it was hoped would turn the Goering group against Himmler's, Ribbentrop's against von Keitel's, and so on. We hoped that more blood would flow in the wolf-eat-wolf reprisals than in our own killings, and that the subsequent distrust and fear would contribute to undermining the régime.

It is an odd sensation in 1952, looking out an open window at the blue Mediterranean and a garden full of flowers, to recall planning murders only ten years ago. We have so soon forgotten Buchenwald, Dachau, and the enormity of the mass murders against which we were fighting then.

Project Skipper got under way with great hopes. But after I left for Africa the State Department howled so loudly against our using a German Nationalist, that Donovan was forced to abandon the whole affair when information had hardly started to come in. Treviranus went back to Canada.

This retreat galled a bit as it was then known to OSS that President Roosevelt himself was keeping his fellow Harvard graduate, Puzy Hanfstengel, on a Virginia farm near Washington with much the same sort of set-up. Hanfstengel was far more compromised than Treviranus, having been an ardent Nazi, a personal friend of Hitler, and openly anti-democratic for over a decade. *Le roi le veut !*

III–HAGEN PROJECT

It galled, too, since the same old State Department was crying 'Communist' at us out of the other side of its face because we wished to use Paul Hagen, ex-German labour leader, in a similar project on the left called *Project Freiheit*. If Hagen had been a fellow traveller, who hadn't in the Europe of the Popular Front? We were convinced he was no longer, if ever he had been, a Party member.

When Allen Dulles published his book, *Germany's Underground*, in 1947, I found that a large proportion of the conspirators against Hitler mentioned by him had been recommended, already in 1942, by us of *Special Activities*. We had been asked to prepare lists of 'reliable' or 'probably reliable' Germans for various desks in OSS. These lists were compiled through the Schwarz-Putlitz Project, the Treviranus-Keller Project, Paul Hagen's group, and through other contacts.

We were attacked for these lists from both sides: it was said they contained 'dangerous Communists', and, conversely, 'hopelessly reactionary generals and Junkers.' But Dulles' book points out that the only sizeable, serious attempt to overthrow Hitler and Nazism was the result of an alliance between extreme right and extreme left – with a few exceptions from the centre.

From incomplete notes and my memory I recognized the following names of conspirators against Hitler's life in July 1944 from Dulles' *Germany's Underground* as old friends of our recommended lists of 1942.

Count Klaus von Stauffenberg, who placed the actual bomb of

71

July 1944 under Hitler's conference table in the Fuehrer's East Prussian Headquarters.

Arthur Nebe, the conspirators' ear inside the Himmler organization.

Julius Leber, Social Democrat, was recommended by Treviranus, who stood politically far to Leber's right.

Colonel General Kurt von Hammerstein was recommended unanimously by all our Germans, especially by Schwarz.

Count Helmuth von Moltke, of the great aristocratic, military family, was the intellectual centre of the conspiracy. He was recommended by Putlitz, by 'Ellen' and by Dorothy Thompson.

Wilhelm Leuschner. I believe it was Hagen who recommended this labour leader.

Ulrich von Hassell, formerly Ambassador in Rome, was strongly vouched for by Schwarz and Putlitz.

Colonel General Ludwig Beck was a 'certain' recommendation of Keller and Treviranus.

General von Falkenhausen, Governor of Belgium and former military adviser to the Chinese Nationalists, was recommended by Putlitz against rather violent opposition.

Carl Friederich Goerdeler, of all our recommendations, was uniquely popular with the oss desks. He had visited America and had an international reputation for his anti-Nazism; he was neither Junker nor too left for the Washington palate.

Albrecht von Kessel of the Foreign Office, recommended by Putlitz and Schwarz.

Count Werner von der Schulenburg, the last German Ambassador to Russia, was recommended by Putlitz and Schwarz.

Hans von Dohnanyi. Treviranus had known him personally. We were considered quite mad for recommending a member of the inner circle of Admiral Canaris' *Abwehr*, the secret intelligence organization of the Wehrmacht. Little did they (or we) suspect that the legendary Admiral Canaris himself was aiding the conspiracy, as was his number two man, General Oster, and that both would give their lives for the anti-Nazi cause! – as would Dohnanyi himself.

Count Peter Yorck von Wartenburg was recommended by Putlitz and Treviranus. Yorck von Wartenburg was the scion of one of the greatest of all the aristocratic, military families of Germany.

Adam von Trott zu Solz, of the Foreign Office, was spoken of in absolute certain terms by Putlitz, Schwarz and a number of Trott's

friends and relatives in New York. He had visited America just
before the war and in a number of secret meetings had warned many
against Hitler. There was in OSS some fear he was secretly a
Communist.

Carlo Mierendorff and Adolf Reichwein were sponsored by
Hagen.

General Alexander Edler von Daniels had been a friend of
Treviranus who was sure of his fundamental anti-Nazism.

Otto Kiep was well known in America as an anti-Nazi – he had
been in the embassy and in the consulate general in New York.
Schwarz and Putlitz sponsored him on our lists.

Our lists totalled nearly two hundred names of politicians,
generals, labour leaders, aristocrats and diplomats. Nineteen, or
nearly ten per cent, of them turned up as important cogs in the
one big and almost successful anti-Nazi putsch during the war
years. Perhaps our lists may have contained some dangerous
mistakes, but Allen Dulles' book proves them, as a whole, to have
been extraordinary.

IV–BULGARIAN PEASANT PROJECT

Out of the residue of my Imro and Agrarian contacts in Bulgaria
for the British, we designed a project to be run from Istanbul.
This project was fiercely attacked by the diplomatic ladies as
'Communist' and dangerous. It is a sad commentary on their
judgment that all the leaders I advised using – except three – are
dead, some executed by the Nazis, others by the Communists.

V–PROJECT BRENNER PASS

One day Big Bill's office called to say they were sending me someone
who had a gadget which might interest us for the skulduggery of
Special Activities.

A man came in with an induction microphone no bigger than a
jacket button attached to a long hair-fine wire with a tiny ear-
phone no bigger than a bean, on the other end. When we pressed
this little gadget against a wall we could hear the conversation in

the next room through a hundred yards of the almost invisible wire. Put within an inch or two of a phone line, we heard, by induction, the conversation being carried over the wire without tapping it – right through the insulation.

I ordered several for experimental purposes – (*Special Activities* had not yet given birth to a technical laboratory for gadgets of all sorts) – and fell to talking with my visitor. He wondered if we had any use for a clever short-wave communications engineer who couldn't get into the army because he was an enemy alien – a Hungarian.

'He's my new son-in-law and he's a wizard at short-wave work. Why, he installed all those difficult communications where wires wouldn't stand the snow in the railway system over the Brenner Pass.'

Now *Brenner Pass* was a phrase to excite any intelligence worker in 1942. Over the high passes of the Brenner, between Austria and Italy, ran one of the Axis' most vital communications arteries.

'He knows the Brenner?' I asked, trying to hide my interest.

'Knows it? He lived on it for four years. He knows every stone, every snow-bank. Why, he has a whole trunk out in Chicago jammed with blueprints and photographs....'

'What's his phone number in Chicago?' I asked, unable longer to hide my excitement.

The next morning Charles Mero and his trunk arrived in New York by air and I was there to meet him.

For security reasons we had to set up a special office for Mero's *Project Brenner*. He, with a commercial artist and a secretary, set to work. The result: two fat volumes with views of the Brenner installations taken from every nearby mountain peak, floor plans of the power stations and transformer stations.

We discovered that the rails of the Brenner were too light for steam locomotives and, because of the poverty of Italy and Austria at the time of the building, were intended only for electric engines. Moreover, the power system was hooked up only in series and not in parallel. Any power break in the line paralyzed the whole system. The two volumes, illustrated elaborately with photographs, blue prints and commercial art work, were presented to Air Corps Intelligence.

We introduced Mero to Major Carl Lohman, head of oss communications. Soon he turned up in 'Q' in an army uniform. In ninety days he was a citizen. Nearly two years later, in Africa, I ran into Colonel Mero of the American Army and OSS. He was chief of all our clandestine communications, controlling hundreds of secret radios in occupied Europe.

VI-THE LIBRARY PROJECT

During the first World War, Colonel House had a strong sense of the historic importance of his missions and collected every scrap of paper he could make away with, published or private, which he thought would interest historians of a future generation. These papers he gave to the Yale University Library, and they proved to be rich material. Already early in 1942, Yale was writing to her *alumni* in government asking them to keep in mind the Yale collection of war papers for World War II.

Certain 'fugitive' documents must be collected at the moment – newspapers, pamphlets, letters, etc. It would serve the purpose of the library to have trained historians placed in the neutral countries bordering on the Axis. It would serve equally the purpose of OSS to have available such excellent 'covers' for agents in these very countries. Trained research historians make excellent intelligence collectors and evaluators.

Putting the two needs together gave birth to the *Library Project*. The government – OSS – would not appear in the picture at all. We would find an anonymous donor to finance the Yale Library in sending these historians, and OSS would reimburse his donations.

The anonymous donor had to be a real person, because we did not feel we could take a certain high official of the university into our confidence. This official had been a pillar and a bitter-ender of the *America First* organization, which had so dangerously played Hitler's game in America before Pearl Harbour.

The contact with Yale was made through Wallace Notestein, professor of history, and a natural conspirator. Only he, Thomas Mendenhall, curator of the war collection, and Norman Holmes Pearson (who later did an outstanding job as liaison with Britain's most hush-hush counter-intelligence) were in the secret.

The young historians, who were trained by OSS, did both of their jobs splendidly, as spies and as scholars.

VII–PROJECT COUNTERFEITERS

Japanese money was made with a special reed. We were told this by experts whom we consulted about making German and Italian Bonds to sell in pro-Axis but technically neutral markets. The State Department stepped with both feet on our idea – 'ungentlemanly warfare', which, incidentally, might undermine the savings of their international pals, 'the good old tried and true governing class'.

But we, at least, learned that Japanese money was made with the special reed. And then happened one of those God-sent coincidences: a lampshade made of these reeds was discovered in someone's house. Traced, it proved to have come from a chain store.

The careful management of the chain stores in the face of the Japanese boycott before Pearl Harbour had put some hundreds of thousands of these shades in storage. Would they sell them to the government? No, they would donate them.

How the money was made and distributed, the extraordinary security measures taken to maintain secrecy of the technical details of a really perfect counterfeit job are better not related – but it did cause the Japanese serious trouble.

VIII–SHIP'S OBSERVERS PROJECTS

Ship's Observers Projects were a technique taught us by the English – always our betters in this field. A listening-post is set up in a port – Lisbon, Buenos Aires, or Seattle. The ships of a neutral country are carefully watched and the sailors tailed when they take shore leave. One or two sailors are discovered to have cousins, uncles, or sweethearts in the city. Upon investigation it is easily found out whether the sailor's contact is 'friend' or 'enemy'. If 'friend', an agent of the post seeks his acquaintance; this agent should be of the same national origin as the sailor to be approached.

On the ship's next trip, if all goes well, the agent is already a member of the circle of the sailor's friends. He has discovered if the sailor is or is not likely to be willing by conviction to work for our cause – or merely anxious to earn some money. The sailor is then recruited and given a little training and his instructions.

In Spanish and Portuguese ships we could often locate a 'friendly

element' through some exiled political group, especially the Basques.*
A few Basques are to be found on every Iberian ship. Exiled Nor-
wegians made our contacts for us on Swedish ships. Many of these
ships put into Axis ports – Bremen, Cuxhaven, Naples, Yokohama,
Trieste, Genoa – after leaving the ports where our posts were
located.

A trusted ship's observer is a valuable agent. In Axis ports he
could observe enemy vessels under repairs; content of cargoes and
their destination; bomb damage; civilian morale; and much other
solid information. In a case of emergency he could carry a message
or even a small object like a radio crystal. If he were a radioman,
or could manage to have some time alone in the radio cabin, he
could discover if the neutral skipper was giving Allied shipping
locations and weather reports to enemy submarines, raiders, or
naval stations.

Important was the definite proof that Spain was refuelling Axis
submarines with oil from our own wells; oil granted as appeasement
to Franco, and under his solemn promise not to allow a drop to fall
into enemy hands.

In the early summer of 1942, there was great excitement in 'Q'
and up at Donovan's office when the Seattle listening post for
Russian ships (Russia was still a neutral in the Pacific war) reported
that American machine-tools, loaded as supposedly lease-lend for
Russia, were being delivered in Jap ports, apparently to make
airplanes and tanks to be used against American soldiers. We

* The Basques were loyal to the Spanish Republic because they had been
given local autonomy by that Republic and because they, rich and poor,
left and right, were anti-fascists. We were fortunate to have in America
Dr Aguirre, President of the Basque Republic, and Manuel de la Sota,
wealthy young Basque shipowner, both refugees from Franco's régime.

When we wished to send Dr Aguirre to South America to help organize
the Basque Ships Observers' Scheme, he was refused exit papers by
Secretary of State Hull. Finally, we had to develop a cover to fool our
own State Department, and Aguirre, a professor of Columbia University,
was invited by South American friends of ours to make a series of lectures.
Hull had to give in to a request from 'our good neighbours' which he
had denied oss. The trip proceeded and President Aguirre did a splendid
job which produced valuable results.

Over fifty of de la Sota's ships served the Allied shipping-pool during
the war, having escaped from Spain.

were ordered on 'highest authority': *drop the subject*; *make no record of it*. When it seemed this might cause a small OSS mutiny, we were finally given an explanation. The Japs were exchanging rubber, real, crude Malaya rubber, in return. Without rubber the Russian armies could not fight on. Our supply experts felt that rubber was more important to us in the Battle of Europe than the machine tools were in the Battle of the Pacific.

IX–PREFABRICATED COVERS PROJECT

When the necessity arose for a given desk in OSS to deploy an agent or a team in a neutral country, it was sometimes seriously delayed by having to find proper cover for the personnel. Good cover cannot be faked – it must be some job or occupation for which a real necessity exists; and the agent must be capable of legitimately discharging the duties of his cover job. It occurred to Bob Ullman of the counter-intelligence department that covers could be created, collected, classified, and stored.

So he began visiting various news agencies, publications, exporting industries, scientific research organizations, banks, shipping and fishing companies, and a long list of others who had reason to send or maintain personnel abroad. He went always to the number-one man since such a decision – to pad personnel with our agents – would have eventually to be referred to him for approval. In this way the security risk was limited to a single person – the head of the business. With something approaching unanimity, all agreed to expand their overseas activities with our men, and many offered, for security reasons, to carry them on their own payroll.

Ullman salted away covers which ran from African coastal fishing fleets to news correspondents, sales managers, and mining prospectors. Geographically they covered five continents and dozens of countries.

X–PROJECT PICK-LOCKS

The British were tops in getting through locks and inside letters and official envelopes without leaving a trace. Our people going overseas should at least know how to open the normal tumbler of a Yale-type lock without a key, and a few similar, if simple, tricks involving the use of only tiny gadgets, easily masked in a pen-knife, pen or a pencil.

Sidney E. Clark, amateur cook and Bach organist, set about establishing, with the help of his wife, a Fagin's den on Central Park West in New York. He turned out, with the aid of the British, *Special Activities*, and the New York Police, some magnificent little gadgets – and his 'students', along with love, laughed at locksmiths. To this den all desks could send their personnel for a few lessons before going overseas.

A medical sergeant was stationed at Sid's School-for-Pick-Locks to give his students going overseas their final immunity injections. When I visited the school one day I saw an eminent member of the New York Stock Exchange and the Racquet Club with his pants down around his ankles, working hard on a Yale lock while the sergeant was injecting his bare bottom with typhoid, para-typhoid, tetanus, typhus, and assorted bugs.

XI–THE RED GENERAL PROJECT

General Alexander Barmine was a deputy-chief-of-staff to Tuka-chevsky at the time of the great Communist purge of 1936. At thirty he was one of the youngest Russians ever to become a general and had commanded manoeuvres in Siberia. He was on a diplomatic mission in Greece when he heard that his chief was arrested, charged with treason, and being prepared to confess. Barmine did not return to Russia.

It occurred to me that oss needed someone off on the sidelines to interpret the strange military and diplomatic behaviour patterns of our Russian ally, who was keeping Britain and America as definitely outside the veil of her security as she did her Axis enemies. Barmine gave unusually cold and unbiased information on Soviet personalities. He was worth his salt alone for his detailed knowledge of Siberia as a possible scene of operations against Japan – which was then not excluded by military planners. The Soviet government would give us no information of value to a planning staff.

In the late summer of 1942, there came into my hands the famous Mao manual of partisan warfare in its Russian translation. This was compiled in the early thirties by the Communist partisans in China, and had become the bible of Communists everywhere on the subject. The purely Communist outfits operating in Spain had used it; it was used as the authoritative text-book in the military section of The Leadership Schools in Moscow. Copies of the manual were numbered and jealously guarded by those who were allowed to study it.

This translation was one of the first important jobs we asked General Barmine to undertake. I remember the expression of surprise on his face when he saw we had one of the revolutionary technique texts from the Moscow Leadership Schools.

Since the way we obtained this book may still be open, it is another story which had better remain untold.

XII–PROJECT IGNATIUS

The Jesuits have the reputation with non-catholic historians of being His Holiness's Loyal Opposition in the church hierarchy. During the war the general of the Jesuits was a Pole, and the German invasion of his homeland stirred in him a fierce hatred of Germany.

Under the Concordat which Mussolini made with the Vatican, that tiny state has full diplomatic privileges as an independent country. The Vatican diplomatic bags (often freight cars) come from all parts of the world to Vatican City without fear of search or seizure.

Father 'X' was brought to us by friendly South Americans. He wished to state that he would be willing to help us 'in any way agreeable with my conscience'.

'How anti-Axis *is* your conscience, Father?'

'Very,' he replied dryly.

I expressed doubts about the political position of the Vatican as a worldly state, as distinguished from the Catholic Church as a religious institution.

'There are loyal Germans in high church positions. It is riddled with pro-Fascist Italians. How can we possibly make use of your offer with any sense of security whatsoever? Why, only four years ago I saw a pastoral letter of Cardinal Innizer to his flock signed, instead of 'yours in Christ' or whatever is usual, with the startling salutation "Heil Hitler, Innizer".'

'The Church gives separate secrecy to the communications and the pouch material of the Jesuits.'

So *Project Ignatius* was written up for presentation to Donovan's office. Father 'X's' offer was only used once, provisionally, while awaiting Donovan's approval – and it worked – the delivery to Rome of a small package disguised as a book.

But Bill Donovan refused the 'O.K. – W.J.D.' I have heard him accused of having rejected it because he is a Catholic. I do not believe that. I believe he and his advisers felt that such a project, should it become known to the enemy, would rebound propaganda-wise to our great discomfort: 'Allies use religious immunity to make war'.... It was a bit like going into battle behind a screen of priests.

Donovan was always rigidly opposed to using the Red Cross or its personnel in any way whatsoever for intelligence purposes, I think with a good deal of justice. The refusal to use a church is really a logical extension of the same thinking. Now, looking back over a period of ten years, Donovan's vetos were wise in almost every case.

XIII–PROJECT 'I CASH CLOTHES'

Our British allies had warned us early in the game of the great danger which lay in overlooking details in preparing a mission to enter enemy territory. Among the most serious and dangerous of these details were the equipment, clothes, baggage, tobacco, everything carried along by a mission.

The British always illustrated this by the story of an agent they had lost in France because the corners of his pockets were full of golden-yellow, Virginia tobacco. They told of another who took with him some arch supporters in his shoes, which had been made in England just before he left and were obviously new.

We needed European suits, overcoats, shirts, ties, socks, shoes, underclothes, handkerchiefs, hats, watches (not made for the American markets), shoe laces, gloves, glasses, penknives, pocket-books, insignia for buttonholes, keyrings, keys, pens, pencils, suitcases, and every possible piece of clothing or pocket gadget which a European might carry. These we needed for all the countries from Norway to Greece and from Spain to Finland.

Project I Cash Clothes was to meet this need. Women's organiza-tions, refugee-aid organizations, charitable organizations, had to be canvassed. Europeans who were not destitute were asked to contribute what they could of their wardrobe and gadgets. Americans who had bought things in Europe before the war were encouraged to give them to us. The project subdivided in dozens of small ones. Each of us wrote to his friends around the country asking them to make such collections and to write to others to do the same. Since no true explanation could be given, the false explanation was that for propaganda purposes we wished to parachute clothes to Europe's needy but did not want to send American things which might get the recipients in bad with the Nazi and Fascist police.

About this time we received a request for old European luggage, especially small handbags, to build into them the almost miraculous little X10, long-distance, short-wave radio, developed by OSS. The first X10's had come through in chic little handbags which looked as if they housed a thousand dollars' worth of Fifth Avenue crystal and silver toilet articles. Where our old, small, European bags came from in such numbers, God only knows. We had many hundreds.

Before long the express-collect packages began to swamp us. Fortunately, we had asked the collectors to instruct the donors to attach to each piece a tag giving the country of origin. The stuff had to be classified, cleaned, assorted, sized, catalogued, and stored. 'Clothes – France', 'Gadgets – Germany,' 'Handbags – Italy.'

*   *   *

These projects, activities, were neither the greatest nor the smallest that occupied me at *Special Activities*. Certain of them, as usable today as ten years ago, are left untold.

Special Activities itself created two other desks, the *Labour Desk*, spoken of before, and X2, as counter-intelligence was called. Our activities cut across every nationality desk – we had projects involving Sweden, Germany, Holland, Poland, Russia, Persia, India, Italy, Bulgaria, Yugoslavia, Spain, Central Africa, South America, Switzerland, Finland, France, North Africa, Syria, Ireland, Turkey, Palestine, Greece, Tibet, Burma, Japan, Norway, Malaya, the Congo, Chad, Britain, and the U.S.A.

We even tried a *Project Penetrate MacArthur* in an effort to get OSS admitted to his theatre, which he had expressly forbidden. We did get one OSS naval officer to the Philippines. To do that required a fantastically complicated conspiracy with Naval Intelligence officers on MacArthur's staff. Our man was captured – not by the enemy – by MacArthur and sent home!

We recruited not only for our own projects but for all the geographical desks. Many of them were jealous of our encroachment on their territories. Others, like Arthur Roseborough's French Desk and Ulius Amos' Greek Desk, welcomed our collaboration and our contribution in ideas, plans, and recruits.

But such a honeymoon could not last forever. Bruce was tired of tribal fighting in Washington and he wanted to fight Germans for a change, so he asked for and was promised the London Office of OSS. Allen Dulles was off to his great successes in Switzerland. I, too, wanted to go overseas. The African landings were maturing – it was already the first of November – and my secret camp of Spaniards in Virginia was ready for its 'graduation day'.*

Early in November the landings took place. A few days later Bill Donovan invited me to dinner at his house in Georgetown. He explained to me the dangers of Spain to the Allies in North African communications and supply. The lone, single-track railway and highway from the Atlantic ports of Morocco to Algeria and Tunisia ran within ten miles of the Spanish Moroccan frontier. Franco was openly declaring that Spain would defend Germany to the last Spaniard, that democracy was degenerate. His Blue Legion was fighting the Russians.

I suggested going immediately to North Africa with my group of Spaniards and trying to establish an OSS unit as an integral part of the G2 of an army in the field. This had as yet not been achieved anywhere. Donovan said 'Yes'.

It was clear now that the days of civilian control of OSS were numbered. Brigadier-generals and colonels and naval commanders, clubmen and bankers from New York, Boston and Philadelphia, began to appear in bulk. Great pressure was brought from above on us civilians to accept commissions, and this week's civilian was next week's major or colonel. Such stalwarts as Art Roseborough and Art Goldberg were fast-talked into uniforms. Carl Devoe sported a naval officer's blue and gold. Bruce was an officer now. Even Donovan became a general – and that may have been necessary – but it also made him subject to the whims of anyone who happened to have one more star on his shoulder.

* See Chapters Eight and Nine for this project and its outcome.

An example of how badly military procedure fits into the work we were doing, was the inspection of OSS made by Lt.-General McNarney, then Deputy Chief of Staff to General Marshal. A knock, with no warning, came on my door in 'Q'. The door opened and the parade started. First, Jimmy Murphy, the boss's secretary, to hold the door open – and then General McNarney, aides, aides' aides, and aides' aides' aides – brigadier-generals, chicken colonels, fig-leaf colonels, a bevy of rigid majors, and then Donovan and Bruce and all sorts and sundry others. Donovan introduced me. Everyone remained standing while General McNarney fitted a cigarette into a long, white ivory holder. An aide's aide's aide lighted it.

'Well, Mr Downes, what are you doing? What's your job? What is all this?' The cigarette swept the room like a teacher's blackboard pointer. It was just at the height of the embassy safe-cracking work. I turned to Donovan.

'Shall I tell him? There are lots of people here I don't know.'

Donovan, obviously embarrassed, replied, 'Of course, if the General wants to know.'

'I'd rather not... unless you insist, sir,' I aimed at McNarney.

'Speak up! This is an official inspection. Certainly, or I wouldn't have asked.' (That special frown soldiers have for civilians.)

'Well, sir, I am stealing codes from neutral embassies. I began with the...'

'Never mind. We'll skip it,' said McNarney, embarrassed.

Several coughs but nobody snickered.

Then McNarney to Donovan: ' Send him over to my office sometime. I'd like to hear the story' – but I was never sent, nor went. The parade filed out.

More people learned of the *Embassy Project* in that ill-advised inspection than we had included in the entire security coverage of the project's personnel, and within OSS itself not half a dozen people had been allowed to know of our work.

*   *   *

'Let's go out and see Lane and Louise tonight,' became a sort of refrain for those who did not like the new militarized and formalized set-up in OSS. Louise Rehm was an excellent cook and Lane a superb bartender. You could be sure that all the guests would be 'in security' – and you could blow off steam.

Lane Rehm, OSS Finance Officer, was recommended for his job by Averill Harriman and David Bruce. They recommended him because earlier in his life he had been called upon to handle large sums of money when what was needed was incorruptible integrity and a lasting contempt for money, and those who worship it.

Donovan was asking Congress for tens and hundreds of millions of dollars in unvouchered funds. Naturally, Congress, the Budget Director, and the White House asked, '*Who* will control the spending? Donovan can't watch every penny.'

The answer was Lane Rehm.

In the twenties, the Harrimans noticed a small, brilliant, shoe-string financial journal published by Lane Rehm. At their invitation he began a career in investment banking. But Lane Rehm wanted to be a painter. So in his forties he quit banking cold – having saved almost enough money to keep one of his Wall Street colleagues in whisky and golf balls.

He and his wife, Louise, bought a farm near Kent, Connecticut, and Lane, between chopping wood and shovelling snow, began to paint seriously. Big salaries couldn't lure him back.

But when he was called to Washington with the country at war, he willingly put aside his paints, his shovel and his axe. They finally got him into a colonel's uniform which was about as *à propos* as a woman's négligé on General Patton.

There was never a scandal with the hundreds of millions of dollars which passed through Lane Rehm's hands. A man in whom he and Donovan had confidence was never, to my knowledge, refused funds or badgered about his expenditure. But he was highly critical of that small minority of useless OSS colonels who sat in requisitioned villas in Cairo and Algiers and Caserta with little to do but drink and whore and decorate one another's breasts. He made it difficult for them to come by unvouchered funds.

Lane Rehm looks like Cotton Mather. He has hard, blue eyes, impossible to look into while telling a lie. A straight, closed mouth, with almost no lips. The stern face of a puritan until he smiles, and when he smiles he couldn't look less like a puritan – for he is gay, and jolly, and civilized – three most unpuritan vices.

*   *   *

It was nearly Christmas before my priority orders to fly to North

Africa came through, and for my Spanish group to follow by ship. I was to prepare the way for them and to find some sort of a niche in army organization tables to use such an unorthodox outfit.

I was not going too soon. George Bowden saw the end of the usefulness of *Special Activities* in the militarization of OSS. It had served its purpose – and might have continued to do so under civilian control of intelligence activities, as the British, the world's best intelligence operators, have always insisted upon. Spying is essentially an unmilitary activity; from the top brass's point of view it just isn't a respectable occupation for 'an officer and a gentleman'.

In OSS, so long as Donovan, Dulles, Bruce, Bowder, Rehm and Goldberg were on my side, I feared no one. But with Bruce in London, Dulles gone to Switzerland, Bowden resigned, Rehm and Goldberg usually away in the theatres, and Donovan himself often absent for weeks, the banker-diplomat-colonel New Order would have made mincemeat of me.

I got away just in time.

*　　*　　*

Probably I had not seen clearly the forest of the huge and successful organization Donovan had built for the trees of our *Special Activities*. Amateurs, we lacked the knowledge of the limits of our own capacity – and the knowledge of how little the lumbering inefficiencies, conservatisms, and jealousies of democratic government will allow individuals or groups to do, especially if their activities be outside the normal orbit of accepted respectable procedures.

But for a group of enthusiastic amateurs, there was a good, solid core of accomplishment; nor were we ashamed of our unsuccessful attempts – some the result of our very enthusiasm and amateurism, some the result of the actual conditions under which we had worked in Washington.

CHAPTER SEVEN

J. EDGAR HOOVER MAKES WAR

'Quis custodiet ipsos custodess'

1942 TO 1943

In January 1942, soon after my transfer from British Intelligence to the new OSS organization, I was called down to Washington to see 'K'. While I was entertained without restraint in the homes of Donovan, David Bruce, and the leaders of the new secret intelligence, they were, at first, wary about having me in their offices.

I understood this well enough since my work for British intelligence had put the FBI on my tail and the no-man's-land between the FBI and OSS was dangerous territory, the more so in my case as I had worked for the British in those pre-Pearl Harbour days when J. Edgar Hoover and his boys had done everything possible to obstruct and embarrass British intelligence in the United States.

This seemed particularly silly in the light of the fact that the President, the Army and the Navy had broken all sorts of laws in rushing aid to England after the fall of France. We were ready to help the English in all other ways in their lone stand against Nazism, but we were unwilling to help their intelligence service operate in America.

When I called at 'Q' Building to see 'K', then Donovan's chief assistant, he came quickly to the point.

'We want, and the request is from the highest possible military level, the codes and the cyphers of four neutral embassies here in Washington, Alphonia,* Betonia,* and Gammonia,* and Vichy France.

'We have reason to believe they are handling information for the enemy. We want to be able to read their cables.

'You will be given a completely free hand, technical advice and aid from the British, and whatever sums of money are needed subject to our approval, that is Allen Dulles and mine.

---

* These were three neutral countries who were playing the game on both sides so as to be sure to be in good with the winners of the war.

'You can count on us for all help and aid possible, *unless you are caught.* Then, we agree, we have never heard of you.

'You may recruit such persons as you may need but you cannot tell them for whom you are working. They must understand that if they are caught you have never heard of them.'

And so it began.

Vichy France was a pushover. Outside the ambassador, M. Henri-Haye – convinced follower of the Axis and of senile Marshal Petain – and his commercial attaché, practically the whole embassy personnel, diplomats, janitors and secretaries, were working for some agency of the American or British Government – and without pay (so far as I know). There was one exception, a certain Madame du Clos, who not only wanted money but love as well, and love not only for herself but for her daughter. The amount of money she wanted was relatively modest. The same cannot be said for the amorous payments which finally occupied a good deal of the time of two of my assistants and the son of an official of British Intelligence in the United States!

To my knowledge, FBI, G2, ONI, Economic Warfare, OWI, British Intelligence, the State Department, and other desks of OSS all had informants in the embassy.

My take was copies of the commercial attaché's mail and cables before they were sent or coded. These were important because, at this moment, 1942, we were negotiating to send economic aid to North Africa, provided the French guaranteed not to let the Germans have raw materials of North African origin. Vichy was double-crossing us. These papers Madame du Clos brought out by the simple method of hiding extra copies in her extensive and well-known bosom and either delivering them to our cut-out (go-between) or mailing them if they didn't seem so important.

After the War Department agreed to send the son of the negro janitor to Officer's Training School, that shrewd old darky's patriotism bloomed out and we had, through him and various secretaries, everything set up to open the safes and photograph the military, naval, and diplomatic codes. But we called it off when we discovered that the various attachés concerned were already voluntarily donating these codes to other government agencies.

Alphonia wasn't so easy. Nor Betonia. With Gammonia OSS never succeeded.

The Alphans speak one of the languages taught widely in our

colleges and universities, and their female secretaries for the most part lived in two boarding houses off Connecticut Avenue. On these two facts we based our attack.

It occurred to me that an office, like nature, abhors a vacuum. That if we should lure away a secretary, the Embassy would have to hire another in her place. I sent a most formidable colleague, one who looks like a Morgan partner, to see the heads of two of our best known women's colleges. Yes, they had capable teachers of the language spoken in Alphonia. If the government needed them for the duration of the war would the college be disposed to grant them a leave of absence? Yes, the college would.

The question was, would any of them know typing and shorthand? Mrs G... did. In fact she had married an Alphan and had lived in that country. She was of Alphan ancestry.

Mrs G... was exactly the right type. Young, about thirty-five, efficient, neat, she felt the war strongly and was possessed of a spirit of adventure. She was soon installed in the boarding house off Connecticut Avenue. She had, she said, come to Washington to find a fat wartime job with a fat salary. She soon became friendly with the girls from the Alphan Embassy.

For two months Mrs G... reported on these girls, every like and dislike, characteristic, peculiarity. We checked and rechecked against reports of other informants, and finally knew these girls better than they knew themselves.

Now the vacuum had to be created in the Embassy office. A large corporation which does an international business and which has foreign language secretaries was approached through its president.

Would he be willing to employ a girl to take dictation and type in the language of Alphonia? It would greatly help the war effort. . . . Yes, he would be proud to, but he would prefer to undertake the salary than have the government pay.

It was arranged that an advertisement describing the young secretary of Alphan descent whom we wished to remove from the embassy in order to put in Mrs G..., be inserted in *The New York Times* the following Sunday.

After breakfast on Sunday Mrs G... invited four girls from the Alphan Embassy to her room for more coffee and some cake sent from home. The girls were reading the movie and style sections when Mrs G... idly picked up the advertising section: *Help wanted.*

'Why, Ella, this is a perfect description of you:—

'Capable efficient young single woman capable of becoming executive preferring career to marriage wanted by big corporation as secretary. Must speak, read, write, take dictation in Alphan and in English. Some French desired. Willing to travel. Salary to begin $400 a month. Rapid advancement probable to right young woman. Apply N. Y. Times 374508 X!'

Ella was thirty, ambitious, efficient, capable, didn't want to marry. She spoke a little French; her Alphan was letter perfect; her dictation excellent; and her weakness, travel.

So Ella went to the president of the big corporation and $400 a month and in gratitude she recommended her 'old friend Mrs G...' to the Alphan Embassy, which was delighted to find such a cultured woman, so loyal to her Alphan blood, so quick and efficient.

Oddly enough, before two weeks were out, Ella took a friend from the Embassy into another job in the big corporation and Mrs G... brought a friend of hers (supplied by us) into the Alphan Embassy!

The Betonians took the same sort of bait.

'Sidney Black' and his wife 'Sarah', rich Philadelphians who had always lived in Paris, where as a hobby they had built up a prosperous business, were in America, fugitives from occupied France. Both were excellent amateur photographers, especially of movies. In need of a deputy to act as cut-out or contact man and general manager of these safe-cracker activities in Washington, I approached the Blacks. They accepted.

The Blacks' cover was that they wished to make, to give to museums, colour films of folk-dances and folk-costume in a number of countries, including Alphonia, Betonia, and Gammonia. It would take some time to plan these expeditions, a year perhaps. In the meantime they were in Washington to work out the details with the embassies concerned. They had a fancy suite at the Wardman Park and entertained embassy personnel of high rank lavishly. Needless to say the Alphans, Betans, and Gammans led all the rest in regularity of entertainment.

The Blacks were soon guests in these embassies. We thus had a first-hand check on reports from lesser informants: janitors, secretaries, male clerks. Besides, it was comfortable and convenient to know that while Attaché X was having his safe searched, his codes photographed or his files copied, he was safely with the Blacks in their suite at the Wardman Park. And, too, if one of them should take it into his head to leave early, the Blacks could telephone directly to his office and give us warning to get out.

From sources inside and out, we soon discovered that the Alphan coding machine was nearly fool-proof. We would need an expert mechanic, photographer, and improviser to copy its functional insides without leaving a trace of our having touched it.

Jimmy was our answer. Jimmy was a young Greenwich villager, employed by an advertising agency. He had the trimmings of the advertising agency set: gin, late hours, a flossy wife. But Jimmy had a gadget brain, a passion for photography, and the soul of a tinker. He could improvise anything out of two hairpins, a tin can, and a pair of pliers.

But we still had to get into the big Alphan safe, which held the coding machine. Mrs G... knew from observation that the combination on the big dial was impossible to read with an Alphan body (the Attaché's) crouched before its tiny numbers as he twirled rapidly.

In earlier activities I had got to know Major 'Fuse', formerly head of the New York Police Bomb Squad and now of Army Counter-Intelligence, working on dangerous political groups in New York City. To him I went for advice.

'Simple,' he said, 'you want Sadie Cohen. Let's go.'

On the way down to Sadie Cohen's shop on West Broadway under the 'el' the major explained.

'Sadie is a safe cracker and his front is a shop where he sells second-hand safes and locks. Sadie's spent a lot of time in Sing-Sing but we always spring him early and hold back an indictment or two over his head so he works for us. When we wanted the Bund's files it was Sadie opened the safe for us. The Japanese Consulate, the same. There's nothing Sadie can't open!'

Sadie Cohen's long narrow shop looked more like a junk heap. Half-way back was a little office partitioned off from the rest by glass, broken, patched, and rebroken.

Sadie sat at his ancient roll-top desk filing a key. He was a little pot-bellied Jew with curly gray hair on which his battered derby sat like a chicken on its nest.

The Major introduced us.

'Val, lootenant,' he said to the Major, 'how's bombs? Vat can I do for you?'

I told him I was from the government, that for the war effort it was necessary to open a certain safe in Washington. Would he do it and how much did he want to be paid.

'Paid!' he screamed. 'Paid. You've come into my place to insult me. Don't I have two nephews in the army? Ain't I an American as much as you? Aren't you ashamed? Pay me? You can't even tank me. Even a ticket to Vashington you can't buy me, or a Coca Cola.'

'Well, thanks,' I said. 'I didn't meant to insult you. I am paid. Why shouldn't you be?'

'No. But git on and tell me vat you vant.'

Sadie listened, like a doctor in consultation, and took notes on the back of an envelope. He recapitulated:

'Two dials, key door inside, Vilton Safe Company – dat is a model of 1925. Vell, you go to Vashington and buy a hard rubber or leather hammer like dey use to beat gold leaf. Tell your sakretary girl to go early to vork one day vit dat hammer in her voman's national bank, her bosom. Tell her to hit dat little dial a smash-banger vit all her might. It von't make no noise.

'Ven de boss comes, dat goddamit safe von't open. De boss vill telephone to the Vashington agency of Vilton Safe Company and de Vilton Safe Company vill send me, G. B. Cohen, to repair it – dat is if you ask 'em to. Having repaired it, I vill know the combinations and vile I am doing it I vill also break de lock on the inside key door and repairing it, I vill see vat dat key is like and ve vill also have a key.

'Dat night ven you vant to borrow from dat safe, I vill come also to Vashington to be handy if something don't go vell.'

So it was arranged.

In our flat near the Alphan Embassy the weird machines invented by Jimmy were set-up in the living room – wooden wheels with gears for winding coding tape past the lens of a movie camera; an enlarger made into a camera for photographing the pages of a book, or files; an elaborate infra-red outfit just in case the security-wise Alphans had made this tape light-sensitive. Another room was a dark-room, fully equipped to develop and print in a great hurry.

About a week later all was ready. We had supplied the hammer and Mrs G... had followed Sadie Cohen's instructions. The call had come to the Wilton Safe Company at ten o'clock and Sadie had been standing by with his tools.

That same night we had both combinations and a key to the inner door.

N-night was set for a few days later – to coincide with a party of the Blacks' at a road house in Maryland where the Alphans concerned would be occupied until late. H-Hour was for 22.30 hours.

At 10 o'clock we received the all-clear telephone call from our agent the janitor.

'Bob' and 'Dick', my two assistants of Alphan ancestry, and Sadie Cohen left for the big job. I sat by the telephone. Jimmy and his assistant gave loving last adjustments to their machinery.

Getting the incoming and outcoming mail from the janitor, opening it by the British quick-freeze method, photographing it and returning it had been easy enough. It had involved a minimum of risk for everybody except the janitor, who had no idea who had given 'Bob' the money to pay-off his gambling debts and settle a paternity case before his wife knew of it.

But entering a foreign embassy clandestinely and 'borrowing' code books and coding machinery was full of risk for everyone concerned. Donovan, 'K', Allen Dulles, were justly nervous. True, the joint chiefs of staff, through their intelligence liaison, had requested the information – the codes. But if we failed, if someone was caught inside the embassy and talked, an international incident of great moment would result.

While Americans were dying overseas, the calculated risk of our thievery did not seem too great. We had taken all imaginable precautions – that is all except one – the possibility of betrayal by someone high enough in the American Government to know what we were doing. Of my own immediate team I was as sure as I was of myself.

The Presidential Directive on Intelligence gave all counter-intelligence in the Western Hemisphere to the Federal Bureau of Investigation; oss was limited to neutral countries outside the Western Hemisphere and to enemy and enemy-occupied countries. These arbitrary geographical limitations were impossible to enforce. Any organization of a secret intelligence nature must be allowed to conduct counter-espionage everywhere to protect its own security.

The FBI, for example, if it is to protect America from sabotage, must be allowed to follow its investigations, no matter to what part of the globe they may lead. It must be allowed to penetrate, with its agents, enemy sabotage and espionage schools to be forewarned. A mere watchman service is not sufficient.

But even under the Presidential Directive, an embassy is foreign and not American soil. OSS had technical grounds on which to proceed.

But apparently Edgar Hoover was out for Donovan's scalp and any type of co-operation was pretty well one-sided. Not only OSS, but the British Secret Intelligence, many of whose investigations were bound to lead to America, were constantly being hounded by the FBI.

'Bob' and 'Dick' had both told me that they thought their apartment in Washington had been searched and they were certain that on several occasions they had been followed. I assured them it was only the FBI checking on strangely behaving individuals in Washington.

A friend of ours in the Department of Justice had warned us that Edgar Hoover believed we were 'penetrating' embassies and that he was annoyed.

All these fears and worries raced round my head as I waited for the three thieves to come back with the loot. We figured that if we had the goods by 11.15, they could be photographed and returned by 1.45 – if all Jimmy's machinery performed.

At exactly 11.15 a key turned in the lock and Bob, Dick and Sadie carried in four big suitcases.

Months of peeking, of sketches, of descriptions, of deductions would now have their test. Our luck was almost too good to believe. The machine was precisely what we had deduced it to be. All of Jimmy's machinery worked. By 1.10 we had taken three thousand four hundred and some odd photographs. For at least a month, until the roll was changed on the Alphan machine, we could decipher their telegrams.

But this dangerous, nerve-racking business would have to be gone through every time the Alphans put in a new roll.

We finished developing and printing just as a hot June dawn broke over Washington. I stuffed the results of so much work and planning and money into an old suitcase and caught the pre-breakfast plane to New York. When Allen Dulles arrived I had the stuff exhibited around his office.

He was delighted but, I think, surprised and a little shocked that we had pulled it off. I could hardly believe it myself.

When next month the Alphans put a new roll on their code machine, we went about our preparations as if we had done it a hundred times – again success.

All went easily until the fourth month.

At 11 o'clock the phone rang. It was 'Dick'.

'We had to get out. We had just got in and were preparing to open the safe when two FBI squad cars pulled up outside the building and turned on their sirens. It awoke everybody. All the lights . . ."

'Tell me later. If you are sure you're not being followed come here immediately.'

In five minutes they came in. They had seen a car following them and had stopped to check on it, but recognizing the FBI car which had often followed them before, they had gone on, parked two blocks from the embassy and walked to the janitor's door. The janitor had just given them their suitcases and they were actually in front of the safe beginning to open it when the sirens had been turned on. 'No one saw us. We scrammed.'

'OK and thanks. Go home and if you are picked up by the FBI refuse to talk. If I don't hear from you by ten o'clock I'll know they have taken you in.'

I called 'K' at his home in Georgetown. He couldn't believe me and told me to come right out there. Together we called Donovan at his home. I don't believe any single event in his career ever enraged him more.

The next morning Donovan went to the White House to protest.

On that level the case was clearly over my head and out of hands. Donovan was in-fighting with the man of whom I had often heard it said in Washington that no President dare discipline him, let alone dismiss him.

Bill Donovan's new OSS was at the moment fighting for existence. On the one hand Army and Navy, with their idea that strategic intelligence is gossip picked up by military and naval attachés at cocktail parties or through handouts of information from the Governments to which they are accredited, distrusted OSS. On the other hand, the FBI, with its police mentality, was jealous. While we were organizing our projects, there was always the danger of the knife in the back from the FBI. Naturally our headquarters was in the United States, a part of Edgar Hoover's private hemisphere, and by necessity most of our recruiting was done in America.

All over the middle Atlantic states and in the far west our volunteers were trained in secret camps. From these camps, by ones or twos, or in small groups, they were sent by parachute, submarine, or infiltration of combat lines into enemy or enemy-occupied territory. Usually they were equipped with radio which allowed them to speed their information to the nearest OSS radio base station.

To prepare these volunteers with false documents of the latest issue – identity cards, food coupon books, travel permits, military service and compulsory work exemption cards – to clothe them entirely in garments made in that part of the world to which they were being sent; to equip them with money, codes, safe contacts – all this was a tedious and long job requiring months of work for many people, just to equip and launch one espionage team. Most of these agents carried suicide pills, and on capture were pleased to take them and die. They lived the life of rats. But few squealed, and those under conditions of torture and drugging which makes it impossible to blame them.

I can tell you, for instance, what Colonel Rauf, Chief of the Gestapo in Milan, devised as two tortures which gave him excellent results in confessions.

One was to have police dogs especially trained, on command, to bite the prisoner in the genitals. The prisoner was stripped and handcuffed behind his back and put in a room with neither furniture nor outside windows. Two of Rauf's dogs were introduced. At a window opening into the next room stood the colonel with the dog trainer – ready to order the animal off when the prisoner promised to talk.

A second method used by Rauf in the famous Hotel Regina in Milan was to handcuff the prisoner's hands over a bar at a height barely allowing his feet to touch the floor. A stick about the size of a broomstick was then inserted in the rectum to a distance of six or eight inches. On this the guards then beat with shorter sticks until the prisoner agreed to talk.

People about to undertake these risks, and those who were preparing them for it, were constantly subject to FBI sniping. Baseless and indiscriminate charges of Communism and disloyalty were brought against them. Even the ships' observer's posts established in neutral Latin American ports were hounded and harassed as in violation of the FBI's sacred Western Hemisphere. The British suffered similar treatment.*

'Does J. Edgar think he's fighting on Bunker Hill against us

---

* See Robert Sherwood's *Roosevelt & Hopkins* for a contradiction of my statement.

Redcoats or has he really heard of Pearl Harbour?' a high official of British intelligence said to me in New York.

*   *   *

'Won't the President do anything about such near treason?' I asked after the sirens blew.

'No,' said the Political Adviser of OSS, 'he won't. No President dare touch John Edgar Hoover. Let alone congressmen. They are all scared pink of him. But we can use this to deal a little, to get some concessions....'

FBI 'concessions' I never heard about. But we 'conceded' the work in the embassies to them, and I was told a couple of weeks later to go to see a Mr Brown in FBI's Washington field office. One by one I turned over the projects and their personnel to him.

The personnel, almost to a man (and woman), came back later to protest. Instead of being treated as patriotic people making war for their country, Mr Hoover's Mr Brown treated them as so many stool-pigeons, as inferior people who had sunk to the depths of being police spies and informers – the classical cop attitude toward the underworld weakling whom they use to trap gangsters.

Nor was interference in our operations in the Western Hemisphere the only obstacle thrown in our paths by the FBI. They invaded, under one guise or another, the theatres of war outside the Western Hemisphere. For example: 'The Case of Charles Bedaux in North Africa.'

Two extremely clever operators for the French *Sécurité Militaire*, Guy and Jacques Calvet (born Cohen) had early in 1942 offered their services to Robert Murphy and the American Vice-Consuls preparing our November landing in North Africa. The Calvet brothers owned a woman's dress shop on rue Michelet in Algiers. It had a number of entrances, being on a flatiron corner. Also, from its cellars you could exit by either of two other shops, whose owners were in the *Sécurité Militaire* organization, as agents of the Calvets.

Here, Murphy and his organization had many meetings with General Mast, Colonel Jousse, commanding the Algiers garrison, and other officers whose co-operation made the actual landings so nearly bloodless. Here, too, Guy Calvet could inform the OSS-Murphy

97

organization just how much the Vichy counter-espionage, *Sécurité Militaire*, knew of our plans and contacts.

In the same store the royalist groups of 'Uncle Charley' d'Astier de la Vigerie made their contacts with our people. These contacts were to prove bitter and expensive to them; after the assassination of Darlan, they were thrown into concentration camps in the Sahara by order of the Giraud government. Murphy, for whose organization they had risked their lives before the landings, would do nothing to get them released.

It was to help this group that Arthur Roseborough, then head of the OSS French desk in Algiers, interceded with Murphy. He begged that they be released as they were American agents and had risked all for America. 'American honour', said Roseborough, 'is at stake'.

'Art, old fellow, if you have nothing better to do in Africa than to worry about those Jews and Communists who helped us, why don't you just go home?'

Jews and Communists indeed! With one exception they were Christians, and not one of them was a Communist. Some of them bore the names and titles of great and old French families. But what if they had been Jews and Communists? They had put in peril their lives, their families' lives, and their fortunes, that America might liberate France. We owed them a debt – and we still do.

To get back to the FBI, Charles Bedeaux and the Calvets. Bedeaux, an American, was widely known as the 'speed-up-king', in honour of a system he had devised for industrial plant management to get more work out of workers for less pay. Decent management and decent labour condemned the system as inhuman. It was finally adopted by Hitler's Germany and (under a different name – Stakanovism) by Russia.

Bedeaux was violently pro-Axis, for the simple reason that he thought they would win the war. He had acted as go-between for a number of French groups and the Nazis.

One of these groups was headed by Robert Murphy's friend Jacques Le Maigre-Dubreuil (whom Murphy later sponsored as Interior Minister in the Giraud Government in Algiers) and Jean Rigaud, a dope addict (who was later to be Giraud's Chief of Police); others were members of the *Comité des Forges* (the big French munitions corporation) and high officials of the *Banque d'Indochine, Banque Worms*, etc.

98

Bedeaux had the idea to lay a pipeline across the Sahara from Dakar to Oran to bring the plentiful and cheap vegetable oils (peanut, cocoanut, palm, etc.) from Vichy's West Africa to Hitler's fat-starved Europe, thus thwarting the Anglo-American blockade.

For these and other strategic services rendered, Mr Bedeaux carried special passes from the High Command of the Nazi Wehrmacht and went where he pleased in Axis-controlled Africa and Europe.

I know all these things because I have read the contents of Mr Bedeaux's files and his briefcase. They made Benedict Arnold look like Nathan Hale.

For Mr Bedeaux was unfortunate enough to be trapped by our landings in North Africa. More unfortunate still for him, Guy Calvet, as a member of the *Sécurité Militaire* of Vichy, knew of many of Mr Bedeaux's activities and, the same night as the landings, went to the trouble to have Mr Bedeaux's briefcase and files stolen.

No one could have welcomed his fellow countrymen with a greater show of patriotism than Mr Bedeaux. He stood innumerable Allied officers innumerable drinks in innumerable bars. Hadn't these fine fellows liberated him from the Huns and their Vichy pimps?

But sooner or later Calvet's reports were bound to reach Washington – they did, and Bedeaux's arrest was ordered. This the French had anticipated and Mr Bedeaux had already spent wearisome weeks in the Algiers jug. No one seemed interested in the prisoner. So I wrote a report. But as I found out later that all our reports of a 'political nature' were being submitted to Robert Murphy for approval, I doubt it ever left Africa.

I advised Guy to have the more incriminating documents from Bedeaux's file and briefcase photographed. 'That buzzard has a lot of influential friends. You'd better hide a couple of sets away to protect yourself when his friends swing into action.'

One day a month or so later, Guy came to see me – across North Africa, all the way to Morocco. 'The original Bedeaux documents have disappeared out of the *Sécurité Militaire* files! They are coming to see me on Friday, two men from the Federal Bureau of Investigation who are to take him back to Washington for trial. How will I explain the loss of the documents?'

As I was going back to Algiers for a meeting anyway, I returned with Guy by air. It was his idea that I should overhear Friday's interview in his shop. He put me in a fitting room and piled up all sorts of junk in front of me – fitting forms, empty boxes, a broken sewing machine, a few bolts of material. I sat on the floor under a table behind it all. The door was left half-open.

They finally came. I heard them present their credentials, heard Guy ask them to be seated. I did not take this conversation down – so the report of it which I give is not verbatim but its spirit and content are quite accurate. The conversation was in English.

1st Southern Accent: 'Mr Calvet, you are an agent of the French *Sécurité Militaire*, are you not?'

Guy: 'Yes, I am.'

1st S.A.: 'You were instrumental in the arrest of the American citizen Bedeaux.'

Guy: 'Yes, I was.'

1st S.A.: 'Did you take certain papers from his room at the hotel and deliver them to the French *Sécurité Militaire*?'

Guy: 'No. An operative of mine took the papers but it was I who delivered them to the SM. I thought it was the safest place to leave them. I have heard they are missing. But they were not in my care once I'd delivered them.'

2nd S.A.: 'We're not worried about the papers. We have them.'

1st S.A. interrupting: 'After all, he is an American, the papers are rightly ours. It is entirely our jurisdiction. The Provisional Government of General Giraud has no authority over Americans whatsoever.'

Guy: 'I know that, I know that. We were holding him for your Government.' (I could hear the relief in Guy's voice.)

2nd S.A.: 'What we are worried about is that we were informed at SM offices that you had these documents photostated and the copies are not there. Do you have these photostats?'

Guy (who was quick to realize that those two wanted *all* the copies of the Bedeaux papers): 'One set, yes. I had four made.'

2nd S.A.: 'You must remember this man is an American citizen. We have a right to all the copies and we demand them.'

Guy: 'That I cannot do. The one I have, yes, I shall give you. It is home in my safe. Would you care to accompany me?'

2nd Voice (angrily): 'That won't do. We must have all the copies. Where are they? We don't want to have to appeal to AFHQ – this is strictly an American affair and we demand those copies. You must remember you have committed an offence under the agreement with the provisional government. Technically we could arrest you for

100

having seized American property and having illegally imprisoned an American citizen.'

Guy: 'I am very sorry. I have made this error through excess of zeal. I thought I was helping you. I have always helped America against Vichy and the Axis....'

2nd S.A.: 'Quit stalling. Where are those other three sets of photostats?'

Guy: 'I cannot retrieve them. Two I gave to American organizations' (Clever of you, Guy, to think this one up under fire), 'one to the British. I am certain two are in Washington and one in London. Surely you cannot object to the fact that your own....'

1st S.A.: 'What organizations were they?'

Guy: 'I have been a long time in intelligence work. I do not tell the names of persons or organizations with whom I deal, not even to their compatriots. You must excuse me but those are the rules of our cricket, I mean our baseball.'

There was mumbling between the 1st and 2nd Southern Accent.

2nd S.A.: 'Let's go get that copy at your house. We have our car outside.'

Guy: 'My brother Jacques is at home. I can telephone him to bring it down.'

1st S.A.: 'OK.'

(I heard Guy go out to the telephone.)

2nd S.A. (to 1st S.A.): 'There's no use scaring the hell out of him. It's probably CIC and OSS – and British Intelligence. We'll never get them back...' (Lowered voices – pause.)

Guy (returning): 'He'll be here in five minutes with the photographs.'

1st S.A.: 'We don't want to take action against you on this matter. But we have reason to believe many of these documents are forgeries – to make a good case. A statement by you to that effect might clear this case up quite a bit. We could then see that no action is taken by AFHQ against you and others...'

Guy (quiet, cold anger in his voice): 'My friends, I am a Frenchman. It is true we had the Dreyfus case. It is true we had the Vichy Government. It is even true that we have the present provisional government of General Giraud. But some of us, most of us Frenchmen, I among them, are ashamed of these facts. And to state that papers are a forgery when I have reason to know the opposite, to swear a lie to protect a dog, that I will not do. I think...'

101

2nd S.A.: 'Nobody asked you to swear to a lie – but you know as well as I do that...'

Guy: 'I know that others who have helped America are in prison or concentration camps only because they *did* help your country. I know you have put over us a government as bad as Vichy, and that none of the ideals you lured us with has come to pass. You cannot frighten me by threatening to put me in prison, too. Good day, I am occupied. I have other things to do.'

1st S.A.: 'As you please. Let's go.'

(Their voices faded into the other room.)

On his way home under arrest Charles Bedeaux, officially under the surveillance of the FBI, committed suicide when changing planes in Florida. He took poison, bought in Florida. How he managed to get it can only be surmised.

Guy came back alone. I climbed out from under my table.

'In the name of God, can you imagine such a thing?' he said.

'Yes, I can, well enough,' I said, remembering the sirens outside the Alphan Embassy.

'I am not afraid. In fact, I am enraged. In fact, I dare them, I wish them, to arrest me ... and thank you, thank you for your advice to copy those documents.'

*　　*　　*

From du Pont Circle to Algiers I was learning more and more.

CHAPTER EIGHT

BLOODY BANANAS I

Food to feed the eyes with mourning
Exile sad, more sad returning!
Slain wert those, whom thou hadst slain,
Found wert thou and lost again.
Lost, in sooth beyond reprieving.
Life, bereft and life-bereaving.
Race of LAIUS, woe is thee!
Woe, and wail, and misery!
Woe, woe, thy fatal name!
Prophet of our triple shame.

AESCHYLUS

The Seven Against Thebes

SPRING 1943

No modern story is sadder than the betrayals of the Spanish people. If there is a real hero of the war he is the forgotten Spaniard, abandoned by democracy in 1936 when the Second World War really began, to a choice between Communism and Franco's Fascinazism.

First, we democrats betrayed the Spanish Republic to the Nazis and the Fascists. Then we betrayed the Republican movement to its Communist minority, and then, when rescue would have been so easy, in 1945, we rebetrayed them by leaving Franco's Government in power as the only Axis oasis in Europe.

I was an instrument, if a small one, in this 'our triple shame', against my will and with the bigger job of 'win the war' to soothe my guilty conscience.

When the Fifth Army allowed us to establish Special Detachment G2, we agreed to undertake any task they might ask of us. We had successfully broken up the Axis drive to sabotage our life-line railway and highway by wholesale infiltration of Axis sabotage schools in the Spanish Zone of Morocco. The reasons for this success were two. First, the work among the Arab Nationalist leaders done originally by Carlton Coon, later carried on by Gordon Browne and André Bourgoin; second, the work of Bourgoin in infiltrating the Axis schools and in gaining the co-operation of the young officers commanding the Berber troops on the frontier, the famous Goumiers – those tall bearded warriors in green jalabas looking like an army of medieval Christs.

Ours was a hard territory to defend against sabotage infiltration. From the little corridor of French Morocco which reaches the sea west of Oran, the frontier of the Spanish Zone swings in an arc southward, following the Moulouya River, and cuts through the high and wild Riff Mountains to Tangier in the west.

The eastern side of this frontier was our danger point: the Moulouya River and the mountainous Riff country. Here our vital transport ran close to the frontier, through the empty desert and under the Scorpion Tunnel. A perfect set-up for sabotage.

By agreement with Spain at the time of the landings in November 1942, no Allied personnel were to approach closer than ten kilometres to the Spanish frontier. So on moonless, starry nights, in the crisp air of the desert, André Bourgoin and I would drive out in a jeep, with no lights, to mend our fences along the frontier. Sometimes we would eat and lodge with an Arab sheik, who would report any unusual happenings on his sector of the frontier, any gossip from activities in the Spanish Zone.

Sometimes we would visit a Goumier outpost, like the one commanded by a lonely and charming French lieutenant, Pierre Chatouville, on the frontier beyond Berkane in the east. The Goumiers, who enlist for life, bring their women with them. The women's camp site is surrounded by barbed wire. When we would arrive about midnight, the Goumiers would be sitting at their campfires in the women's compound, singing to flutes and tom-tom drums the sad and lace-like songs of the High Atlas from which they come. Chatouville would meet us with a drink. We would sit in his little garden and discuss his sector. Sometimes nothing had happened. Sometimes he would have a prisoner or two for us, Arabs who had tried to pass the frontier. Sometimes only a body – for the Goumiers were quick with their knife or their rifle if a challenge was not answered or the stranger tried to run away.

In fact, one night we owed our lives to Bourgoin's knowledge of Berber. We had left Oujda at dusk and made several stops at our outposts. We wanted to visit an Arab of the clan of the Caid Mimoun who had reported that a European dressed as an Arab, travelling on foot towards Oudja, had passed one of his shepherd boys. A runner of Mimoun had come to Oujda to alert us.

We were worried. We had had word from our radio in Melilla that Wiedemann, German espionage chief in the east of the Spanish Zone, was to come to Oujda, under our very noses, to visit the Pasha of Oujda, long his friend, and now the good friend of General Mark Clark. (General Mark Clark had a bad habit of making politically dangerous friends from Morocco to Naples, Rome, Florence and on north.)

We had warned G2 about the Pasha of Oujda, but headquarters staffs are always reluctant to criticize their co's friends and his private life. The French *Bureau des Affaires Indigènes* and the household of the Sultan himself had both agreed, off the record, to pack the Pasha off to the southern Sahara for his health and ours, if we would get the Fifth Army to make an official secret request. This we were never able to get for fear of offending Clark.

Driving across the desert to the house of the clansman of Mimoun we steered by the North Star. That far west there is no longer the Moulouya River to prevent one driving into the Spanish Zone by mistake. Somehow we missed the tiny village. André became worried that a light ahead was a Spanish outpost. We decided to stop and reconnoitre afoot.

It was so dark that we lost one another several times, although we were only a dozen feet apart.

We knew we could return to the jeep by keeping *Stella Polaris* directly over the suspicious light ahead.

Suddenly the light went out.

'*Purée de merde!*' whispered André. 'We'd better go back to the jeep or we'll never find the thing in the darkness.'

We missed the jeep. For an hour we wandered around.

'We'll be here until dawn when those *salauds d'Espagnols* will see us. *La fortune est une espèce de putain.* Probably we are on their stinking side of the bloody frontier.'

I heard a sort of gargle from André and, as I turned my head to look hopelessly in the dark, an arm encircled my neck from behind and I was on the ground, my mouth covered with a cloth. I was afraid to struggle.

There was a mumbling. Then André's voice in Berber, a little breathless but, as always, authoritative. More mumblings and orders in Berber.

As suddenly as I was thrown down I was pulled to my feet. Someone handed me my colt. André was still talking in Berber. Then to

105

me in English, 'You all right? We are just two hundred metres from the Spanish line.' The Goumiers had followed us from the jeep. When they were convinced we were about to cross into Spain they captured us – if we had struggled we would have had our throats cut. Orders are orders, and our orders to the Goumiers were that 'no one crosses the frontier'.

Like cats in the dark they led us to the jeep. One mounted behind and guided us to the house of Mimoun's clansman. With hot buckwheat cakes and honey, sweet green China tea and mint, I recovered my nerve.

The shepherd boy was interviewed and questioned. His master wanted to beat him for not having captured or killed the European. We begged him clemency and hurried back to Oujda by dawn to hunt Wiedemann in the Medina. We never found him. He returned safely to Melilla to laugh at us.

He had, in fact, entered Oujda in the Pasha's car, travelling on petrol given to that dignitary by orders of the Commanding-General Fifth Army.

'*Merde de Kous-Kous*,' was André's only comment.

Sometimes, however, the shoe was on the other foot, and it was ourselves who outwitted and outplayed our Axis enemies across the line. We found that Karl Frick was running the German sabotage school in Almeria in Spain and arranging for the supply of Axis submarines in Spanish ports: the same Karl Frick who had set off Black Tom in New Jersey, the biggest sabotage coup of the first World War. This formed the basis for a strong diplomatic protest in Madrid by Allied diplomats.

Friederich, the German Vice-Consul in Melilla, was, we discovered, a representative of the S.S. Intelligence Organization (S.D.) of Kaltenbrunner and not of Admiral Canaris' *Abwehr*. From our agents we knew every habit of his day. He made André's and my life uncomfortable by offering large sums for our heads. Friederich, his house and sabotage school were blown up.

We uncovered Wiedemann's chief intelligence chain into Morocco and Algiers. It centred around the Spanish Consul in Oran and Sidi Bel Abbès, Señor Rocca. First we 'convinced' their Arab messengers to work for us and, finally, shut the system up.

Wiedemann and his assistant Kruse also had a radio station in Beni-Saf, a little town on the coast roughly half-way between Oran, the port, and Oujda, the headquarters of the Fifth Army.

106

We long guessed there must be a station in our midst, since our opponents were no fools. One day our base-station radio at Special Detachment G2 picked up strong signals in code. My operator, a veteran of the Spanish Civil War, thought it had the characteristics of a Spanish naval operator, but did not think it was Spanish naval code nor sent from a ship's radio. We had often asked for direction-finding equipment, but there we never any to spare. Now we improvised one by hiding normal receivers in two French automobiles.

The trail ended in Beni-Saf, over the line in Algeria, and thus, technically, outside our territory. We put a watch on the house and notified AFHQ in Algiers. But the agent got wind of our surveillance and prepared to run. My Spanish terriers were not so easily evaded: the body of Wiedemann's agent was identified as a Spanish ex-naval wireless operator named Lopez. We kept the radio for our own use.

Our infiltrations of the German sabotage school for Arabs in the Moroccan town of Melilla were successful, and we had information of every sabotage team before it was sent out. Usually these teams contained one of our Arabs. Not a bridge was blown, not a rail removed, not a tunnel damaged, despite the fact that our life-lines of road and rail ran through the desert only ten miles from Spanish territory.

*　　*　　*

Fifth Army was afraid of a surprise attack through Spain. General Orgaz had 100,000 native and Spanish troops in Africa, as well as the Spanish Foreign Legion. German airborne troops and parachutists might be flown in, as they had been to Crete. Between the Italian Navy, and the guns on the Spanish shores of the Straits, these narrow waters could be easily closed to Allied traffic. While the fortress of Gibraltar could always close the Straits, it was powerless to keep them open.

With this in the mind of the staff at AFHQ in Algiers and at the Fifth Army in Oujda, I was requested by the G2 to do the following:

1) Keep a close watch on Spanish airports and report any lengthening of fields, storage of fuel, building of bunkers, or other evidence that the Luftwaffe is preparing to use these fields.

2) Report on German civilian movements in Spain – especially

in and about airfields, ports, military establishments, and transportation facilities.

3) Keep a close watch near Algeciras, on the European side, and Melilla, on the African side, for the installation of new coastal guns, and for the shipment of such guns, their ammunition, etc., to Africa.

4) Make contacts with Spanish military leaders with an eye to encouraging possible desertions of whole units to our side through political promises or monetary corruption.

5) Make frequent reports on Spanish battle order, especially in the southern port areas and on the African side of the Straits.

6) Open contact with the anti-Franco republican elements in Spain and in exile, with a view to organizing a partisan movement to operate behind Spanish-German lines as soon as the Germans enter Spain, prepare to sabotage railways, airfields, bridges, etc. etc., to impede the transfer of any great force into Africa. But to act only when, as, and if the Germans entered Spain.

This was a big order. Normally, it would have taken from six months to a year to prepare it, to train the personnel and to deploy them with any degree of security and proper communications.

Fortunately, 'K' and Bill Donovan had allowed me to form a Spanish group early in 1942, which was ready in time to follow me to North Africa in December. I recruited these Spaniards through Alvarez del Vayo, last Foreign Minister of Republican Spain, with whom I had worked at *Free World*, and Dr Aguirre of the Basques. They found me veterans of the Civil War, specialists in espionage and partisan warfare. Others I found in Mexico City through the members of the Spanish Government in exile there. Del Vayo gave me letters of introduction to the ministers in Mexico and I flew down. General Donovan, too, found me recruits among the American veterans of the Abraham Lincoln and International Brigades.

In discussing the projected Spanish outfit, I insisted that if trouble came in Spain even trained men and equipment would not be enough. We should need a deposit of dollars, or better gold, ready on the Iberian Peninsula. There might be a general for sale – and a general with his troops at such a moment would be a bargain at any price. So it was arranged with Colonel Lane Rehm, OSS Finance Officer, that some Fort Knox pay-dirt, to be exact, $6,000,000 in old European gold pieces, be deposited with the

108

American Finance Officer at Gibraltar. Moreover, quick payment would be essential to the usefulness of the gold: the normal procedure of receipts had to be waived. But how would the hypothetical Spaniard identify himself when he came for the little bags?

I own an antique Navajo Indian ring, an odd turquoise containing a strip of matrix, set in a crude, lopsided silver mounting. It has a different number of flutings on either side of the setting. Mr Gray, the finance officer leaving for Gib, saw the ring. He was given a colour photograph showing the number of flutings on one side only, but showing clearly the odd green-blue stone marked with a vein of rust-coloured matrix. He memorized the number of flutings on the unphotographed side and a code number – 123. Gray was instructed to give all or part of the gold to anyone presenting my original ring who, in reply to, 'Who sent you?' would respond '123'.

My special Spanish group was entirely independent of the Spanish Desk in oss. The desk was dealing with Spain on a different and far more 'genteel' plan; quite properly, it was composed of people with a certain sympathy for Franco's régime. Theirs was a kid glove job of great value in preparing overall reports for all government agencies, and, once we had a direct route to get these reports from Madrid, they were also valuable to G2, Fifth Army. I know that the Spanish Desk personnel in Spain put many doubts in official Spanish heads of ultimate Axis victory, which tended to discourage Spain from intervening openly – as when Goering tried to promote an attack on Gibraltar.

Ours was a non-kid-glove job with a pair of brass knuckles always available. We did not succeed in great measure, partly because Spain did not come into the war, partly because of bad luck, partly because of poor management, and partly, too, because British Intelligence sold us for a mess of diplomacy at a crucial moment.

I had chosen a young American captain, and a lieutenant, demolition experts, to officer my Spanish group. They numbered about twenty. But as soon as I left Washington airport, bureaucracy took a big bite out of my group.

The bright, energetic, young demolition officers were detached, raided by the Far Eastern Desk, and sent off across the Pacific to be killed in China. Instead we were sent a nice, big, jolly college boy in a major's uniform, a tuck-shop cowboy of the rah! rah! rah! for dear ole Siwash variety – useless for my purposes, but who might have made a crackerjack combat officer. Two others, enlisted

109

men of first order, had been detached with no explanation offered.

Immediately upon arrival in Algiers the group was taken, over my protests, to do special sabotage jobs behind the Tunisian front. A colonel commanding OSS troops wanted to make a showing quickly as a paramilitary operator to win some praise at AFHQ. Actually, he knew no more about infiltration and paramilitary work than Gracie Fields. Here was a specialized group, recruited and trained at great cost in time and money, all experts in Spain, knowing the language, and with experience in guerrilla warfare from 1936 to 1939. They were being sent to do the work of an ordinary patrol, or at most of a Ranger infiltration team.

I was enraged. But it did not do me any good. The same colonel controlled our communications with HQ OSS in Washington. My protests to Donovan went unanswered because they were never sent.

I lost two good men in Tunisia, bringing my group down to fourteen. But the Germans had the good grace to capture my Joe-college major, so I figured the score was about even.

But I needed more Spaniards – and good ones. I asked permission to visit the Vichy concentration camps four and five hundred miles south of Oran in the Sahara at and near Colomb Bechar. It was already – in February, 1943 – a disgrace that AFHQ, under advice of Robert Murphy, was allowing the Giraud government to continue these torture holes which compared in horror and inhumanity with Buchenwald, Dachau and Mauthausen. In these camps were the remnants of the Spanish Republican Army to which France had offered asylum; Germans, whose only fault was that they had enlisted in the French Foreign Legion to fight against Nazism; and a smattering of other nationalities.

Some press reporters unknowingly turned the trick for me by threatening to write about the camps as part of their campaign to stop AFHQ from using military censorship to hide the Vichy nature of the Giraud government. And because no American had even seen these camps, someone had to see them before the Press, and I was allowed to go with an Englishman of SOE (Special Operations Executive) as my duenna. With a truck and a command car we left Algiers early in February. In the truck were the last of my Spanish group; the others were still in Tunisia.

In all the camps we visited we experienced the same pattern of events. First the sadistic bullies who ran the place tried to convince us that they had mostly criminals who were being used to build the

110

Transahara railway from Oran to Dakar. When we still insisted on interviewing the prisoners, they gave us a Lucullan feast and tried to flatter us, and to squeal on one another. In the meantime my Spaniards had gone through the camp and we began to know the disgusting truth.

The prisoners slept on concrete shelves with one cotton blanket each (the Sahara is bitterly cold at night). These shelves were less than twenty inches apart. Diet consisted of water, cabbage, and carrot soup twice a day, with daily allowance of about twelve ounces of bread to do for both meals.

For this they were supposed to work for ten hours on the railway construction. If they worked overtime they were paid a sum in cash, but were only allowed to spend it in the shops run by the guards or on the whores managed by the guards. In the shops they could get overpriced cigarettes, biscuits, and a little watery wine. From the whores they had got, about fifty per cent of them, venereal diseases.

Punishment was called being '*frit*', or fried. It consisted in being put in a coffin-sized concrete box with a hole over the nose, and exposed for a day to the Sahara sun. About half of the '*frits*' died. Beatings with bull whips were the least of the tortures, which, as in so many German camps, took on a peculiarly sexual quality.

We were in all eight persons, including my Spaniards. Between us in four days we interviewed just under two thousand prisoners. Of course these interviews were superficial but they gave us a line on certain groups for future use.

Of all the nationality groups in the camps, the Spaniards had stood up best. They, it is true, had been part of an army that had gone into the camps as a unit, and they had retained their dignity, their discipline, and their hopes. The Austrians and the Italians, as groups, were broken in spirit and body. Austrian boys who had escaped from Hitler and enlisted with courage and determination in the French Foreign Legion were pitiful to see. Their lower lips quivered and they wept like girls on being left alone with one of us, away from camp guards and camp brutality. One poor youngster tried to kiss my feet. Almost incoherently they poured out stories of the horrors and brutalities to which they had been subjected. The Greeks, Yugoslavs, and others were not much better.

How different the Spanish! On entering they clicked their heels and saluted. They were formal and cold and suspicious of us. I told one, after hearing the story of his war record in Spain, that I thought I could use him and might take him out of camp with me.

'I refuse to go before the others,' he said. 'I shall only leave here as part of the Spanish Republican Army or on the orders of my government....' He was a little runt of an Andalusian whose ribs showed through his torn undershirt, demonstrating the degree of starvation he had experienced.

'But I have here credentials from your government.'

'If we judge them to be authentic we are at your disposition. My commanding officer will look at them.' His ugly little face shone with both pleasure and anger.

In time of war, give me Spaniards!

We discovered that the mortality rate was running at five per cent. A life expectancy of under twenty months!

Back in Algiers with my list of potential recruits, I tried to interest the American authorities in closing these camps. I had no luck. It was not until General de Gaulle took over from Giraud that, by mere force of his decency and popularity, these camps were closed. Then de Gaulle did a real job of it and court-martialled and shot the worst of the camp managers and guards.

In the meantime I was allowed to take out special individuals for my own work, provided an equal number would volunteer to enlist in the British Pioneer Corps (labour force)! But since the British had no special documents from the groups which these Spaniards considered their government – Negrin, Del Vayo, and the ministers in Mexico City – they refused. Furthermore, the British insisted that they should enlist as individuals 'in His Majesty's Forces for service anywhere at His Majesty's pleasure.' This snag was never really resolved.

So I only obtained the release of a small number on various excuses, such as sending for them for questioning, and then just not returning them to the camps. Others I helped to escape.

For these few, Mike and his brother Jim – once members of the Abraham Lincoln Brigade and originally recruited by General Donovan – opened a clandestine communications school in an old villa on the sea outside Algiers. Their results were so superior to those of the joint British-American school across the bay, despite all its magnificent equipment, that within a month other oss desks were begging us to take their students. To refuse would offend, but the Spaniards were so touchy about their security that we had to refuse.

Later, in the summer, when General de Gaulle closed the concentration camps, we got the rest of the recruits we wanted and
the whole Spanish effort was removed to Oujda in Morocco, where
I had gone to initiate *Special Detachment, G2, 5th Army*. It was
safer there.

With the help of André Bourgoin we located an ideal place for
the Spanish 'Finishing School', about fifty miles south-east of Oujda.
It was a mountain on the edge of the desert with good water on its
summit amid a great grove of oaks.

We opened 'Fifth Army Meteorological Station', as the sign over
the camp cheerfully lied in large white letters on a red background.
Here the original 'Spanish Group' from Washington, recruits from
the concentration camps and the Mike-and-Jim Radio School
assembled. In all, there were about fifty men and a dozen instructors.
A cleaner and more beautiful camp than this one (set up by the
remnants of an army defeated four years before) I have never seen.
Communications, codes, street fighting, demolitions, battle order
identification, enemy weapons, all the usual courses were included
in the curriculum.

I remember the night I went up to tell my camp commanders
that we had the go-ahead from Fifth Army on the six-pointed project
in Spain as insurance against a not improbable German attack from
that quarter.

From Oujda I had brought a dozen bottles of Spanish brandy for
a special ration to the camp. We ate under the great oaks. On the
horizon twinkled indistinctly the lights of the oasis of Oujda where
Fifth Army Headquarters were. Off to the north-west, imagined more
than seen, were the outlines of the Riff Mountains in Franco's zone
of Morocco.

After dinner two guitars appeared and the Spanish brandy and
a couple of goat-skins of wine. Each part of Spain sang its songs.
The sunset afterglow became dimmer and the clear desert stars
became more, brighter, and closer overhead.

Then the Andalusians did a series of *Flamencos* – the weird,
Arab-like, falsetto songs which are their heritage from Islam and
the court of their masters, the western Caliphs in Cordoba. These
songs slide off in long, jewelled stalagmites and stalactites of wailing
notes, like the arches of the Alhambra where the Caliphs lived in
Granada.

José took me into his office as camp commandant. 'The *Flamencos* make me too sad. I wonder how many of these who have suffered for so long will die to carry out these six jobs the Army has asked us to do?'

I was silent.

'I cannot bear *Flamencos*,' he said, nodding towards the great oaks from under which came their long, sad notes, 'they remind me of 1939.' He poured brandy.

'We had a guerrilla band in Catalonia – I am a Catalan – but with us were two Andalusians, boys, no, really babies, brothers fifteen and seventeen years old.

'Our band was small, twenty men. We were operating just behind the Fascist lines to sabotage transport.

'One day with four wounded we had to climb a mountain to find a small town with a doctor where there were no Fascist troops and where we could find some food and get a little sleep.

'We came to the little town and the doctor cared for our wounded. He said two of us could sleep in beds in his house, and we sent the two babies, the brothers from Andalusia.

'They were like little girls, these shepherd brothers from the Sierra Nevada Mountains.

'They knew nothing of politics, but when their father saw the Moorish troops of the Fascists he sent his boys off to fight for the Republic.

'Well, about four o'clock we sent again for the doctor. One of our wounded was dying.

'He came, it was useless and he left.

'Those babies came down at dawn. Soon the doctor came back excited and talked with our commander.

'He came out and told the two brothers they were under arrest and he took their guns away.

'The doctor had said that the two boys had raped his daughter of only fourteen years while he was with our wounded in the night. She had resisted and they had smothered her. She was dead.

'We were silent and sad all day. In the afternoon, late, our commander called us all together for the trial of the little brothers.

'They admitted what they had done and they cried, but they did not cry like men cry but like babies cry.' The *Flamencos* reached a high pitch outside – José finished his brandy.

'Our commander said that things like that the Moors or the Fascists did. That we must set an example to the people of this little town, to all of Spain, who had helped us.

114

'The two little brothers would be shot the next morning before we left to return to the valley.

'We were sick at his words. The brothers did not cry any more for they had become men during that trial.

'The priest came to see them. He told the commander he was wrong. But we knew he was right. You cannot make war against things you do not like and then allow your own people to do the same things.

'When that night came no one had eaten. We were all sick. The commander said we must dig a grave for the boys of Andalusia. It was like digging not in the dirt but in our hearts.

'Outside the town on a little hill we took turns digging. Then the commander brought the boys out. They had asked the priest for a guitar to hear a last time their music, their *Flamencos* from Andalusia.

'We were still digging by the light of an old kerosene lantern when they arrived. One, the older of the boys, sat down on a rock and began to play the guitar. His brother stood behind him, with one hand on his shoulder, and sang, sang *Flamencos* like an angel. Their faces, so calm, so baby-like, were lit by the lamp and the singing was not loud enough to cover the grating of the shovels in the stony earth.

'At dawn we stood them down in the hole and shot them. They did not cry but as we covered their bodies we cried.

'When I hear a *Flamenco* again I always see their baby faces in the weak light of that kerosene lantern and hear the angel voice of the little one…and hear spades scraping in the hard mountain earth.'

José and I talked of the approaching departure of the first team. As carefully screened as was every man in this camp, we could take no chances on one of them being a plant. They must go out of here to a series of little isolation camps to be briefed for their big job.

The first two would go on foot to Melilla, then by boat to Malaga. There they would locate our 'safe address' and make contact with whatever was left of a Republican underground. One would stay and one come back. Then he would go back again with two radio operators and their set, landing on a beach north-east of Malaga. André had already procured me the blank forms for their identity cards and discharge papers, for they were to pose as discharged soldiers.

From then on, the chain begun, other landings would follow. Other cells would branch out and seal themselves off, security proof, from their parent cell once they had radio contact with us.

We decided to put the first pair over the Moulouya River at the Sheik Si Hamet's north of Berkane. The two men selected were first moved to a house near Oran and later to Tlemcen on the Oran-Oujda highway. Here they were briefed, studied maps and reports for a week. At the end of the week they could each reproduce the map-section from Berkane to Melilla in considerable detail from memory.

The old address from Mexico City of the 'safe' Republican in Malaga was committed to memory. If he were no longer free or living they would have to find a safe address for themselves.

It would have been better had one of our oss people in Spain arranged all this, but against this was the fact that the Spanish Desk agents must be kept in ignorance of these activities of oss Fifth Army. Besides, security is almost in inverse proportion to the square of the number of people who know.

CHAPTER NINE

BLOODY BANANAS II

. . . the laurel also bears a thorn.

W. S. LANDOR

The full moon was a disadvantage to a crossing of the Moulouya. Worse, the river was in flood which made it extremely dangerous to swim, a rush of yellow water, full of whirlpools, dead trees, and Spanish barbed wire.

But we decided not to wait. Time was too pressing.

André and I arrived with the two Spaniards, Manuel and Juan, at about eleven o'clock. Si Hamet's stone house stood on a rocky knoll overlooking the Moulouya River. Sloping away on all sides were his fertile fields (fertile so long as we gave him army Diesel fuel to run his irrigation pump). His house had a courtyard with a wall on one side and three rooms, one floor high, on the other three sides. Outside the wall was a stone barn, barely big enough for his three horses, two mules and several donkeys. Pieces of farm machinery, rusting in the open, after the American fashion, stood here and there between the courtyard gate and the barn. Mud and manure and muck were everywhere, but Si Hamet, six feet tall with long grey eyes, white pointed beard, and high cheek-bones – a really beautiful man of seventy – was always immaculate in white and topped in a white turban.

After kissing us ceremoniously, Si Hamet led us into the centre room – the one 'public' room of the house. The room on the left was for the women (three wives and an unknown number of daughters), the one on the right for the men, Si Hamet and his seven sons.

Si Hamet was always at our disposition. The highly-sweetened green tea, flavoured with mint, began to arrive. But the moon? The river was angry. He looked at the two little Spaniards (small even for Spaniards) with disgust.

Si Hamet hated all Spaniards without exception and almost all Frenchmen.

'Those,' he said to André, 'will be swept away by the river like sick mice.'

'That,' replied André, pointing at me, 'demands they cross this night despite the moon and the flood. He has told you and proven to you how great is his affection for you. You have told me how great is your affection for him. He represents here the mightiest country in the world, and from its generosity it has sent you oil that you might irrigate the fields, yellow pills to cure your sons and your clansmen of the fever, tea and sugar that you might entertain as befits your station. If he wishes to sacrifice the lives of two miserable Spaniards, why should you object? But it is important that they arrive over there; important to him and you, for you are revenging the slaughter of your clansmen by those pigs the Spaniards. Your big sons, the black giants whom all admire, whose lives you have already risked for us, and for which we love you and thank Allah, these two sons could carry these miserable little Spaniards across Moulouya as a shepherd boy carries the new-born lamb on his collar.'

'By Allah, it shall be so this night,' replied Si Hamet, bowing gravely. 'Now let us eat and I shall even give to eat to those, so dearly I love you both.'

At about 1.30 a.m. he sent the younger sons who had served us our meal to awaken the two great, black sons. When they came in Si Hamet gave them orders more like an officer than a father. They were, if not twins, nearly of the same age, and of the same great height and breadth of shoulder, bigger than Joe Louis and much blacker in colour.

Then Si Hamet gave his sons a sort of blessing and led us to the door. We six, André, the two Spaniards, the two Arabs, and myself took a long round-about route to the river led by one of the great sons.

The moon was high and brilliant but the river was invisible under a ground mist. As we came closer to the bank we dropped to all fours so as not to be seen in silhouette from the Spanish side.

We crept into the cover of the ground mist. The leading son raised a hand and stopped us. He motioned to the Spaniards to undress. I gave them each a pat, a weak sort of send-off, a few words of encouragement in French. They grinned. They had little use for encouragement.

The brothers took the Spaniards' clothes and rolled them tightly into little wads which they inserted into sheep bladders. These they tied at both ends and fixed them with raw-hide to the Spaniards' necks. Then the brothers undressed and left their clothes with us.

118

As they stood there in the fog-diffused moonlight their great, muscled, black bodies seemed like bronze figures in a fountain, rippling and playing with moonlight for water.

Solemnly each of them picked up a little, white Spaniard and hung him around his neck. The contrast made the Spaniards smaller and whiter, and the brothers more gigantic and blacker. One of the brothers pointed to his Spaniard and laughed silently; his mouth was suddenly full of white moonlit teeth. They turned without a word and entered the icy water.

There was no sound but the river thrashing in its bed until a dog over on the Spanish side began to bark. Si Hamet's dogs replied.

Time seemed to be swimming against the current of the mad Moulouya.

'I am worried they didn't make it,' I whispered to André.

'I am not worried. They are resting for the return.'

I looked at my watch. Already an hour.

Suddenly one of the naked black brothers appeared in the mist. He was winded, but he spoke in short spurts to André as he wrapped his jalaba about him.

'All is well,' said André, 'they made it. The other has gone to the house. They landed below here.

'*Comme je disais, ceux-ci sont des tigres, des tigres noirs.*'

We detoured back to the house. My mind was with the two little men. Was everything prepared properly? The identity cards, the discharge papers? These they couldn't use before Melilla – two days and two nights in the mountains with no story that would resist questioning.

They are Spaniards, I thought, that's half the battle. What courage and guts and discipline will win, they already are assured of. Good luck, Juan and Manuel – may the tough war-god of the Iberians look after you.

Back at Si Hamet's: more tea and compliments. A few curses on the heads of all Spaniards and most Frenchmen. More tea, hotter and sweeter. A ceremonial kiss. *Bara Kalaufic Bisef,* good-bye and great thanks. May Allah be with you...(and with you too, Juan and Manuel).

Dawn was pink over the Algerian mountains – over the Fifth Army Meteorological Station – and as we reached Oujda the Mouezzins were calling to prayer.

I suddenly felt that I, too, wanted to pray. For it dawned on me to question my right to send Juan and Manuel to gamble so lightly with death, and the odds so heavily against them.

*   *   *

In searching for code names for the series of projects to carry out the six-pointed programme requested by G2 5th Army, we decided on fruits. Juan's and Manuel's phase we called *Pineapple*. The mission already in Melilla we renamed *Apricot*. The follow-up in Malaga with full personnel and supply, was to be *Banana*. We planned for Cartagena, Cadiz, Algeciras, Barcelona, Madrid – *Orange, Grapefruit, Apple, Cherry* and *Lemon*.

Banana was to be the parent operation – in Malaga. From here the other cells would set out. *Banana* would provide their reception committee on some southern beach, hide them for a few days and help them on their way. But their exact destination was to be unknown to *Banana*, for security reasons. Once established, only our Oujda Base Station would know where they were. However, OSS Algiers would monitor their communications to make sure of maximum reception.

Through the good offices of Colonel Arthur Roseborough in Algiers, we received assurance that a Royal Naval vessel used by British Intelligence would effect *Banana's* transportation by sea. I did not like, for security reasons, using the vessel of another organization for so delicate an operation as a clandestine beach landing. But the British were foxy in this war – being poor in supply and manpower they knew that 'he who controls G2 and communications controls all.'* So in our work, the British insisted on a monopoly in clandestine parachute flying and in clandestine beach-landing craft. Fortunately, we had our own communications.

In two weeks Juan returned. He had been picked up naked by some agents of the CI Corps near Berkane after losing his clothes in the Moulouya crossing. He was cold and miserable and wrapped in an army blanket. He had left Manuel with a small, rather intellectual and moderate Republican group in Malaga – one of the 'safe addresses' I had obtained in Mexico City.

Banana was now ready for launching. The team of eight – two

* Wm. J. Donovan, commenting on Eisenhower's staff set-up in Algiers – 1942.

radio operators, two guerrilla warfare veterans, two pure military intelligence observers, and the two political intelligence operators – was in an isolation camp and briefed. I could not be in Algiers for the sailing; I was in London seeing Dr Juan Negrin, but Arthur Roseborough and José put them aboard the *Prodigal*, an ex-Portuguese trawler used by the British for such expeditions.

In four days Algiers flashed me in London:

'*Prodigal* returned *Banana* delivered without incidents receptionists contacted 13871* returned.'

Now our base station stood by at the appointed daily-varying schedule and waited.

Four days of silence. Then on the fifth afternoon, after my return, it came:

'Established *Banana*'.

*   *   *

Dr Juan Negrin, the object of my trip to England, was one of the most interesting personalities of the 'thirties. He had been a non-political, socialite doctor of medicine in Madrid – and above all *bon-vivant* and *gourmet*. Only when he had seen his country hell-bent for Fascism had he put down his stethoscope to mount the political platform.

Negrin, himself, opened the door of his simple, elegant apartment in Grosvenor Square. He was as simple and elegant as the apartment and a little too perfectly dressed – rather like a chic Park Avenue doctor. But he was fat and jolly and easy to talk to.

On the table was a Yorkshire ham, some excellent bread and Huntley & Palmer's biscuits. A decanter held the driest, most fragrant Manzanilla that I have ever tasted. Rareties all, in wartime England! Over ham and biscuits and sherry I told him how magnificent I had found the remnants of his Republican Army in the concentration camps.

He believed we could put a strong partisan movement in action, capable of harassing any Francoist-German operations, using the people we had already prepared to head it. He was optimistic about sabotage and about subversion in the ranks of Franco's armed forces – but he was completely the realist about any general uprising.

* 13871 was Manuel's code number-name.

121

'The Spanish people are tired – they are sick of civil war – that is Franco's only real strength,' he said.

Throughout the conversation, I sensed strongly that without saying it in so many words, he was warning me, advising me, against giving key posts to Communists.

When I thanked him for putting many of his best people at our disposal, effectively under our orders, to work without reserve, as if they were working for their own government, he waved aside my gratitude.

'Our paths for the moment are parallel, our enemies we have in common, what will defeat Fascism and Nazism will in the long run help Spain. I cannot allow myself to believe that Franco will survive in a world of the victorious democracies....'

I wanted to contradict him after having seen the Darlan-Giraud-Murphy type of thing in North Africa under Anglo-American auspices. But I didn't.

At least I didn't agree with him and he apparently saw what my silence meant. A deep Latin shrug of his shoulders and an elevation of his eyebrows made me understand that he too had serious doubts.

With further help and assurances of co-operation I hurried back to Africa to follow up the fortunes of *Banana*.

*   *   *

Banana messages were coming in regularly. Reports on the available political resistance; on Spanish battle order; on German activity at the airports; a long list of priceless information.

The first step in the six-point programme was succeeding. The information about German activity at the Malaga airport, brief as it was, excited G2 Fifth Army. They asked a list of particulars which we radioed on to *Banana*. A second report on Spanish artillery – units and commanders identified – moving out of Malaga by sea was snapped up and air reconnaissance was requested to follow the two boats concerned.

Cadiz, *Grapefruit*, we set up without using *Banana*, through the help of a neutral but friendly consulate. These arrangements I had been able to make in London. The *Grapefruit* team of two men entered Cadiz as citizens of a Spanish-speaking country and set themselves up as exporters of brandy and wines – or something similar.

122

Trouble began with the *Banana* radio about the time we had *Orange* and *Apple* nearly ready to send along. They discovered that all but one of their crystals were useless. They could receive but not send. Fearing even this would break down, they sent Juan back over his now familiar route, Melilla to Moulouya and Berkane. This time he crossed the bridge quite dry, having convinced the Spanish customs that he was a brandy smuggler and paid them accordingly.

Banana's request was for a relief landing to send them two new radios, other less peaceful equipment, and to replace three of the men who were ill or nervous or both. They suggested we send *Orange* along with its equipment at the same time. They had made contacts for reception and cover inside the naval base of Cartagena.

Banana suggested two nights when their reception committee would be on the Green Beach. If we failed to see their signals from Green Beach on either night it would mean that the beach was 'hot', and we should try Yellow Cove on the third and fourth night.

The dates they had chosen did not give us much time, but we hurriedly packed *Orange*, prepared *Banana's* relief supply and isolated the new personnel, known as *Banana II*.

Arthur Roseborough undertook our arrangements for *Prodigal* through British Naval Liaison at AFHQ, with the usual OK of British Intelligence. Sailing of *Prodigal* was set for forty-eight hours before first landing contact. José, with a convoy, gathered up the missions and their waterproofed packing-cases – a truck and a weapons-carrier full – several days in advance. They were lodged in 'Columbia University', our Spanish hide-out near Algiers, and fitted out with Spanish clothes, cigarettes, lighters, wallets, money, razors, blades, and the bric-à-brac of pocket and suitcase – all obtained through dry, painstaking, risky sub-projects. They were given their Spanish identity cards and other necessary documents.

Early on the morning they were to sail I arrived from Oujda by air.

Arthur Roseborough* assured me all was well.

---

* I know of no individual who fought this war with such intensity and loyalty to the very best of American ideals as Arthur Roseborough. He not only headed the OSS French desk in Algiers with unusual imagination and efficiency, but was always ready to work hard for someone else's projects as well. He felt strongly that our purpose in this war was not merely to defeat the Axis, but to bring in our wake decency, justice, and democracy of the Jeffersonian brand. It hurt Arthur's pride and it

Prodigal was standing by in the harbour. Port clearance had been granted. We had only to load – and *Banana II* would be on its way, carrying with it the beginnings of *Orange*.

Arthur Roseborough and I with José and the *Banana II* convoy arrived at the appointed dock at H-hour, midnight. Blacked out, Algiers harbour was smelled and heard more than seen. In the starlight a dozen big ships were outlined – black against dark blue – otherwise, one only smelled gasoline, and Stockholm tar, rotting garbage, and fresh paint.

Arthur, following instructions, cupped his hands and called three or four times:

'Ahoy, *Prodigal.*'

Silence, smell, slapping water, a Cockney singing, but no reply from *Prodigal.*

'Of course they don't answer you, Art, you sound like a landlubber. Listen to me!

'Ahhhhh-hoy *Prodigallllllllll.*'

I tried three or four times.

Finally, a sleepy voice came from close by, 'Who's hailing *Prodigal?*'

'Colonel Roseborough of AFHQ,' responded Art.

'Excuse me, sir. I'll come ashore.'

We heard a boat lowered; pretty soon oars breaking water. A dinghy drew up and a British Naval Petty Officer stepped ashore.

'I am Colonel Roseborough. Captain "W" arranged for *Prodigal* to load certain personnel and material tonight.'

'I'm sorry, sir,' said the petty officer, 'but we're not loading tonight. All the officers except the lieutenant have taken shore leave, sir. Shall I wake the lieutenant?'

aroused his militant indignation to see corruption and political reaction confirmed in power by American authorities on the excuse of military expediency.

He foresaw our struggle against Communism, and is as anti-Communist as Senator MacCarthy, but he knew reaction is a poor weapon against Stalinism. He felt that reform and a 'wholesale exportation of Jeffersonianism, Lincolnism, and F.D.R.ism' would defeat Communism in the world. For this reason he stood up like David to the Goliath of the political side of AFHQ. He did not have David's luck and he was slaughtered. Arthur Roseborough went on to a brilliant career in combat intelligence with airborne troops.

'If you please. Tell him it is important.'

'Don't tell the boys who are going,' I told José, 'it will upset them. They are pretty well keyed-up.'

'There was no mistake with Captain "W". I confirmed with him again this morning,' said Arthur.

'Some goddam high level snafu,' I suggested, 'thank God we have a night's leeway. The first appointment is the day after tomorrow. If they can get away any time tomorrow they can make it.'

'Loading a group like this isn't so good in daylight,' protested José.

The lieutenant arrived. 'Colonel Roseborough? Colonel, didn't Liaison at AFHQ notify you? We were all ready to load *Banana II* tonight. We had a cancellation order at about 17.30 hours.'

'Postponed until when?' I said, 'we have a deadline to meet.'

'I'm sorry. It has nothing to do with us. It wasn't a postponement, sir, it was a definite cancellation.'

'I'm going to see Captain "W", the liaison officer, tonight,' said Arthur, and added rather tartly, 'you'd better get your officers back aboard because I assure you *Prodigal* will sail before daylight. I'm going now and wake "W" at home. You'd better go back aboard and try to send someone for your liberty officers.'

'Yes, sir, good night, sir.'

'Good night.'

I sent José to take the boys back to 'Columbia University', and to tell them the ship had motor trouble and would be ready to come alongside at dawn.

'You don't suppose it's internal sabotage, you know that Colonel...'

'No, he hasn't got the guts. No, I smell a full-grown Foreign Office rat. Or maybe a triple play, Hoare* to Hayes† to Murphy.‡ British Intelligence may have reported that they got us *Prodigal* for *Banana I*. Foreign Office may have notified Sir Sammy, he may have told Hayes; and Hayes asked Murphy to stop "agressive actions likely to drive Franco further toward the Axis".'

* Sir Samuel Hoare, British Ambassador in Madrid.

† Carleton Hayes, United States Ambassador in Madrid.

‡ Robert Murphy, personal representative of the President, with the rank of Minister and ploitical adviser to General Eisenhower.

'But that doesn't help those poor devils stranded in Malaga – what's more, waiting on a beach!'

Art stopped before a villa. 'You'd better go in alone, Art; he knows you.'

I waited nearly an hour. Finally, Art came out.

'It's hopeless, I'm afraid. Nothing less than an appeal to London will give us *Prodigal* or any other British ship.

'It's not an order from AFHQ but directly from the Admiralty in London. No British vessels are to take any further clandestine landings to Spain. It's a solid order.'

'But those ships are no longer commanded by the Admiralty,' I said, 'once in this theatre. They are under Cunningham who takes his orders from Eisenhower, who takes his orders from the Combined Chiefs of Staff. That's the agreement. You know as well...'

'I'll go to see Bedell Smith tomorrow morning. But you'd better not be too hopeful. This play wasn't Hoare to Hayes to Murphy. It was simpler: it started with a leak from British Intelligence to the Foreign Office. Those old ladies were shocked.'

'They don't want the Spanish Government upset – so they asked their fellow old-school-ties at the Admiralty to stop you *and you are stopped*. Nice system, eh? Fine security we have with a gossip of old ladies in London. Oh, hell – that's the way it is.'

'I cannot believe it somehow.'

Next day Colonel Roseborough called on General Bedell Smith, Chief of Staff of AFHQ. The excuses were long and wordy. The meat of them was that AFHQ did not consider the matter important enough, 'to warrant making an issue all the way back to the U.S.-British Combined Chiefs of Staff in Washington.'

Wasn't there some American vessel available in the theatre?

General Smith supposed there was but it would be a part of Admiral Cunningham's Naval Command. Couldn't be detached without the same appeal to the C.C. of S. in Washington.

With the *Banana* radio now probably all the way out of commission we could only advise them of the catastrophe by the long, dangerous trip for Juan. We sent him off. But the *Banana* personnel in need of radio parts and money was sweating out four nights on beaches. And on the fourth they would know we had let them down. Their morale might collapse.

Our *Banana II* group and the *Orange* boys, waiting idly in Algiers, wouldn't accept for long our obvious excuses. Already

126

the next night their loss of morale showed in their eyes. The fine edge of men prepared for a mission was gone. We were expending their fellows in Malaga. Wouldn't we some day equally expend them? So I decided to tell them the truth. I was right. It made them wild with anti-British anger, but it recrystallized their melting morale.

We would start our own Fifth Army Navy, we decided. It would probably be too late to save *Banana I*, but action only is tolerable in such times, and establishing an outlaw, pirate fleet, was action.

José and a French agent of ours went off to Oran to buy a fishing boat for cash. We had two Spanish Republican Naval Officers in our group. They knew where others were in Oran and Algiers. André Bourgoin would get us a French civilian permit for a fishing boat. These were OK-ed almost automatically by the Allied Naval Authorities. But we would be flagless. To get to the Spanish coast, out of bounds for French fishing boats, we would have to run the gauntlet of our own navies as well as the Spanish.

And so I became admiral of a navy; it consisted of one ten-metre French fishing boat, decked over, two row boats, and a half-dozen rubber landing rafts. Its home port was a sandy Mediterranean beach on that tiny corridor of French Morocco, which reaches the sea between Algiers and the Spanish Zone. Its local garrison of OSS troops and Spanish sailors lived in thatched huts built on the beach.

But it was too late to save *Banana I*. And Juan never returned from his overland trip. He did not arrive in Malaga.

* * *

In October in Italy I heard the end. One free survivor had told it – and the Foreign Minister of Spain had also told it, angrily, to United States Ambassador Carleton Hayes in Madrid. Patching the two stories together, this is about what happened.

Not seeing *Prodigal* on the nights appointed they had stayed another two nights. They had caused suspicion, being so long in the area. Political police had followed two of them separately to Malaga. These two had been kept under surveillance. Three days later a meeting had been called by the local *Banana* organization chiefs. Of course it is against security rules to call such a meeting, but their condition was critical. They needed some new documents, radio, money, and above all they had received a telling blow to morale.

127

So nineteen of them came together in one house to discuss what to do, whom to send to Africa, and by what route to send him. The police had seen nineteen people enter. Such meetings are forbidden in Spain as they were in Germany and are in Russia. A raid alarm was sent to police headquarters. Falangists, the S.S. of Spain, came too. Fifty or a hundred in all, with machine-guns, tear gas, hand grenades, and tommy-guns.

Apparently the meeting had been called where the local group had their largest store of arms. There had been added a hundred pounds of our plastic, some grenades, and a dozen sten-guns. An open battle, or rather a siege, resulted. Of *Banana* and their local organization one escaped, eight were killed and ten were captured – all wounded – to meet a worse death later. Of the police and Falangists, twelve were dead and about an equal number wounded.

Plenty of evidence (the stens, the grenades, and the plastic) was found to connect the group with the American Army.

Essentially, the story which the Spanish Foreign Minister presented to Mr Hayes was correct. Of course the sparks flew in Washington. General Donovan was on the mat. State Department was indignant. Inter-departmental protests and demands for scalps flew around Washington.

General Donovan replied, with the backing of Fifth Army, that all I had done was known in advance to Fifth Army. That it was part of a security measure taken by Fifth Army. The General was not aware of the fact that an American army in the field, with a dangerous open flank, had to get permission from the State Department to take measures for the security of that army.

The protests died down. Proper apologies were made in Madrid. Franco, for his own good reasons, among them not being any love for American democracy, did not come into the war.* Our six-point programme proved unnecessary and ended in a disaster – but, had Spain come openly into the war, had General Orgaz led his troops against Fifth Army, had they closed the lifeline from Casa to Oran, had they closed the Straits, had a German Army moved into Spanish Morocco to outflank us....

* The most important reason was apparently the influence of Admiral Canaris, Chief of German Intelligence (Abwehr), on his old friend General Franco. Canaris advised Franco that Hitler would inevitably lose the war. (See *Chief of Intelligence*, by Ian Colvin. Victor Gollancz Ltd., London 1951.)

We would have been overjoyed to have one Spanish Division of Moors come over to our side, to have known what airports to bomb, to have an efficient and armed guerrilla movement, under our orders, in the Germans' rear.

It is sometimes a fine line between being heroes or heels.

CHAPTER TEN

PINK EYE'S STORY

'Why sometimes I've believed as many as six
impossible things before breakfast.'
THE WHITE QUEEN
Alice Through the Looking Glass

1943 TO 1950

'Pink Eye' was his OSS code name dating from the preparation of our landing in North Africa in 1942. He was an agent for that little group of American amateurs who engineered so ably (under timid cover from the State Department as Vice-Consuls) *Operation Torch*.

Pink Eye is a tiny, plump man, almost an albino, elegantly, even dandyishly dressed. He has one brown and one blue eye startlingly placed in a pink, baby face. He has the air of a man who looks far younger than he is – probably fifty or fifty-five. His wife, a former Austrian opera diva, is at least a head taller than little Pink Eye. Her hard, inscrutable face has traces of great past beauty. They are always accompanied by two French bulldogs, fetishists for human feet; both of them, like Pink Eye himself, are watch-eyed.

Now, the first commandment of espionage is to be inconspicuous. Imagine him, complete with white suit, pale blue tie, wife in nearly six feet of red dress, dogs in fur collars, and all four sharing a mountain of pastries in a Roman sidewalk café, and there you have a small measure of his inconspicuousness!

Pink Eye is always jovial, always festive, and his ill-mated eyes glitter and sparkle. He is one of that rare breed of professional 'agents' celebrated in fiction by E. Phillips Oppenheim and Eric Ambler. He has few convictions and fewer ideals. He is as cold as ice and as expensive as diamonds. He practises with all teams and plays in none.

The North American Vice-Consuls had warned me against Pink Eye, but all of them liked him. I like him too. But liking him makes me feel akin to Darby the Taylor-bird in Kipling's *Rikki-Tikki-Tavi*.

I first met him one evening early in 1943 in Fez. We had a native

131

house there, under the direction of Gordon Browne, for dealing with the leaders of Arab-Moroccan Nationalism. This Fez house was as romantic and bizarre as Fez itself – a city directly out of the Arabian Nights, its streets too narrow for any vehicle, teeming with life and death and with conspiracy, commerce, great wealth, and great poverty.

Lamidu the Jackal, Gordon's Berber majordomo, fugitive from a feud murder done years before in his village high in the great Atlas Mountains, his face alight with hashish, bowed in little Pink Eye, huge Mrs Pink Eye, and the two fur-collared, watch-eyed dogs.

We rose from the floor, where one sits in Fez, and I was presented. Within five minutes he had told me that he was largely responsible for the success of the landings; that he loved America; that I was an extremely sympathetic, capable, and shrewd person; and that at last he had found someone worthy of his efforts and we should team-up and defeat Hitler.

Now this was not said crudely, in fact it wasn't even *said*, but it was his message to me, hinted at between the lines and italicized and emphasized with here a wink, there a chuckle or a knowing nod.

Then the pumps were turned on. She in her rich contralto, he in his persuasive tenor. What were our plans? What was this Fez house all about? Very flatteringly, all they wanted to know was where Downes, Browne, and FDR were planning to strike the Axis next! At that moment we were sufficiently ignorant to be in no danger of giving away any military secrets. Later, unfortunately, that was not to be the case.

All during that spring I saw the Pink Eyes off and on, either during my trips to Algiers or Casablanca. Pink Eye was still drawing at least his OSS salary and as each new innocent came over from 'Q' Building in Washington he would continue his pumping operations.

After the Axis African surrender in May came our successful landings in Sicily in July. In July the big shots of Fifth Army Head-quarters in Oujda were called to Algiers for the Planning Board of the Salerno landings, code-named *Avalanche*. Pink Eye we carefully kept away from Oujda lest he find some scrap of information, or missing jigsaw piece usable by the Fuehrer's or Marshal Kesselring's headquarters.

My suspicions of Pink Eye were greatly aroused by his curiosity every time I saw him in Casablanca, curiosity as to just exactly what we were doing on the Spanish frontier. I always supplied him with true information when it was unimportant and plausible lies when necessary.

Pink Eye, I became convinced, was still in touch with the Germans. To this day I cannot prove it. But an authentic double agent, known and controlled, is the most valuable of all espionage heavy artillery. For after feeding the enemy a long series of useless truths, you may, at some vital moment, feed him the 'big lie' when it serves your purposes best. After two or three 'big lies' a double agent often becomes useless as the enemy realizes his duplicity. At this point he may well meet with a fatal accident, or simply fade away.

If Pink Eye was in touch with the Germans, I never found out how. We knew that General Noguès, French Governor of Morocco, was in touch with Vichy over a telephone line to Tangier with voice scramblers. But General Patton, politically as ignorant and dangerous as he was militarily brilliant, would never let us cut these wires. Perhaps this could have been Pink Eye's channel of communications. Perhaps a radio in the Medina of Casablanca. More likely the Spanish Consulate in Casablanca.

At the end of July, Colonel Howard of G2 Fifth Army and his counter-intelligence officer, Major Art Blom, sent for me to come to El Biar, a suburb of Algiers, to assist them with certain problems of the Planning Board for the Salerno landings. I was to help them with matters pertaining to the geography and the iconography of the country south of Salerno. Also I was to prepare to take with Fifth Army D-day convoy about twenty men with transport, communications, and supplies. Another fifty would come in on D+5 day convoy. We were to include enough Italians recruited in North Africa (anti-Fascists, Freemasons, Communists, and anarchists) to make up teams capable of infiltrating the enemy lines with walkie-talkies or the little oss radio set. These were to supply not only strategic (long-term military and political intelligence) but also tactical, geographical, and sanitary intelligence, and to set up counter-intelligence groups to supplement the cic Corps, which had neither the means (unvouchered funds) nor the personnel for carrying on counter-espionage beyond the enemy lines.

In Oujda we had shared offices with the cic Corps, and we used one another's ci files. We were able to give them communications, transport, and civilian informants far above the niggardly supply

133

and cash funds allowed them by the army, which was not at all convinced that counter-espionage was valuable.

At the Planning Board, behind the barbed wire and elaborate security arrangements in El Biar, I was told the whole *Avalanche* story – day, hour, place, and strength. I resolved that until after the embarkation early in September I would, first, not drink, second, cut off all social contact outside the security group of the Planning Board and my own outfit, third, *keep my mouth shut.*

That is with everybody except Pink Eye. For I had determined to plant a 'big lie' with him, hoping it would grow to bear the Nazis some bitter fruit.

I sent for Pink Eye late in August to be flown from Casablanca to Algiers. He arrived and I installed him in a little house which we had requisitioned some time earlier for another project. I delegated two well-trained Spaniards to keep him under surveillance, day and night. He was to be allowed in the Villa Magnol, one of the two OSS headquarters, only when accompanied by a staff member of the organization.

I took him to dinner at the best black-market restaurant in Algiers. At dinner I brought up the subject of languages. Now, Pink Eye knew that I knew he spoke perfect French, Italian, and German, and good English. I asked him what languages he spoke. He told me these four and added that he had a fair knowledge of Spanish and the Balkan languages. I changed the subject to his wife's opera career and little by little led the conversation around to Yugoslavia, Albania, and Greece. I asked if he had ever been to Belgrade.

'Wonderful people. We loved them. Gem of a city. Such caviar! The Islamic population is restless, you know.'

I sounded him out on his ideas of Tito versus Mihajlović, of the Greek partisans versus the Royal government in exile, on the hatred of Italians in Albania. We discussed the hotels in Athens and Dubrovnik and the lack of them in Albania.

'A fine place to break into Europe,' he said, 'cut the life-lines of the Axis armies in southern Russia, keep the Communists out of the Danube Valley.'

I tried to look guilty, like a poor poker player putting on a pair-of-Jacks-face when he has a full-house pressed against his chest.

'So I've read. So the press says Churchill thinks, but of course I wouldn't really know.'

Afterwards I took him to a café, indoors, with bright lights, for I wanted to watch his pink face and his grinning ill-mated eyes when I planted the 'big lie'. We found a table surrounded by empty ones. I could talk.

'Pink-Eye, would you care to go with me on an amphibious operation in the coming months?'

'Me?' he replied, 'me?' – and he laughed and stared deadpan for a long time at his white manicured hand holding a glass of fake, saccarined anisette.

'You could do as fine a counter-intelligence job as you did in aggressive intelligence before the Casa landings last year,' I said.

'I couldn't accept without hearing more about it. I'd be no good on a landing-beach...'

'Never mind that. You would not come in until D+2, or D+4. We need you. *There are so few people with a working knowledge of these languages.*' I had launched the 'big lie' as casually as I could – to Pink Eye I could only mean the Balkans. I went into a long discourse about the kind of counter-intelligence group I wanted him to lead. But I watched his face. Poker-faced as he was, he was rolling the phrase 'working knowledge of these languages' around the palate of his brain, like a gourmet with a truffle on his tongue. He wasn't listening to me. He would let me know in a week if he felt he were capable of doing the job which I had 'honoured' him and 'flattered' him by offering.

I had to hurry off to Mostaganem to put our Germans and Spaniards, who were going on the Salerno landing, behind barbed wire in two leak-proof camps, patrolled by MP's. Their last training and briefing of necessity gave away the nationality of our landing beach and its general location. We had ourselves penetrated enemy training camps often enough to know that the chances of our having a Nazi 'plant' among our recruits, however well-screened, was real and dangerous. So they were all watched night and day. No one groused. Volunteers for espionage missions are, in fact, usually grateful for every evidence of security and secrecy as it augurs well for their own safety on future missions.

One of my American colleagues whom I had left in charge of Pink Eye and his Spanish guards telephoned me the bad news. *Pink Eye had broken through the ring of security and knew where and approximately when the landings would be.* I hurried back to Algiers.

135

Art Roseborough told me the story. Pink Eye had gone, as was permitted to him, to the Villa Magnol one day in the company of a member of the organization. He wanted to see 'X', who had been his chief in pre-landing days, and discuss the advisability of his going with me on the mission. At least that was Pink Eye's story and we were stuck with it.

'X', pompous, ambitious, and rather fond of the bottle, did not 'have security' for the Salerno Planning Board. That meant he was not supposed to know where or when the operation was taking place. Through his friends at Allied Force Headquarters he did in fact know.

The day Pink Eye came to see him he had given a heavily liquid luncheon party to a friend, a fellow officer of the same company in the first World War. The most charitable thing to say is that he must have been tight. He was putty in the hands of an expert like Pink Eye. Pink Eye implied that he already knew where the landings were, that I had told him. 'X', shocked, believing that I had broken security, gave away both the date and the fact that the landings were 'near Naples'.

My own conclusion was that Pink Eye was too dangerous to the safety of hundreds of thousands of Allied soldiers and sailors to live. I thought we should kill him. André Bourgoin agreed.

My duty was to advise both General Donovan and Colonel Howard, my boss at Fifth Army and responsible for security of the whole *Avalanche* operation, what had happened. 'X' would have been court-martialled and I probably would have been sent home. Colonel Howard and Major Blom, on whose responsibility I had been given 'security', would have been on the mat before General Clark, and before the British Colonel Hill-Dillon, who was Counter-Intelligence Officer of G2 on Eisenhower's staff at AFHQ. Hill-Dillon had never liked either Howard or Blom and would, I believe, have been delighted with the opportunity to embarrass them.

Roseborough and my Spaniards assured me Pink Eye had not been out of their sight since he had so successfully pumped 'X'. To this day I think I was right, but I was persuaded against my better judgment to leave Pink Eye alive, under unofficial 'house arrest' in Algiers. I was promised he would be kept under twenty-four hours surveillance until D-day, September 9.

Only after the landings did I learn that these orders had been countermanded by 'X' when I had left for the embarkation, and

Pink Eye was released and allowed to return to Casablanca a week before the actual landings 'as his wife was ill'! Back to Casa where he was free to communicate with...anyone he chose.

Naturally, I didn't take Pink Eye with me. But somehow he got to Italy.

The next time I saw him, he was oozing prosperity in Milan during the weeks after the German surrender of May 1945. He was close to that unsavoury group of Allied Military Government hangers-on which had moved north, following Colonel Charles Poletti from Sicily to Milan. Their chief was a bogus duchess. Their business was in shaking down Italians who had to have, for any of a thousand reasons, a permit from the Allied Military Government. I have no proof whatsoever that Charles Poletti shared their take or that he even knew the nasty, profitable games they were playing.

Pink Eye invited me for a drink in the swank Principe e Savoia Hotel which served this group as office and club. I accepted. He was annoyed because the CIC had locked him up for investigation several times. His story was that he was working for the British which I was sure was untrue. We avoided talking of Africa.

In 1946 and 1947 I often saw him around the elegant Caffé Doney in Rome. He was even more prosperous and, with dogs and wife, lived at the expensive Grand Hotel.

'I want to write my memoirs, Donald. I shall call them *Pink Eye's Story*. Will they sell? Will you help me?'

'Will you tell the whole truth?'

'Well, not exactly,' he laughed, 'one has to live.'

Has to live. I wondered if he meant 'earn a living' – or 'stay out of the grave'.

'Who are you working for these days, Pink Eye?' I asked.

'Oh, everybody,' he giggled with his mouth full of cream puffs, and gave me an exaggerated wink.

'You know, Pink Eye, before the Salerno landings, before I left Africa, I had some plans for you that might have cut *Pink Eye's Story* short.'

'So I heard, so I heard,' he said gaily and divided another cream puff between the watch-eyed dogs. 'Quite right you were, quite right you were. Of course I have always been faithful to America.' He winked again. 'But how could you know? You couldn't take a chance. Proper solution...,' he drew his index finger across his fat neck like a knife and licked a little whipped cream from his lips.

'But you must help me publish *Pink Eye's Story*,' he added.

Quite suddenly in 1948 Pink Eye, his monumental wife, and the two sexy, watch-eyed dogs with their fur collars disappeared from Rome.

You cannot hate Pink Eye any more than the curator of snakes in the Bronx Zoo can hate his best adder. You can't even dislike him. Knowing him well, at times you can doubt his very preposterous existence; you can feel you dreamed him after reading Eric Ambler.

You can even feel sorry for Pink Eye, loose, homeless, friendless, harried by his operatic wife and his horrid dogs. You wonder at the strong cages he must have built in his brain to restrain his fears. I confess that I wish him well.

But I hope he isn't living in, say, Berlin or New York, or Hong Kong.

Even more I hope 'X' isn't a big shot in the Central Intelligence Agency in Washington.

CHAPTER ELEVEN

DARBY'S RANGERS

'Darby was a wonderful battle leader. There
is no praise which you can give him which
will be too lavish.'

GEN. A. M. GRUENTHER

SEPTEMBER 1943 AND APRIL 1945

Just after sunset on our second day ashore on the Salerno Beachhead, the jeep full of colonels came for me.

'Is there a guy named Downes here?'

I managed a weak yes.

'Pick up your stuff quick and jump in, you're going out to the command ship. General Gruenther wants you. There's a PT waiting at the beach.'

My fruitless trip to find an HQ site for the generals was over. I must have done something terrible and was going to be sent back. What had I done?

We cut across fields at a dizzy rate and, I thought, with a dizzy disregard for mines. General Gruenther wanted me, and Alfred Maximilian Gruenther, one of the world's best contract bridge players, was General Clark's Chief of Staff.

I had seen little of him, a smallish man with cold blue eyes and nondescript brown hair. I never heard anything but praise for Gruenther as a military man. I remember a colonel in Mostaganem before our embarkation saying, 'Fortunately for everybody General Clark will be so busy with his Public Relations Officer running *The Mark W. Clark for President Club* that he will leave Fifth Army's war to Al Gruenther – and that's bad news for the Krauts and the Eyeties.'

The command ship, *Ancon*, a Panama liner done over by the Navy, was an HQ ship for big amphibious operations. She embodied every modern device known to man, and some secret ones besides. She was air-conditioned, connected to shore by radio teletype, soundproofed, and she bristled with anti-aircraft guns and radar. She had a twenty-four-hour-a-day restaurant where spotless negro mess boys served steaks, French fries, ham and eggs, apple pie, ice cream, and excellent coffee. She was the most beautiful and polished temple of efficiency in all the world.

An office-boy colonel guided me down to the command room in the bowels of the ship. He opened the door like Jeeves and showed me in. On the opposite wall a huge detailed map, a so-called 'situation map', kept track of every unit ashore. The information came in on one of those magnified teletypes such as you see in fancy brokers' offices to give latest prices to the customers.

Then I spotted little Gruenther. He was sitting in a corner, engrossed in a game of bridge with a British war correspondent, a British naval liaison commander, and his own sergeant. Between plays he looked sharply at the map, at the teletype, and back at his hand. Every once in a while he called a captain from a desk at the far end of the room and gave an order almost in a whisper. There was a sense of relaxation and normal execution of business in the room. No one ran, no one shouted.

Later, in the offices of lesser lights on *Ancon* I was to see nervousness, indecision, and real fright. But this, the brain of the whole landing operation, might have been the bridge room at the Yale Club on an off night – except it was too clean and too orderly.

Finally, my colonel-guide dared go up and announce me between hands. Gruenther glanced in my direction, grunted, and politely waved the colonel away. He gave some orders, played another hand, explained to his sergeant-partner why he should not have taken a certain finesse.

Then he swung around his chair and called me. 'You're supposed to know the country on the Peninsula over at Amalfi. Do you?'

'Yes, sir, pretty well.'

'Well, Darby's over there with three battalions of Rangers and the Germans are giving him hell. He's got a shock outfit that's supposed to operate for short periods only and for special assaults under some other outfit's staff. But he is stuck; we can't relieve him. In short he's got no G2 and no G4.* Howard at G2 recommended you. Want to go up?'

'Yes, sir. I intended to establish my outfit at Amalfi, anyway.'

'Damned funny thing sending a civilian to G2 for a combat outfit at the front.' He laughed.

---

* G4 Supply, transportation, etc.

'Listen. Don't think you have any orders superior to Darby. He doesn't have to take you. Maybe he'll say no. It's a thin front. He's got a few men. Danger of infiltration. Danger of sabotage of his supply. He's got no transport either, you'll have to improvise that. He's afraid of the civilians. They're hungry and he's got no food for them and no civilian affairs officers. A.M.G. won't be ashore for a week. Now go up to Howard's office, get some particulars from him, some orders, and tell him to find you a bunk, a shave and a bath here tonight, you're pretty dirty and crumby looking. Thanks, good luck. You'll like Darby. He's a great officer.'

He turned back to his bridge and I went up to Colonel Howard's office. I got a bath, a shave, and a bunk. But I wished I were back on shore. *Ancon* had the hell shaken out of her all night by close-misses from air raiders. I didn't sleep at all. But I am sure Alfred Maximilian Gruenther slept like a baby and dreamed of big slams doubled and redoubled.

The next morning a PT was to take me to Maiori where Colonel Darby had his headquarters. But it was late, and while I waited I saw the first radio-controlled bomb launched by the Germans. It seemed a tiny fighter plane circling around, while its mother ship, invisible to us, was hovering in the stratosphere.

It caught the cruiser *Savannah* squarely in her forward turret. The magazines exploded and catapulted the bodies of sailors out of the turret like coloured stars from a fireworks fountain. General Gruenther came up to see the wounded *Savannah*, deep down by the bows, back away at full speed astern, like a dying Moby Dick.

All of us on deck behaved like chickens, dashing from group to group with inexpert conclusions and wild guesses.

Gruenther stood calmly watching her back away. I went up to him.

'General, can I ask you a personal question?'

'Sure, why not?'

'How could you keep your mind on that bridge game when you had all that on shore to play, to manipulate last night?'

'An operation like this is a good deal like bridge anyway. You've got to decide and play fast. Bridge keeps my brain awake and helps me forget what a mislead could mean on shore there; what kind of cards we're playing with, how high the stakes are. This is a game you've got to keep your nerve in' – he waved toward shore.

'Thank you, and good-bye, sir.'

'Good-bye. My best luck to Darby.'

141

He went below. My PT was announced.

I went aboard and we batted hard water towards Maiori. The familiar silhouette of the mountains of the Sorrentine Peninsula rose high out of the sea, an old friend welcoming me. And there on those lemon terraces, rising thousands of feet from the steep, narrow valleys and the sea to the brutal monolithic crags of the mountains, among enchanted chestnut forests, Americans were fighting, hiding, killing and dying. I had to say it to myself to believe it – 'In the land of Sirens and Fauns.'

I saw again over my shoulder that fantastic endless fleet. It was divided in two by the figure of a sailor, clean and starched-looking, standing in the stern with his face, a young face, set in lines of fatigue and determination. The sailor seemed gigantic, standing on the horizon rather than on the PT. Nothing in the world could stop him, no one could hate him.

The PT ground up on the pebbly, steep beach of Maiori. A couple of soldiers were swimming near a landing barge of supplies. A few townspeople sat idly under the oleanders along the sea wall. There was no real evidence of war or signs that less than seventy-two hours ago men had landed here by force.

I jumped down and the starched sailor handed me my musette bag and carbine.

'Thanks,' I said, and added, 'for everything.'

One of the soldiers who had been swimming came out of the water. I went up to him.

'Where's Colonel Darby's HQ?'

'On the corner. There's only two streets in this burg, so there's only one corner. You'll find him in there with the seven dwarfs.'

'Thanks.'

''Scuse me, but what the hell is that uniform you got on? – civilian?'

'Don't know,' I replied, 'I'm on my way now to ask Colonel Darby what I am.'

'Dontcha know?'

'No, I don't. Thanks again.'

'Well, so-long now.'

In a tiny summer boarding-house and restaurant I found Darby and three of the seven dwarfs. A sergeant dressed in parachute boots, pants, and an undershirt received me. I told him I had come from General Gruenther.

142

'Hey, Colonel, sir,' he called out, adding the 'sir' obviously to impress me, 'there's a...' (to me) 'what are you?'

'Civilian.'

'...there's a civilian, an American here who says he is from General Gruenther.'

'Send him in.'

Colonel Darby was the Arrow-collar-ad in the perfect Abercrombie and Fitch uniform. He was so clean and shaved that he shone. His uniform was creased to a razor's edge. His tie was perfect. His nails were manicured. I saluted, shook hands and handed him my orders... *You will report to* CO *Ranger Battalions in or near Maiori for such duty as that* CO *may require. These orders effective until cancelled either by yourself or* CO *Ranger Battalions'*... or words to that effect.

'Sit down, Mr Downes. What do these orders really mean?'

'First, regards from General Gruenther and Colonel Howard. Second, I am, most erroneously, believed to be an expert on this part of the world. General Gruenther said you didn't have any G2 or G4 and he thought maybe a civilian could improvise, be of more help than anyone bound by the rules and regulations...'

'I'm damned proud of my outfit. Everyone of these guys is a volunteer. They are tough; they know how to fight; and, by Jesus Christ, they know how to die. I let 'em wear phoney uniforms and choose their own weapons, but there is no part of the army with better discipline – *when we need discipline.*

'If anybody but Gruenther had sent me a civilian – nothing personal y' understand – I'd have sent him away so damned fast... I'd have thought they were making fun of me. But not Gruenther. That's a real soldier, Gruenther.'

'He says the same thing about you, Colonel.'

'I'm glad you told me. It means something coming from him. Well, you can stay...and I need you.'

He explained his difficulties. He had less than two thousand men and something like thirty miles of mountainous front to hold – not only to hold, but to use as a base to raid and fire on the German communications, which skirted the far side of the mountains on the plain of Vesuvius.

The Germans had reserves – best part of a division of Panzer Grenadiers. Darby had no one behind the front; no one to unload supplies; no one to patrol the roads from the waterfront to the fighting front on the passes high in the mountains; no one to control the civilians; not even any decent wireless contact with the command ship.

'And I don't depend from any corps or division. I'm just a sort of afterthought, a floating kidney of this operation. Now they tell me there is no relief, no reserves in sight. Just hold on. Hold on to what and with what?'

'Why don't we put civilians to carrying supplies to the front?'

'I've got no money to pay them. You can't conscript civilians – forced labour, Geneva Convention, all that.'

'I have plenty of money, Colonel, and when that runs out I can open the banks around here and take what they've got.'

'Hell, you can't do that. That's looting!'

'Sure I can and I'll leave them a receipt. Somebody'll pay them some day, or OSS can pay 'em out of secret funds. Who cares? This is a matter of necessity. I am a civilian. You soldiers are expendable at the front; I am expendable behind the front. The most they can do to me is send me home.'

Then I told him my plans to move *Special Detachment G2* into Amalfi when possible, when it was no longer a no-man's-land. He had no idea what we were supposed to do. I told him our programme to infiltrate radios and agents by land, sea, and air to the north, to Naples, to Rome, to gather all types of long-term intelligence.

'And,' I added, 'to do any jobs of tactical intelligence for army, corps, air, artillery, down to companies, if they need us and want us.'

My human mule teams, all volunteers, began unloading supplies and toting them to the front or dispersed dumps that same night. Over three hundred men and boys worked ten hours a day. Mortar shells, tins of water, cases of rations, ammunition boxes, medical supplies, all were carried, if not quickly, carefully and safely to the front, about 2,400 feet high above the town. Over fifteen miles by road.

These people are used to carrying packs in the mountains, a usage some three thousand years old. Even today many peasants live 2,500 steps below or above their work. Cases of lemons, bags of earth, flour for the mill, all supplies are transported in this way – on the heads of men, women and children.

I paid them $1.00 a day for adults, $0.75 a day for children, and since they were hungry – the whole peninsula was virtually starving – I gave them two cans of 'C' ration (meat and beans) a day as fuel, provided they were opened and eaten on the spot, at noon and at sundown.

OSS never criticised my spending unvouchered funds in this unexpected way, although it reached a sizeable sum in three weeks. But later, Allied Military Government lodged a bitter protest at HQ Fifth Army, saying I 'had broken the agreement with Prime Minister Badoglio not to inflate Italian civilian wages'!

Even now I can see that long line of men and boys in rags winding up the Chiunzi Pass, each with his load of from fifty to over one hundred pounds, with steadiness and patience from sun up to sun down. Much of the material they delivered under fire at the very front. One dollar a day 'might upset the delicate balance of Italian economy.' I had hoped we had come to Italy, among other reasons, to upset the indelicate disbalance of Italian economy.

Colonel Darby was pleased with results, including the 'looting' of the Maiori bank, and he closed his West Point eyes to my grossly unmilitary behaviour.

War is not very West Point anyway.

I not only grew to admire Darby but to like him, and to like the seven dwarfs, too.

The seven dwarfs were his seven senior officers. Of course, Darby was 'Snow White'. His radio and generator sat under the palms between the HQ and the beach.

'Snow White calling Dopey, Snow White calling Dopey, over.'

'This is Dopey, over.'

'What is new up there, over.'

'Nothing. They've stopped dropping mortars on us. We have no new wounded to report, over.'

'We've sent you a hundred rounds for your mortars and twenty cases of rations; have they arrived? over.'

'No, over.'

'Good night. Call us if you need us. Snow White will be up there to-morrow morning, over.'

'Good-night, Dopey signing off, over.'

'Snow White signing off.'

'Snow White calling Grumpy, Snow White calling Grumpy...'

This spit-and-polish dandy with three battalions of men who looked like hobos in mismatched uniforms was more beloved by his men than any leader, military or otherwise, whom I have ever known. He was alternately as kind as an indulgent mother, and as tough as a Prussian drillmaster. I have seen him cry when a soldier went in for an amputation, and cry publicly and unashamed. I have heard him tongue-lash a soldier in a really brutal manner for a small forgetfulness.

To me he was always extremely fair, but often curt and brusque. He never gave me an order with a *please*, and usually it had a *right now* appended.

On the other hand when he wanted my advice he was courteous, almost exaggeratedly so. He would invite me in, offer me a drink and a smoke, and spread the maps on the big dining-room table.

'Could you help me?' he would begin. 'In your opinion is it possible to infiltrate that town after dark? Have you been there?' He always heard me out in silence. We sent a good many local infiltration teams through the lines to obtain precise tactical information for him. He was always astonished at their ability to pass. He usually had the jitters after they had left, and was certain that my agents wouldn't return; he thought they were killed, or captured, or had gone over to the enemy. When they would return or walkie-talkie back the information, he was almost childishly gleeful, and behaved as if I had performed a miracle.

Darby, a brilliant West Pointer, was ignorant of the possibilities of well-organized espionage and sabotage. He had not even a *Saturday Evening Post* reader's knowledge of civilian partisan warfare. But he was honest, alert and hungry for knowledge. He was easy to help; he made co-operation possible and effective. Most generals, I discovered, were at least as ignorant as he about intelligence matters, but lacked his virtue of curiosity and the desire to experiment and to learn.

One night Colonel Darby called me down to Maiori from Amalfi, where I had in the meantime established my HQ for OSS, Fifth Army, and our clandestine radio base-station. He was worried and excited.

'The Krauts must know every move we make. Their snipers are too accurate and their mortars can see our supply dumps over the mountain tops. They must have agents and a radio on this side of the hills. For God's sake find it. I lost half my gasoline today, and worse still I had nine wounded. Now the British wireless spotters tell me they have D-F'ed an enemy transmitter in this town.

'I don't care if you tear the whole town down. Find that radio. Right now.'

'I'll do my best,' I replied, 'I have about twelve available men in

Amalfi of whom seven speak Italian. How many Rangers can you give me?'

'Will a hundred do?'

'Yes, thanks; at ten tonight?'

'OK. Here at my HQ.'

Poor Maiori. The Germans had been dropping an odd bomb on the beach every night hoping against hope they would find some target. The town folk were afraid and every evening, about an hour or two before the habitual raid time, they left their homes to sleep in the fields or caves on the hillside. Our search was thus made much more difficult. Many houses were locked; others were open, but the family had carried away the keys to the various chests of drawers or cupboards.

But a search is a search, and if you are hunting for a radio no greater in size than a shoe-box you have to search in, over, under and behind everything. We had about 500 houses. We had to open every drawer, look under every bed, probe the bottom of each vase of tomato sauce, look up the chimneys, sound the walls, and fine-tooth-comb everything, including the back-houses.

To do this without keys required axes. Axes make a hell of a noise and destroy treasured property of a lot of decent, poor towns-folk who've struggled for generations to acquire it. Already the town was upset because we would not allow the churches to clang their bells every few minutes as is their habit. We had had an unfortunate experience in Sicily of a priest signalling to the enemy with his bells.

I established four teams of twenty-five Rangers each. An Italian speaking Ranger officer I put over one, an Italo-American sergeant of mine over the second, Marcello over the third, and Ugo over the fourth.

The town is composed of one long street beginning at the main Amalfi-Salerno highway and cut by many dead-end side streets. Two groups were to start up the valley and work one on each side of the main street, towards the waterfront. One squad was to start up the highway towards Amalfi, one towards Salerno, and these two also were to work toward the cross-roads, Ranger HQ.

One man was to be stationed in each little dead-end tributary street with orders to arrest anyone coming out of a house after the search began. Our signal to begin was to ring the church bells at 11.30 pm.

To Ugo and Marcello, being native-born Italians, responsible men in their fifties, recruited from among the anti-Fascists in French North African concentration camps, I gave the more important assignments, the two sides of the main street.

Ugo was an anarchist – anarchists are the intellectual cream of the Latin countries. He had been a professor at the University of Rome. As a good anarchist he hated all governments, but hated Fascism especially, because it pretended government was more important than any or all of the individuals governed. He had escaped to Tunisia, where he had preached anti-Fascism among the 200,000 Italians there. Vichy, of course, had clapped him behind barbed wire.

Ugo was gentle, a dead shot with a Tommy-gun, sentimental, and wore a ferocious bristling beard almost red in colour. He always spoke formally as in a class-room. In Africa he had said, 'You need not worry that as an anarchist I shall refuse orders. We anarchists admire discipline when it is directed towards the destruction of evil,' and he had lived up to his promise.

Marcello looked like a fat Ben Turpin. He was a Communist and a Mason. He carried these two mutually contradictory beliefs to the point of religious fanaticism, sealing each in some peculiarly strong logic-tight compartment. Usually in cross-eyed people, one eye crosses. In Marcello, each eye looked over the bridge of his nose at the other.

Marcello was bellicose and somewhat of a bully to his inferiors, but a slave to those qualified to give him orders. He was as big as Ugo was small, heavily muscled but clumsy. In a pinch, lacking a Spaniard, I'd take Ugo.

When they were half-way through their jobs (I had been visiting all four teams), I had to take over from Marcello. Apparently, destruction for its own sake intoxicated him or gave him some deep, almost sexual, satisfaction. The Rangers with him, being young and out from under Darby's discipline for a few hours, took to this game. They were literally splintering everything, axing down doors before trying to force them, making kindling wood of furniture which wasn't even locked. Later, when I inspected the houses Ugo had searched, I found negligible damage; nothing unnecessary. Those townspeople living on his side of the street were as calm the next day as those on Marcello's side were lamenting and protesting.

At best it is humiliating and degrading to rout peasants out of their beds; paw over their few miserable possessions; expose their poor hoard of rag-like clothes and wormy dried fruits; pry open a box to find it full of pressed funeral flowers, twenty-years'-old wedding candy, the curl from a dead child's head, and a faded cheap print of the Virgin signed 'with big kisses from mama.'

Ugo came to me afterwards. 'Sir,' he said, 'I nearly disobeyed your orders tonight. I wanted to shoot Marcello.'

'So did I, let's try to forget it,' I replied.

'If you do not need me any more tonight I should like to walk on the beach and sleep there. I would rather not see him. I shall be at the Luna early, before you are up. I must continue to work with him, but I ask to be free tonight to control myself.'

We didn't find the radio, but we did find its aerial under the eaves of a house empty since we landed. And plenty of evidence that someone had slept there and eaten German iron rations for at least a week.

British Direction Finding reported three days later, 'The Maiori clandestine transmitter is off the air.'

The fact that our quarry had escaped worried Darby more than his original belief that the radio existed. My opinion was that the Nazi spy had listened in on Darby's chats with the seven dwarfs; on at least two such chats he had discussed 'there's a Jerry with a radio in this town some place.'

He often called orders out of his window to jeeps going up to the front. I have heard him describe a new distribution of his mortars with his map spread out before him under the palm trees in front of his HQ and civilians less than ten feet away.

Once or twice when there was no one around I took the liberty to criticize his security. But his only reply would be 'Good God! Did I really do that?' It seems to me a weakness of all professional officers who are not G2 specialists rather than any failing of Darby.

Darby saw I was short-handed and offered me a driver for my jeep. Jimmie, about twenty-one years old, a lanky hill-billy from the Great Smoky Mountains, turned up with a note from the colonel.

He's a good driver and the best shot in my outfit with a heavy calibre machine-gun. He had about fifteen pieces of metal taken out of him Friday, so I'm giving him ten days' driving for a rest. Keep him out of mischief and you'll find him a good man – Darby.

Jimmie soon made my jeep look like a monitor. He put a pipe

149

through the cowl just front and right of the driver's seat, and using this as a swivel, mounted a 25 mm. machine-gun he'd salvaged from a wrecked plane.

Driving on the tortuous Amalfi road he'd spot a cave half a mile away, jam on the brakes, and say, 'Bet I kin put the first burst in there' – and he would, but the jeep had to be firmly braked or the recoil would drive us backwards.

One day coming down from Agerola to Amalfi, the most snake-like and dangerous descent in Italy, he spotted a German fighter coasting in very low, actually below the mountain tops and not much higher than we.

The fighter was either sneaking away from superior numbers or had been badly hit. Before I knew what he was shouting about he had run the jeep against a wall to stop it short, and was firing. He put a long burst directly into the fighter's belly and it began to smoke.

We didn't see it hit but we heard it, screened behind the cliff which rose over our heads. And from farther down we saw the smoke and flame.

No child on Christmas morning was ever so pleased, so excited.

'Wait till I write Lee that. Holy smoke. Right in that lousy Kraut's guts. Gee wiz, Mr Downes, you'll tell the kunnel, won't youse. I'll write Lee tonight.'

I promised to and I did. But Jimmie thought I was very unreasonable not to give him a day off to climb the mountain to look for his plane.

After the fall of Naples, Jimmie went back to the Rangers. He was killed in the tragic ambush at Cisterna on the Anzio beachhead below Rome. That ambush nearly wiped out the Rangers. And Darby was too tied up in his troops, part mother and part commanding officer. He never recovered from that ambush. After it he was invalided home. Nervous breakdown, his surviving officers called it. I think it was closer to a broken heart.

He had said to me one day, 'Did you ever see such a crowd of men! Every one a volunteer. I really believe they are the finest body of troops ever gathered together. Training them was more fun than work. They don't surrender either. They fight for keeps.'

But when they didn't surrender, trapped by tanks at Cisterna, something went out of Darby.

I saw him for a moment in Italy just before he was killed by a stray shell in the last weeks of the war. He had aged and the spring and life were gone from his walk, from his eyes.

150

CHAPTER TWELVE

THE BOSS

. . . he hath counsel and understanding.

JOB XII, 13

SEPTEMBER 1943

Outside of a confidential trip for President Roosevelt in the Balkans before we were at war, and the nature of his highly successful work as a corporation lawyer, William J. Donovan was a 'secret intelligence' amateur when war with the Axis became inevitable. Most countries have had decades, sometimes centuries of experience with highly-specialized secret-intelligence organizations, abundantly supplied with funds for which no accounting need be made. The U.S.A. was a 'secret intelligence virgin.'

Donovan turned to our British Allies, the most experienced nation in the world in intelligence matters. He frankly asked their aid and advice and they – with their backs to the wall in 1941 – unreservedly and energetically supplied him with both.

With a wide Presidential directive and with British advice, Donovan set up OSS, a huge secret intelligence and secret operation organization. He had the good sense to realize that the cloak-and-dagger boys, like myself, the secret missions, the conspiracies, the sabotage teams, the uniformed raiders, and all the theatrical side was relatively unimportant compared with an organization capable of interpreting facts for use of the President, diplomats, generals, admirals, planners and all.

So Donovan created a 'Research and Analysis Department.' Here quietly working were thousands of the most learned brains in the country. Everything from the beach gradients in the Bay of Salerno to the religion of the natives on some obscure Pacific atoll, or the habits of sea-birds on Ascension Island, was their business.

There is nothing 'wild' about Wild Bill Donovan, and whoever gave him that nickname was both misinformed and did him a great disservice in his political and military life. His most noticeable weakness was that his heart often ruled his head.

I remember the days I spent with him in Amalfi, Capri, and Ischia, when those Lotus Lands near Naples were the front. I had established

151

the OSS Fifth Army Headquarters in the old Hotel Luna in Amalfi – once a monastery founded by St. Francis of Assisi. He arrived in a sort of Churchillian baby's jumper suit with his general's insignia and a musette bag – no luggage. The hero of Chateau Thierry was wearing his Congressional Medal of Honour ribbon, won in 1918.*

He wanted to see the beach-head, already nearly two weeks old, to smell powder, to sleep in a fox-hole and eat K-rations. Instead he found our outfit luxuriously installed in the Hotel Luna within rifle-shot of the fighting. Don Antonio, the proprietor, was prowling into no-man's land for good fresh Mozzarella cheese. We had, all ninety of us, fresh sheets on our beds. The chambermaids wore spotless uniforms; the waiters served in dinner jackets.

The General was disappointed. He mumbled something about this being a hellova way to fight a war, and added a footnote about congressional investigations. Major John Roller suggested digging him a foxhole under the mimosa tree in the rose garden, but no one quite dared offer to do it.

The next day Donovan wanted to see the Bay of Naples (still held by the Germans), which probably meant being under fire, and to visit Capri, because he had promised Mrs Harrison (Mona-the-best-dressed-woman) Williams to protect her villa. We ordered one of the three PT boats the Navy had put at our disposal and shoved off early the next morning after a good night's sleep (despite a naval barrage overhead) and an extravagant breakfast of grapes, eggs, bacon, fried fish, coffee and butter.

First, we whizzed towards Capri, 'to see Mona's villa' and 'do something about it.' On the way I got the bad news. I was to remain in Italy as head of counter-intelligence only. Colonel 'G', whom Donovan as well as I knew to be a good-natured incompetent, but a man politically important in New York, was to head all OSS activities in Italy. There would be a breaking-down of Special Detachments of G2 into Secret Intelligence, Secret Operations, and my new command, Counter-Intelligence.

I was in agreement that we needed an overall head in Italy to stay at HQ of Fifth Army. I wanted to be more active, to set up additional missions of my own to operate beyond the lines, and had no objection to the counter-intelligence assignment.

* In the 1914–1918 War Donovan was the only officer to receive America's highest decoration for bravery.

But I refused to serve under Colonel 'G'.

The second piece of bad news was an order 'from highest political level' that we could use no more Italians, in any capacity, who would not take a new oath of allegiance to the Italian Royal House of Savoy. This I resented even more than Colonel 'G'. How could we betray all the Italian democrats, almost to a man rabidly anti-House of Savoy, by insisting that they swear allegiance to the ridiculous little king who had saddled them with Fascism and thumped for Mussolini until military defeat was inevitable? Again I refused.

This refusal Donovan took much more seriously.

'This is wartime and those are orders,' he said.

'Thank God, I am still a civilian. Soldiers have a military code of honour they won't violate, I have a civilian's conscience still and won't violate it.'

My tone was both insubordinate and nasty. Our arrival at Capri changed the subject.

We went to 'Mona's villa.' It was an elaborate Grand Rapids horror grafted on a naturally beautiful island where only simplicity is tolerable. It annoyed me. Donovan said as we left, 'I wish you would arrange to requisition the villa. We don't want it ruined by a lot of British enlisted personnel – and they'll have this island.'

'I've not enough men to spare,' I said, in a not very respectful tone, 'you'll be at Fifth Army Headquarters tomorrow, ask them to do it. I don't want to fight a war protecting Mrs Harrison Williams' pleasure dome.'

Donovan looked at me and didn't say a word. My Irish was up in a way that, in retrospect, I am not proud of. I was facing an Irishman also capable of getting his Irish up. He was my elder, and my superior. But he held his temper, all except his eyes.

That conversation was interrupted by our leaving for the Island of Ischia via the Bay of Naples, where there might be mines, German E-boats or shore batteries. The commander of the PT put on some real speed, and real speed in a PT pounds hell out of the passengers.

Donovan went up to the prow. Naples was burning, great columns of black and grey smoke reached the sky. Vesuvius was smoking too, but it seemed modest in comparison with poor, broken Naples.

He called me to him. 'What is that over there? What is this over here?' He balanced himself without support while I hung on to everything available for dear life.

Under his steel helmet, his great shaggy eyebrows covered his pale blue eyes. His face was stern and set with anger.

I wanted to say, 'I'll take it all back. I'll requisition Mona's goddamn villa and serve if necessary under Charlie McCarthy' – but I couldn't. That night we returned to Amalfi. Donovan asked me to come into his hotel room.

'Listen to me, Donald,' he said, 'believing what you said today, taking the stand you've taken, you cannot stay in Italy.

'I appreciate the work you have done, a fine job for your country, first in America and then Africa. On the *Banana Mission* disaster I stood behind you and it was no easy position to take.

'There are reasons, many of which I cannot tell you, why I have decided to put Colonel 'G' here.

'G2 at Fifth Army speaks very highly of you. You have played the game with them and they are your friends.

'It's hell on the front back in Washington, too. There's Congress, there's G2 War Department, there's Naval Intelligence, there's the FBI all gunning for us because we have a new idea. A necessary idea for modern war. It's like the old generals opposing Bill Mitchell and airplanes. So I have to compromise every day. I counted on you to compromise too. But you won't.

'Now I envy you your ideals and your willingness to stick to them cost what may. In government you can't do that. You are lucky you can. I wish I could too.

'I shall not hold against you anything you did or said today. I think you're a case of 'intelligence fatigue' – it's three years now. And, besides, you've just been over a landing-beach. You're nervously exhausted. What's more I think you are physically ill; you look green.

'You did a job at Fifth Army. It is our only functioning unit with a combat army in the field as an integral part of that army's make-up. I appreciate the ground you broke, so if you want to stay in command until after the fall of Naples, you may. It is your due.

'Then I'll get you high-priority orders back to the States. Go to a first-rate civilian hospital and have a check-up. Get your health and your nerves back again. When you are ready and well, come to Washington. I'll let you go any place in the world, except Italy, to do whatever job interests you most – you can have what personnel and funds you need. I still have great confidence in you and a real affection for you. I am leaving early tomorrow morning.

154

'Good night – and when you get to America ask my secretary for a letter, she'll have one for you from me.'

You just can't help loving a guy who can make such a speech to you, disagree as you may with some of the things he does. I admit it gave me wet eyes.

To complete the record, that letter with his secretary in Washington had in it his personal cheque (and a fat one) to cover my hospital bills.

He was right, too – I had amoebic dysentery, a really nasty disease. After I was cured he lived up to his word and I went to the Middle East.

I do not think that there was another American in 1941 capable of creating a functioning secret intelligence organization overnight. His raw materials were thousands of enthusiastic amateurs. Maybe seventy-five per cent of the effort was fruitless. To my knowledge there were projects in the remaining twenty-five per cent which contributed enormously to winning and shortening the war, to saving many thousands of Allied lives. It was smart in those days to say OSS stood for *Oh, so social*. It is true Donovan had a lot of stuffed shirts and straw men around him, social, financial and political. But they mended his political fences in Washington and had he not used them his organization would have died before it was born.

Donovan was never intolerant of failure. He was always intolerant of laziness, half measures, dishonesty, and double dealing. Those in whom he even suspected these sins got summary justice. Those in whom he had confidence could see him as much as they wanted, even if it meant, as it often did, that he worked twenty hours a day.

In the eight months I was in 'Q' Building in Washington in 1942 I saw him nearly every day. Some days three times. At six o'clock in the morning he would dog-trot in a sweat shirt to Washington from his home in Georgetown. At his office, 'The Kremlin', he bathed and dressed. Before he went to bed at around 1.30 am. he had worn out three shifts of secretaries, and he was then well over sixty years old!

Above all this, the old man had imagination and wasn't ashamed of it. Nothing was too fantastic for Donovan, if you could convince him that it had a chance of success, or that it would harm the enemy. Some stuffed-shirted general or some kid-gloved admiral afraid of being ridiculous, some timid diplomat from a State Department career, would never had the courage to give the OK to most of these projects.

It might be the counterfeit Japanese currency from old lamp-shades in Massachusetts. It might be to blackmail a German general in Africa. It might be a plan to make an OSS agent of the wife of the German Ambassador in a neutrál country. It might be to poison the cattle in Bulgaria. It might be to trade new American clothes for the old European clothes of refugees.

'Do you think it has any chance of success? How much will it hurt the enemy?'

OSS, Donovan's own creation, with the stamp of him on it, with the spirit of him in it, became à vivid and compelling force in many critical moments and places of war.

He's a great guy and he did an extraordinary job, and I think I know what gave him the patience, the courage, and the energy to carry on over all obstacles. He loves his country more than any man I know.

But, my God, sometimes he can make you want to knock his teeth out, too. Like about Mona Williams' villa.

CHAPTER THIRTEEN

BELLA NAPOLI

. . . only she doth carry
June in her eyes, in her heart January.

THOMAS CAREW

AUTUMN 1943

I left Amalfi to enter Naples on my birthday, 30 September 1943. Naples fell on 1 October, pitiful and lovable in her ruins.

In Naples in the weeks preceding our entry, the only unplanned, spontaneous partisan movement in Europe flared up. The Germans, as always, had behaved perfectly as individuals and like swine as an army. The water supply was cut off; sewers were plugged; civilian medical supplies destroyed; funerals forbidden; property uselessly burned. All this not by irresponsible individuals, but by command of various headquarters higher than divisional.

With me when I entered the city was Adolfo Omodeo, president of the University of Naples. He had always been one of Italy's few democrats – and unfortunately for Italy he died shortly after the war.

Omodeo was at his summer house in Positano when we landed. He was delighted to find himself on the same side of the line as his sympathies. He (with Croce's son-in-law, Craveri) was of great help to us and he wrote the letters which some of our infiltration teams took through the German lines to Naples – letters to the city's sanitary engineer, the engineer of the waterworks and others. These letters requested all the technical information needed by Fifth Army engineers to order pipe, valves, and pumps from America to make the city tick again.

Naples was the first big European city to fall to us. The Nazis had made it as much of a liability as possible. Fifth Army sanitary experts, the medical corps, and the commanding general were all inexperienced in meeting so great a problem: a city of a million people with typhus, unburied dead, no water, no power, no fuel,

157

no sewage, little medicine and less food, with most of its housing and all of its transportation facilities unusable. It was a mess.

A few days after the city's fall the repair materials arrived. In short order Naples had water and sewage; the typhus was wiped out; medicines and, above all, wheat were available. The city, which might have been a disastrous liability, was, instead, calm and easily controlled, so that its great port was soon functioning again.

We had heard that the German command had burned the city's famous collection of ancient and medieval manuscripts, one of the two or three greatest in the world.

Omodeo was convinced it couldn't be true. No civilized people would order the destruction of so important a part of 'the intellectual treasure of western civilization.' Our report said it had been done because of 'suspected partisan activities of certain university students.'

We drove towards the smoking city, past Castellamare di Stabia, Pompeii, Torre del Greco, Portici – names highly seasoned with historical flavours – now so ruined as to be almost indistinguishable from the ruins Vesuvius had created eighteen centuries earlier.

The whole city was heavily scented with the sweet heliotrope odour of unburied dead – tens of thousands of bodies lay under the rubble of two years of bombings. Thousands of others lay on the streets and behind shuttered windows.

A hot September rain had turned the air into steam, and it continued to fall like a tropical downpour. As we skirted the impassable port area, we began to see the Neapolitans along the streets and among the rubble – ragged, hungry, hollow-eyed with sleeplessness, but cheering and laughing through their tears. An old woman ran out to the jeep and offered us a dry and dirty piece of bread and a half-withered pink dahlia. We accepted, tried to smile our thanks, and drove on.

'She thinks the whole world is hungry,' said Omodeo.

Near the wrecked railway station we began to see boys from fourteen to twenty with little strings of red, Fascist hand-grenades hanging from their belts, kitchen knives, shotguns, German Lugers, tyre irons, and bottles of petrol. Even gentle, tired Naples had turned against the Nazi!

One group wanted us to see a German tank full of its dead which they had ambushed the night before as it passed along via Roma in retreat.

158

I took Omodeo first to his beloved library.

It was true. The interior was a charred shambles, still stinking of burned old leather and petrol.*

He bit his forefinger until I thought it must spurt blood. Then he put his face in his hands and sobbed quietly, like an old, lonely woman who has had bad news.

I left Omodeo and went to my rendezvous with others of my unit in Piazza Municipio. Ski and Irv and Bourgoin were already there. There was good news, only one of our agents in Naples was missing. There remained the problem of a house to bed down my outfit, now considerably increased in size. A big *palazzo* was necessary. I remembered the name of Achille Lauro from our list of Fascist big shots in Naples, 71 Via Crispi. Why not his house? 'Our object all sublime....'

I sent Lieutenant Ski to scout the place – to advise its occupants, if any, to leave and to attach our usual *Requisitioned by G2 HQ Fifth Army – all others keep off*, to the front door.

Ski came back in a half-hour – 'That guy says we can't have his house. He has to stay there and, besides, he says he has lots of friends in England and America. He did say you could have a couple of rooms for office space on the ground floor if you need them.'

I decided I had better discuss Gerarch Lauro's hospitality with that great owner of Fascist newspapers and merchant ships himself.

Number 71 Via Francesco Crispi is a temple to essential Fascist vulgarity, and looks like nothing so much as a movie lobby in the gilded days of the opening of The Paramount in New York. The further you proceed from the circular foyer in green marble with the insignia of Lauro's fleet worked in the marble floor, the more institutionally ugly it becomes.

I remember the bathrooms, one mauve marble, one pale green, one, I believe, pink – each with twin fixtures, so the great man or his guests could wash, empty their bowels, or use the bidet in company.

---

* Destroyed in the burning of The Library of the Italian Royal Society and the National Library by order of the German Command: The Greek and Roman Papyri from Herculaneum; 4,000 unique *incunabulae*; and the world famous Luchese-Balli Music and Theatre Collection – in the two libraries nearly 2,000,000 rare books, pamphlets, and manuscripts were destroyed. The German Command prevented by force the Fire Department from trying to save a single volume!

159

I arrived with a couple of jeep-loads of my outfit, hungry, wet to the skin, and armed to the teeth. I put my carbine modestly under my arm and knocked on the vast glass and iron-barred door.

Finally, a far too elegant butler approached the door – obviously made up to look like some counterpart Mr Lauro had seen in an English country house. Without unlocking the door he spoke through a small opening – or break in the glass, I don't remember which.

'Whom do you wish to see?'

'I don't care to see anyone, I want to come in!'

'Whom shall I tell the Signore wants to see him?'

'Listen,' I said – angry because I was afraid my tough looking tommy-gunners would laugh at me any minute now, 'if you don't open this door *subito* I shall be forced to drive a jeep through it and a bullet through you.'

This last part was the 'open Sesame.' The great door swung back and all eight or ten of us piled in. Vicious looking, cross-eyed Marcello had his ugly tommy-gun aimed at the old family retainer's elegantly clothed belly.

Ski was sticking the requisition sign on the glass door when the 'Signore' appeared on the eight-abreast marble stairway which seemed to lead down from the two-dollar seats in the loges (smoking permitted) to the Rudolph Valentino Memorial Lobby where we stood.

We stood in a semi-circle and awaited him. He still looked a young man, but even young men under Fascism who were in with the boys, played ball with the party, greased the right palms, could become heads of great monopolies or owners of a huge fleet of merchant ships. He had learned well the superficial airs of an aristocrat if not the tastes. He bowed and extended his hand:

'May I welcome you to Naples? And who is it I have the honour to receive as representative of the great army of American Liberators?' (All in good English.)

I told him my name but I did not care to take his hand so I bowed, and added:

'We need your house, Signor Lauro; we shall have to requisition it. Naples is still a combat zone, my men are wet and must have a place to sleep. We have work to do and here is a dry place in which to work.'

'Oh, I can give you two or three rooms...'

I told him that wouldn't do. I had nearly one hundred men to put up and our work was of a nature requiring complete possession of the house.

160

'I am sorry I cannot oblige you,' he said, with smackable greasiness of tone, 'but why should it be my house and not another?'

Trying to be a little patient, but I admit somewhat enjoying the situation, I assured him it had to be *someone's* house – his was big, centrally located, and he was obviously a man of sufficient means to be able to find and pay for other quarters.

'My daughter and I are alone. She is a gently reared girl. I cannot just take her anywhere.' I thought of young girls I had seen in Piazza Municipio offering to give themselves to soldiers for a few cans of rations to take home to hungry parents and baby sisters!

My politeness wouldn't wear any thinner, it broke.

'I regret I cannot waste time in discussion. You will be out of this house in two hours. Those are orders. Naples is an occupied city. It is your house rather than another because you are an important Fascist. By Presidential Proclamation Fascists, not Italians, are our enemies. It is now eleven o'clock. At one o'clock you will be out of here.'

He was no longer polite. 'I have friends, important friends in England, in Scotland, and in America. If I refuse to leave?...'

'You will be thrown out physically. If you resist you may be shot...'

'You'll find out very soon to whom you are talking. You will regret this,' he had begun to scream.

'Under those circumstances I give you one hour, not two. Now, hurry up and get out of here.'

He turned and fairly ran up the stairs.

We began to search the house. It contained enough hoarded food to feed a normal family several years – while 1,000,000 Neapolitans were starving. Forty hams, barrels of beans, half a ton of spaghetti, canned butter, American spam and canned beef (captured from the British in Africa), a hundred gallons of olive oil, about 500 pounds of flour, about 500 pounds of sugar; down to Russian tinned caviar and vodka, the present of Goering! For drinks, French champagne, Scotch whisky, French cognac, various liqueurs – and in the cellar another room full of canned goods.

A chauffeur went to the garage and brought out an Alfa Romeo roadster and a truck. He and the butler began to load the truck with food.

'Ski,' I said, 'go requisition those two cars. Take out the distributors and hold on to them.'

161

Again suave, Lauro descended the stairs. 'You'll permit us to eat our luncheon before we go?'

'You will be out of here,' I replied 'at twelve o'clock. It is now twenty to twelve. Also I regret to say we need your car and your truck. You may use the truck to carry you and your suitcases wherever you want to go but you will take no foodstuff out of this house.'

'This is impossible. We will starve. There is nothing to eat in Naples. You only wish to humiliate me.'

'The army will have emergency American rations for the population within twenty-four hours. You will not starve – but nearly a million Neapolitans have been hungry, starving, these last three weeks, and you have had this house full of food beyond any possible personal need. You say I wish to humiliate you – you are quite right – now it is almost twelve o'clock – *get out!*'

His daughter came down the stairs and joined him. They left without another word.

The food (less Goering's caviar and a ham and a dozen bottles of champagne for our supper) we gave to hungry Neapolitans. This handout filled Via Crispi with an hysterical friendly mob.

We used 71 Via Crispi for a month. Then the navy took it. Lauro's girl-friend's villa on Posillipo was occupied by General Ridgway. Lauro went into the jug as a dangerous Fascist. Despite several generals' attempts to release him, he spent eighteen months under lock and key.*

---

* Lauro's post-war career is typical of Italy's recent history. He is again Lord of Naples. The favourite of the Christian Democratic Government and various American Marshal Plan agencies, he has had all sorts of gravy in the form of ships and loans thrown his way.

The US Government has gone so far as to give him for a small fraction of their value (and that a loan) two aircraft carriers which are now the fastest passenger liners on the Australia run, outbidding Allied ships for the trade.

Lauro has become the White Knight of the House of Savoy and led his monarchist party into an alliance, in 1952, with the Neo-Fascists, his former associates in the régime of Mussolini. With such slogans as, 'Throw the Anglo-Americans out of Trieste by Force', this alliance carried many southern cities – including Naples, of which Achille Lauro is now mayor. The story in Italy is that he spent over two million

162

It was still early after Lauro's excellent luncheon. I wanted to find Marchesa Sgazetta – she had always symbolized the virtues and the vices of Naples for me. Down the via Partenope and the via Caracciolo, that magnificent waterfront, with its green parks, great tourist hotels, its view of smoking Vesuvius and the hazy island of Capri across the bay, I drove past dead ruins – the Germans had burned every hotel before leaving the city!

Luca, the Marchesa's son, a pilot in the Italian Air Corps, had come to us in Amalfi – odd chance that it should be I, the one American in 140,000,000 Americans whom he had known before the war!

Now I had flour, sugar, coffee, cigarettes and some canned goods in the jeep for her. There she was, in her ground-floor window, just as before the war, with her breasts resting on the window sill, looking out over the water towards Sorrento. Her hair just as blonded, her hands just as puggy, her speech just as vague, her hospitality just as warm and her house just as messy.

The same dead palm was in one corner. The same green-flowered damasked tablecloth with gold fringe and stains of tomato sauce, red wine and coffee.

But her eyes were different. They were the eyes of a woman who had suffered and who had known fear. Her daughter and little two-year-old grandson had been caught in the street by an air raid. A bomb, a big one, had fallen near. That was in 1941. The little boy was muted by the shock. He would probably never speak again.

She tried to be gay. She crossed her legs and patted her lemon-yellow hair, she re-made her lips, heavier and more off centre. She laughed, and made a wry face at the American coffee. She dug up her last spaghetti and cooked it for me, using the legs of a broken chair for fuel. She blamed on the war the bad service of the same

dollars on the elections, offering thirty thousand lires (just over forty-five dollars) for every vote polled by the Monarchist-Fascist combination in Naples.

After the election Lauro shocked Italy by carrying on a public telegraphic exchange with the deposed king, addressing Umberto as His Majesty, King of Italy.

Now he is serving as a valuable recruiting agent for the Communists in their clever campaign, 'Beware of the Lauros and their American and Christian Democrat friends – only *we* can prevent the return of Fascism.'

bad servant she had apologized for in 1936, 1937, and 1938, and the service was no worse.

She laughed. She told jokes. But her eyes could not lie. She was exhausted from terror.

Naples was ominously quiet.

Outside 71 I found young Lorenzo, a Neapolitan of the *Giustizia e Libertà* movement. He had come through the lines to Amalfi two weeks before to beg arms and explosives for his small group. Finally, we had convinced him that information was more important than dead Germans. So we had landed him back near Posillipo with a Spanish radio operator.

'Are you looking for me, Bill?'

Lieutenant Bill Hoagland was with him. I noticed Lorenzo's head was bandaged.

'Haven't you had enough?' I continued looking at his head.

'No, sir,' replied Lorenzo, 'you see, I did want to stay six months with Maria, my wife, until she had the baby, but ... she was killed... the day before I returned. She was stealing arms for our *ragazzi* from the Germans. I should like to sign one of your contracts – for the whole war. I do not want to be here in Naples. I will go anywhere; do anything; here it is full of Maria; we must defeat them – *ammazzargli*; I will cross the lines as often as you want; I will go anywhere.'

His and Bill Hoagland's faces were lit now and then when they drew in on their cigarettes.

'Do you want him, Bill?'

'Yes, sir, I do.'

'OK, sign him up, he's yours. You're lucky, he is experienced. And he can have Carlos again as a radio operator.... You'd better get that head fixed up ... there must be some medics in Naples open for business.'

'We'll go take a look for them,' said Bill. '*Ciao.*'

They walked off through the big iron gates of Lauro's Palace into the blacked-out night. In two months they were both dead.

Lorenzo was caught in Cassino and the Germans gave him the works, including the uglier and more sadistic of trimmings.

Bill died on a mountain top near Cassino of jaundice – and he need not have died had he been less loyal. He was waiting for Lorenzo to return – it was their rendezvous point, a little hut, cold and wet and half the roof gone.

164

Lorenzo was overdue, but Bill knew that loyalty is the basis of the trade of spying. So Bill waited two, three, four, five days, each day weaker. On the sixth day he died.

Lorenzo was already dead in the courtyard behind the S.D. office in Cassino.

* * *

Inside Lauro's I found André Bourgoin. With him was an ugly little woman with a club foot and kind eyes; she could have been thirty or she could have been fifty. Bourgoin excused himself from his strange spinster and took me aside.

'Most extraordinary woman I ever heard of,' he said, 'a tigress. She brought over eighty parachutists from the Avellino drop back safely through our lines, and that took four days in the mountains – with that foot! When HQ of 82nd Airborne wanted to pay her, she refused money.

'She is a schoolteacher, she says. The Italian group has talked to her. Mondo will see her again to-morrow. If they say she passes I want to send her back with a radio and operator.'

She did pass and André did send her.

After the war, when André visited me in Rome, I heard the rest. She was coming up to Rome to see him.

'You remember the schoolteacher with the game leg in Naples? Ah, she is coming tomorrow. I am a father of two war veterans and as near sixty as fifty years old. *Mais celle-là; elle m'aime!* The love letters!' André flushed. 'She made five passages of the lines, back in 1944. On her first trip she and her operator were holed-up on the second floor of a pensione by *des salauds* of the Gestapo, a major and two men.

'She opened a window, put one of her hand-grenades live in the radio to destroy it – threw it out the window. Quiet as a cat, she told the operator to jump. He did. She waited till they broke the door to throw her other grenade – *la tigresse!*'

I carefully chaperoned André (on his request) during her visit, she fifty, he fifty-five. She eyed him like a cat, like a cat on heat!

* * *

'Donald,' said Luca, as I prepared to get some sleep in one of Lauro's brothel-like beds that first night in Naples, 'Mama wants

165

me to ask you, Donald, if you can get me the Italian agency for some ready-made American teeth. She has a friend who is a dentist and he says American teeth are the best, that if we get an agency we can make a sack of money – and hardly any work. All the dentists will come hunting for us.'

'I'll try, Luca.'

The Germans left us alone that night. I had been excited, and wet, and busy, for twenty hours. I slept undisturbed.

Already by nine o'clock of the first morning the black markets, confidence games, and swarms of commercially-minded children, for which wartime Naples was to become famous, were in action. Crowds awaited each incoming motor column ready to do business.

Trading was brisk – offers ran high on cigarettes, blankets, woollen shirts, shoes, socks, and canned rations. For sale were sex, wine, all sorts of German decorations, helmets, buttons, and sidearms.

The soldiers were cheated – soldiers are always cheated.

The sun, Naples' compensation for all her miseries, returned. The bay was blue as ever, Vesuvius as black, and the pines as green. Long queues were forming for water, for DDT, for rations. Some stood outside the engineer's offices waiting for work – but most of Naples curled up on some wall or just on rubble and slept in the warm October sun.

But for me these were to be sad days. I had taken my stand, right or wrong, with General Donovan and I had to leave. By the nature of its security and its mutual trust a small espionage unit is like a family with strong sentimental ties. To say good-bye to it is not easy.

A number of the officers wanted to go if I went but I made them understand that their loyalty was to their agents across the lines; to leave them 'orphaned' over there in the hands of new officers who knew them only as a number and a wave-length was unfair and might prove disastrous for morale – and morale is ninety per cent of a spy's armour and equipment.

Looking back eight years I am still convinced I did wrong to be right – there was a loyalty greater than any ideal. I should have stayed under anyone, however incapable, made whatever promises were necessary about oaths to the House of Savoy, and then used my ingenuity in circumventing both.

Somewhere between Naples and Washington the amoebic dysentery started, and until January I was hospitalized in California.

CHAPTER FOURTEEN

THE WHITE HOUSE BLUES

SPRING TO AUTUMN 1944

Spring 1944 found me in Cairo and Beirut – General Donovan had kept his promise. I had not been allowed into Turkey to play my Bulgarian game with Julius Amos' Balkan Desk. The Turkish advisers of the OSS mission in Istanbul thought I was too 'uncovered' by my operations of three years before – and they were convinced that the Germans knew all about my Imro and Bulgarian Peasant Party activities: they possibly did, and probably the objection was valid.

All our Bulgarian activities based on Cairo were being directed by Americans who thought the Peasant Party leaders dangerous radicals. The result was that OSS Cairo had done nothing. But now the OSS Cairo colonels took time off from the sahib life of the Nile to conceive of a Bulgarian project to calm the agitation in Washington, reiterated in innumerable cables from General Donovan, 'What are you doing about Bulgaria?' – or words to that effect.

There was around Shepheards' Hotel a lieutenant named Donovan (no kin to Big Bill!). He had some vague job with JICA, one of the small, liaison intelligence organizations. Donovan was a lad who craved action and was disgusted with the bickerings of the soft war in Cairo. The colonels decided to use him for their Bulgarian project.*

Their scheme was to drop Donovan, in uniform, with a sergeant and a couple of radio men, 'to the Bulgarian partisans'. He was all enthusiasm and came to see me to talk over the idea.

I asked two questions: (1) How many of the mission speak Bulgarian? (2) To what partisans and where are you to be dropped?

Donovan didn't believe any of them spoke Bulgarian. He didn't know to what partisans or where. I urged him to return to the OSS Cairo office and find out particulars. I warned him I had reason to believe that we were not in touch with *any* Bulgarian Partisans.

---

* Ulius Amos, OSS Balkan chief in Washington, had no responsibility for this affair.

167

In a couple of days he came back and said the OSS colonels had promised to find him an interpreter; they would drop the party in some wild part of the country known to be 'full' of partisans, and the party could undoubtedly find them.

'Shall I go?' asked Donovan, his earlier enthusiasm somewhat dampened.

'I think you have one chance in ten of surviving. And if you survive to find some partisans, I think the mission has one chance in a hundred of being valuable. You know nothing of either Bulgarian politics or background. It is something like sending a ten-year-old boy into a professional football game and expecting him to make a touchdown on every play.'

'They'll think I'm yellow if I back out. The transfer from JICA to OSS is already approved. They could even court-martial me.' He had plenty of guts but enough brains to see that he was being made the victim of a colonels' Cairo holiday.

Well prepared Mission dropped to Bulgarian Partisans 8–29–1944 stop standing by for communications stop personnel Lieutenant Donovan and.... that would indeed sound well in Washington.

'Don't worry about a court-martial. Call me as a witness, call Carl Devoe or Gordon Browne, call anybody who's been out here or who knows anything about preparing and dispatching a mission and the little colonels would be laughed out of court and out of uniform.'

So Lieutenant Donovan said 'no' to the project. He was not court-martialled, and he didn't die, and four or five others didn't die uselessly either.

I wanted to get out of the Middle East and back to Washington. I had had a bellyful of Greece and of Bulgaria as handled from Cairo – a mixture of unlovely British scheming and American ignorance. Maybe in Washington I could upset some small apple-carts with a little truth.

So I flashed Big Bill's original orders which ended 'and return to Washington by air when he so desires.' By the middle of September I was there. 'Q' Building was an impossible mass of tangled red, white, and blue tape. Donovan's Kremlin had ossified into impenetrable layers of committees and colonels. Only Donovan and Rehm remained human, when they were around, and not inspecting India or France or Italy.

George Bowden came on from Chicago. 'It's no use attempting

168

to change the set-up. It is what it is and that's why I got out. Those birds in the Kremlin aren't going to recall their buddies from Cairo or Caserta, or from Delhi or anywhere else.

'On the political side, it's equally useless to feed your information through oss channels. There are too many axe-men on the way up who'll chop it up and throw it in their secret waste to be burned. They are not interested in Mediterranean politics any more – the interest now is all in military information.

'Sit tight for a few days. Run out to California and see your sister or go up to your family in Maine. I'll wire you when I want you.'

So I went to Maine and ate lobsters.

Finally George's telegram came. I left that day for Washington and met him at the University Club.

'One of the President's six administrative assistants, those whom Mr Roosevelt said "must have a passion for anonymity", is Lauchlin Currie. He is in the White House itself and if he can't get your dope to headquarters, nobody can.'

'How do I go about it?'

'I've arranged it like this. Bill Donovan will continue you on oss payroll, but on a written request from Currie he'll lend you to the White House on a month by month basis.

'Let's go. Currie's expecting us over at the White House offices in the old State Department building on Pennsylvania Avenue.'

I met Lauch Currie and I knew him intimately for four months. I had a desk inside his office. On George's recommendation I had access to much of the secret information and plans which crossed his desk. After the war when I heard Congressional Committees befouling him with all sorts of synthetic congressional manure, it first made me laugh and then made me sad. To label level-headed, hard-money Currie a Communist is fantastic.

With George Bowden as catalyst and inquisitor I told my observations on the Mediterranean to Currie. I told him about British policy in Italy and Greece and the facts I had observed which made me believe the Tory part of the Coalition Government was planning to replace the oriental colonies and Egypt, which Britain was sure to lose, with a series of puppet Mediterranean monarchical states.

I told him how different our *Pericles Mission's* reports coming out of Greece were from the official British line, and how completely out of sympathy and touch Greece was with the Royal Greek Government in exile in Cairo.

169

'You must write all this, properly documented, for F.D.R.,' said Currie, 'you can have the use of all the secret reports you need for documentation.'

So began the 'two-pages-double-spaced-in-blue-ribbon' reports (requirement for all reports meant for the eyes of the President). As I recall there were four blue-double-spacers on Greece.

While Currie and I awaited some reaction to come down from across Pennsylvania Avenue, I began a series on Sicily. There was evidence that Churchill (not through his own war cabinet or through the Combined Chiefs of Staff, but directly through British Intelligence channels and the person of Major-General Lord Rennell of Rodd, then head of Allied Military Government in Sicily) was encouraging with materials and funds the Sicilian Separatist Movement – to separate the island from Italy.

I had no way of knowing if there was some secret agreement between President and Prime Minister by which the latter had been given a go-ahead to detach Sicily from Italy and set it up as a kingdom under British protection. For the sake of the reports I assumed not and I began, far away from the documents concerned, to give what information I had and what was obtainable in Washington.*

The Separatists (and their British contacts) based their campaign largely on Sicilian popular sympathy for the United States: few are the Sicilian families that have not more than one brother, father, cousin, or uncle in America. America has always been their promised land whither a lucky minority has been able to flee from Italian governmental indifference and exploitation, landowners' oppression, or the horror of the sulphur mines.

One began to see on Sicilian walls in 1943 and early in 1944: 'Sicily the 49th State of the American Union.' 'Sicily the 49th Star in the Stars and Stripes.' 'Down with Italian exploitation.' 'Long live America. Down with Rome.'

Crowds began to display tiny American flags, much to the surprise of the Office of War Information, usually charged with American propaganda. Investigation showed that these flags had been manufactured in the Casbah of Algiers 'for an English officer.'

* When Currie had the White House and other files searched for information on British political activity in Greece and Sicily none of the reports which to my personal knowledge had been sent in by oss and jica officials abroad could be found. Such a wholesale disappearance of documents seems more design than coincidence.

170

Arms seized by Italian *carabinieri* from the Separatist secret dumps proved to have come from U.S. lend-lease supplies to Britain.

These Sicilian 'double-spaced-blue' reports were further documented by the names of OSS officers who knew what was going on in Sicily.

Four of these followed the four Greek reports across Pennsylvania Avenue.

My next and last subject was a political estimate of Italy. I made one report on the responsibility of Marshal Badoglio for many of the crimes of the Italian Fascist Government. The Marshal was then our current Darlan. These crimes included countenancing and approving the murder of the brothers Rosselli, anti-Fascists, by agents of Italian Intelligence (SIM) on French soil before the war broke out.

Our continued use of Badoglio was focusing Italy's all too abundant native cynicism on the U.S.A.

My last report on Italy was called *Labor Omnia Vincit*, and told of the situation in Italy of labour organization. This, like every report I wrote in the White House, ended with a warning that if we did not take the side of democracy and reform, we should have to contend with a large Communist Party in the period after the war. I pointed out that our strongest case before the Italian people and our chief appeal to the Italian people was a moral one.

Days grew into months and there was no acknowledgment from the White House proper that my reports had even arrived there. Currie could get no information. It was election month and the White House could find little time off from fighting the Republicans.

At this moment State, War, and Navy were contending against Treasury, F.E.A., Justice, and the remnants of the New Deal for the control of post-victory Germany. The real difference was not whether Germany should be returned to an agricultural state, as Morgenthau was accused of sponsoring, but whether Germany should have a civilian or military government of occupation in the American zone.

My chief interest in a 'civilian' government for Germany was the intelligence side. Currie asked me to draw up a table of organization for such an outfit and to suggest names for its administration. This organization was to have a desk corresponding to, and for supplying specialized information to, each of the civilian departments – Justice, Denazification, Transportation, etc. In addition it was to have a desk on Nazism, one on German politics, one on the activities of ex-Wehrmacht officers; one on each of the Allied powers; and one special one on Communism and Russia. Of course it called for a counter-intelligence branch to control all security of the American civilian administration and a small 'operations unit'.

For its head I suggested three names: Allen Dulles, Arthur Goldberg, George Bowden. I must admit I hoped that I would be chosen for the desk on Communism and Russian affairs, or if that was out, on the Nazis.

But the decision, we soon discovered, had already been made in favour of the State-War-Navy plan – a wholly military occupation. The decision had been made in the usual exasperating F.D.R. method of avoiding a decision – at least openly, and letting his lieutenants, whole governmental departments, carry on exhausting and costly intragovernmental warfare under the illusion that their projects and programmes were going to be given an equal day in court.

'On 20 October 1944, Roosevelt dismissed all *specific planning for the treatment of Germany: he said in a memorandum to Hull "I dislike making detailed plans for a country which we do not yet occupy", adding that the details were "dependent on what we and the Allies find when we get into Germany – and we are not there yet".'*

By November we had specific knowledge that the State-War-Navy plan was irrevocably in and the civilian plan irrevocably out – that after Mr Roosevelt gave the above directive he and the State-War-Navy group did the exact opposite. They made 'detailed plans for a country which we do not yet occupy', and the plan for civilian control was never even given a hearing.

On my Greek and Italian reports there continued to be no reaction.

Finally, one November day Currie called me over to his desk.

'The Boss has never seen one of your reports. They have gone into Harry Hopkins' scrap-basket. It is just impossible to get any information before the Boss that "Dubarry" doesn't want him to see.

'He's back strong again after being out of favour last summer.

---

* *Roosevelt and Hopkins, an Intimate History*, by Robert E. Sherwood Harper Brothers 1948, pages 818–819.

172

It has been months since I've seen the Boss without Hopkins around.
'If you want to keep on for the record's sake...'
So I stayed on a few weeks 'for the record's sake' – but my reports had little heart in them. I hoped Lauch Currie might find a hole in the curtain around the President. He went over to the weekly cocktail-tea the Boss gave for his staff, but he was definitely out of touch with the throne.

* * *

Both Currie and George Bowden suggested I return to Italy, but in a position allowing me to write for the press. They wanted me to report on political conditions to Currie. George arranged for me to be allowed oss communications. Currie armed me with a White House letter – sort of credentials – to use in emergencies.

He also introduced me to the owner-manager of a news-agency and under an assumed name I did a series of articles predicting Russian-American disagreement and competition in post-war Germany. The news agency liked them and offered me a job to go back to Italy as a war correspondent. I accepted and offered Donovan, with considerable regret and nostalgia, my resignation.

* * *

I sat down, after I left Donovan's office in the Kremlin, to a beef-stew and coffee in the 'Q' Building cafeteria. It might have been in War or State or any other government department. The oss of 1942 was gone. However much the country and the military had made fun of us, however much we had laid ourselves open to it, there had been something of the Minute Men in those people Donovan had used to create oss out of nothing after Pearl Harbour.

My coffee was cold; I got another cup. The war was nearly over, and then in every country town, almost at every cross-roads, they would erect bandstands, athletic fields, civic centres, and just plain ugly war memorials. On them they would put the name of the local boy who died on some Pacific island; under his name might be the little major from New Hampshire I saw die in the Paestum sand dunes, or the two charred boys in the bulldozer, or someone who died late in the show, putting a bridge over the upper reaches of the Danube. Or maybe the next one on the list just died drunk, driving a jeep full of whores off the coast-road cliff into the sea below

173

Leghorn, or maybe he was shot by an MP while stealing tyres from the dumps in the forest of Tombolo.

In a sense they are all equally casualties of war – no one of them less a hero, less deserving of his letters carved in the marble or cast in the bronze on the village square. It is more war that kills and maims than the enemy's bullets and bombs. And Washington, inevitably, necessarily, had become a machine for feeding war, for killing and maiming. However high the ideal, that is war's ugliest face and peace wears it for some time after the fighting stops.

As I finished my coffee, if I did not precisely foresee Senator McCarthy, I foresaw something like him and what he stands for as the scar to be left on us by the war.

Those boys in *Banana*, and in *Sparrow* and our other missions who didn't and wouldn't come back, they were mostly foreigners, many of whom had never even seen America. But they had died for America in a sense more truly than our Americans themselves. To a man they had volunteered. I recruited several hundred of them. I trained many of them.

When a man goes on an espionage mission he has need of the highest morale, of a sense of moral justification, of a faith in what he is about to die for, considerably greater than a soldier. The soldier is carried along in a social movement, from home to training camp, and from camp to battle. He is one of many and he knows that someone, his family, is proud of him.

The spy must go secretly. Society does not protect him, he is not in a stream of social duty surrounded by his peers. He is alone, furtive, and he remembers that 'dirty' is always the word coupled with spy. The people on whom his information will, if he is success-ful, rain bombs and death are his own.

He has to *know* he is right, to have a morale of gold, and faith of steel.

Most of the 'bodies' – as the British call agents – or 'Joes' I sent out had such a morale founded on what they believed to be the fundamental goodness of America, and a faith in our justice and tolerance. And goodness, tolerance, and justice were their armour, and I think in 1942 and 1943 these really existed for most Europeans only in America.

I wondered then what these 'Joes' would think of Washington and 'Q' Building and the White House.

I wonder now what they would think of Senator McCarthy.

So I bought a bottle of Irish whisky and drove out to Lane Rehm's.

174

CHAPTER FIFTEEN

HOME TO ITALY

The spider in the laurel spins.
HERMAN MELVILLE

JANUARY TO JUNE 1945

The s.s. *Mariposa* had just the necessary twenty knots to make it across the Atlantic without escort. A couple of blimps stood watch in the sky for the first twenty-four hours. A couple more met us between the Azores and Gib. Some planes dropped a few depth charges off our starboard side, and we entered the Mediterranean.

On board we slept twelve and twenty to a cabin and ate one meal a day in transport fashion, but the trip was a vacation and a lark in February 1945 because everybody on board knew the Germans might collapse any day now. That is, we knew it on the blue southern ocean, but the GI's in the snows on Futa Pass and sogged in the rains along the Rhine didn't know it – and the poor bastards in the Pacific not only didn't know it, but didn't give a damn.

Somehow I didn't feel I was going back to the war at all. I was going home to Italy. I had a guilty conscience about Italy. It had been wrong to leave in 1943 – too many people and ideas had been let down: the temples at Paestum, for one, Cellini's Perseus, for two – and there was *Mamma* Sgazetta, the 'Guys and Joes' of Special Detachment G2 Fifth Army, the *Giustizia e Libertà* organization. I would see them all now and try to make some amends – at least by writing the truth about Italy.

The Mediterranean was as blue as ever. We stopped in deserted Oran – the soldiers gone, all except a few to keep the black market and the bars going. I saw Leland Rounds, one of the best of the original vice-consuls who had prepared the African landings in 1942. Lee was still fighting the gallant fight against Vichyism and generally clearing up all the messes we others had left behind – half-finished projects, well-meant promises, even to taking care of our personal effects. He was pessimistic.

175

'What with Darlan here and Badoglio in Italy I guess it will be Goering in Germany and Quisling in Norway.'

The profile of Capri and Ischia and then *Papà* Vesuvio, oddly without his smoke plume. Luca Sgazetta and Achille Lauro? What had happened to them? The poor proud city I had left sixteen months before must be regaining her character and strength, even her productive laziness and gentle sloth. I could see cars like tiny bugs buzzing along via Caracciolo and the British white ensign flying from the Castell' Uovo .The port was miraculously cleaned up.

Naples in the late winter of 1944–45 was one of the worst shocks I have ever had. The Neapolitans seemed more ragged and miserable than when the city fell; they were not lovable as then, nor gay and tired as before the war. They were hard, furtive and sneering.

It is not pleasant to be ashamed of your fellow countrymen and the uniform of your army. Ashamed was the least an American could be in Naples in 1945 – ashamed and angry.

American combat troops behaved well in this war wherever I saw them. Our base-section troops, who ran the supply ports like Naples and Leghorn after the fighting moved on, behaved disgracefully. Germans, on orders, committed mass atrocities in Italy – as individuals they behaved well. The British were distant and cold – but usually correct. No one competed with American base-section troops for bad behaviour, except the French Moroccans and General Anders' Polish Legion.

In Naples the wild scramble to sell government property into the black market went almost unchecked. Discipline was a farce. Italians were treated like a stupid and inferior race. Drunken soldiers filled the streets most of the night. Sex was against any wall, in the light or in the dark, with or without the consent of the object.

My first night ashore I heard a kid about ten years' old bargaining with an MP patrol for the use of his sister who he boasted was only thirteen. Not ten feet away a soldier was selling a half-jeepful of cigarettes to a black marketeer; another soldier was vomiting into the gutter.

When I tried to include this episode in a story on Naples to my agency the censors in Rome killed the whole piece. I doubted anyway if it was my job to underline Sherman's definition – *war is hell.*

Mamma Sgazetta was back in the old groove, serving coffee on the same green table cover with the same grease spots, and with the same dead palms in the corner of the room. The mute child, older and bigger, was a more monstrous casualty of war than as a baby. Luca talked again about the agency for American false teeth, but had an eye on the lushness of the black market. Couldn't I introduce him to some officer in the Base Section, '*con il quale potrei fare qualche affare?*' He was surprised, a little contemptuous, that I, '*quasi un generale*', couldn't pull off a deal in penicillin or tyres or sugar.

'Everybody's doing it, you make millions.'

After many protests about the scarcity of petrol, Public Relations of the Base Section gave me a battered old command car and a driver to go to Paestum to indulge my nostalgia. I took only Luca as *Mamma* 'had a liver' that day.

First, I wanted to see Annunziante who'd given me chickens for a stew, my second evening ashore in September 1943. I had been called away by General Gruenther's jeepload of colonels before I had tasted it, but I still remember the generosity of the gift of a peasant and of his old father who had lived in Brooklyn at the turn of the century and I remember too the smell of that stew.

As Luca and I drew up to Annunziante's rambling sixteenth-century farmhouse we noticed an immense Fiat limousine in the roadway surrounded by nodding peasants, geese, turkeys and goats. The car was so parked that we didn't see the little king, Victor Emmanuel, and his aides, until we drew up alongside. These aides were passing eggs along the line of their ascending rank and the little king was holding each up to the sun and then putting it in a basket.

Observing all protocols the party re-entered the big black car and left in a crunching of gears and a cloud of white dust.

Annunziante welcomed me back. He had a sad tale of a month in a British jail in Salerno because of the U.S. Army canned goods which the banqueteers of the fourteen chickens had given him. British MP's had found them in his house a month later.

'They took me for a thief. I was humiliated. They thought I stole those few miserable cans of fruit and those five kilos of sugar. I told them your friends had given them to me but they would not listen.'

'What was he doing here?' asked Luca, meaning the king.

'The great king who told us to follow Mussolini,' answered Annunziante with a mock courtly bow, 'and who invited the German pigs into our country, he comes here, sixty kilometres from his house in Vietri, to buy eggs at fifteen lire an egg; in Vietri they cost seventeen lire.'

'And,' I added, 'using thereby some twenty-five litres of American gasoline, of which the army is short at the front, and which costs more than the eggs!'

'*Stronzo*,' said Luca, and spat.

'He is too small to be a *stronzo*,' replied Annunziante, '*è una cimice*' (he is a bedbug).

We turned to more hopeful subjects – the wine from the mountain above Eboli and some cake made that morning by the mama of Annunziante. He showed us the tunnel which led from his land, the ancient *Porta del Mare* of Paestum, to the temples themselves.

'Under this land which I work with my family is a great city of the Greeks. We find their coins and utensils of their kitchens and toys of their babies. *Pazienza*, we shall also be under this ground. *Un po' di vino, signor Colonnello?*'

The beach was still littered with bullet cases turned green by the sea air, rusted tins, the metal parts of life-preservers and gas masks, unopened coffee powder, and the twisted skeletons of a couple of landing craft. It was quiet and hot in the spring sun.

The next day I went to Caserta and Rome. Rome was a great splotch of gold, green, and orange in the March sunset. Rome was undamaged and smug, comfortable, even smart. Her palaces, ancient ruins, and churches were untouched by and indifferent to the little creatures in uniform who lolled about the cafés or sat bored in various administrative offices. The battle which had passed north but nine months before was already forgotten. Like an old woman who has had too many lovers, Rome could not recall distinctly even her last conqueror.

There was no black-out; the shops were full of food; the student priests darted here and there in her streets like multi-coloured water-bugs. The old ones (Rome seems never to have priests between the extremes of youth and old age) stumbled along, fat and unhurried, with more life in their darting sensuous eyes than in their gouty feet. Their heads, like spectators at a tennis match, followed the groups of young soldiers who passed.

Allied Commission, housed in the Fascist Ministry of Corporations, was the centre of Roman life. The aristocrats introduced their daughters as secretaries and clerical help and waited for the plums to drop in their laps – they did – in the form of coffee, sugar, and permits for petrol where the conquest was easy; in import and export permits, coal for the black market, and big-time business deals in the case of old and ugly colonels who found the going hard.

Beautiful, seductive, and eternal as she is, Rome was not a pretty picture under the Anglo-American occupation. The Murphy-Darlan mentality was in full swing and the puppet governments of Badoglio and Bonomi were encouraged to continue the old Fascist bureaucracy from National Police to Treasury, from Commerce to Army and Navy. Only a common hatred for the German held the various colours of Italians and Allies together. But as the German defeat became more and more inevitable and closer and closer, the conspiracies multiplied.

In the struggle to control the wreckage of Italy the Church had by all odds the greatest chance to win. It had its priests already dispersed in every hamlet with great power over the people. Official America was behind the Vatican; many American Catholics were in high administrative positions, and the American Protestants were easily convinced on the grounds that the Church was the most militant form of anti-Communism. The Vatican had no idea of sincerely carrying out that minimum of reform necessary to take the wind out of Moscow's sails.

The representative of one of our biggest news agencies, dressed in the uniform of an officer of the U.S. Army, was going round Italy signing up newspapers for long-time contracts to his service. He told editors, 'The army and the occupational government want you to buy this service. It will make it far easier for you to continue to get your AMG permit to publish.' PRO officers knew of this and laughed it off as a good joke on the 'Eyeties': *If you don't oppose my racket, I won't expose yours* seemed to be the tacit agreement everywhere. All struck me as united in cynicism and opportunism. I wanted to get to a zone where there were combat troops, where the war was still being fought, and to leave Rome to the division of the spoils.

In Florence I found my old friends of Fifth Army – Art Blom, Green, Merke and Howard – now moved up to Headquarters of 15th Army Group. All upped a couple of ranks, with Howard now a general, they were still doing the same fine job, the extraordinary quality of the chief of staff (General Al Gruenther) as before making up for the deficiencies of the commanding general and his immediate intimates of the *Mark W. Clark for President Club*.

179

Since Oujda, General Clark had annexed a new PRO officer named Grogan. Colonel Grogan, in censorship, was adding to the phrase 'Fifteenth Army Group' the prefix 'General Mark W. Clark's' without the permission of the correspondents. When 'American soldiers yesterday entered the town of Omega', they became on fiat of Grogan 'General Mark W. Clark's American soldiers'. The story went the rounds of the war correspondents in the bar of the Excelsior in Florence that when Grogan was groggy one night, habit got the better of him and an agency dispatch left for the States as follows:

At Mark W. Clark's dawn today General Mark W. Clark's 15th Army Group troops entered Bologna where a high mass was said in the Cathedral of Mark W. Clark's Holy Trinity to celebrate the liberation of Mark W. Clark's city. General Mark W. Clark attended. The Cardinal Archbishop was also present.

In fact, the fall of Bologna, Italy's most Communist city, was, unfortunately, used as an excuse to push forward the ruling House of Savoy. Grogan's press release of that day gave twice as much space to Umberto, whom Clark took on a tour of the city, as it did to the Allied and Italian troops and the partisans, who, together, had captured it. The release used some eighty words to describe Umberto's resplendent uniform, bringing forth the usual anti-Grogan and anti-Clark groans from the press. It was a most inopportune time and place to show off Umberto – he was hooted down and stoned in the streets of Bologna. Grogan, it seemed. was no better at making kings than at creating presidential timber.

At G2 Fifteenth Army Group after the fall of Bologna I heard that contact between Caserta (AFHQ) and the German Command in Italy had been made to work out the details of a Nazi surrender. My informant, better unnamed, swore me to secrecy, adding: 'I gather it was your OSS boys in Switzerland who have negotiated a surrender.' Allen Dulles and maybe Gerry van Arkel! That Allen Dulles should have engineered this, the most brilliant coup of the war – the surrender of over a million German troops – was no surprise to us who knew him.

'So there won't be any last redoubt in the Tyrol for us to crack.'

Those were weeks of excitement, victories and uncertainty, darkened dramatically by President Roosevelt's death. The cynical say he died at the right moment to affect Europeans emotionally at the end of an exhausting war. There is some truth in such a

180

statement, but I do not believe enough to account for the almost universal hysteria in Italy. Men and women wept on the streets.

An old unemployed refugee living in a hole in the ancient walls of Rome hung a flower and sign outside his entrance, *L'Amico è morto. Chi c'e per aiutarci?* (The Friend is dead. Who is there to help us?) I went up to him and asked what he meant. 'Ah, *signore*, I was afraid of the war, but without him I am afraid even of peace, should it come.'

Currie was no longer at the White House – my mission died with the President. I must paddle my own canoe as a correspondent.

Towards the end of April rumour had it that a great insurrection of partisans in the north had begun. The Italian Partisan Organization, unlike, I believe, that in any other occupied country, had a unified command of all parties including the Communists. The man chosen to run it was Ferruccio Parri about whom 'Mondo' (Raimondo Craveri) had told me down on the Salerno beachhead in the first days of the landing.

No one could be more typical of the little *bourgeois* intellectual of Europe than Parri, known clandestinely as 'Maurizio'. The lower middle-class intellectuals had opposed Fascism from the start, and Parri, along with the brothers Rosselli, had been early organizers in the 1920's of the *Giustizia e Libertà* movement. The Rossellis had been murdered by orders of the Italian State, Parri spent nine years in prison or *confino* (forced residence in distant, obscure towns).

'Maurizio', with his face half of St. Francis and half of Abraham Lincoln, and his huge shock of white hair, became the symbol and the idol of the resistance. He was a leader of few words, kind, even sentimental, but also relentless and without fear. Hunted by both Nazis and Fascists, he stayed on in Milan and directed his CVL (*Commando Volontario della Libertà*), the partisan high command. No other resistance leader in Europe, living in enemy occupied territory, ever commanded an organization as big as Parri's – nearly 200,000 men actually in the field; Communists, Royalists, Christian Democrats, Socialists, his own Party of Action (*GeL*.) and a host of non-political groups.

Outside the armed forces in the hills and forests, the cities and towns were infested with SAP's and GAP's: the former sabotage cells, the latter terrorist cells, each from three to seven members. These wore no uniform and continued their apparent normal civilian

181

occupations. But they kept factories and transport in a constant state of disorganization and made it unhealthy for small groups of Nazi or Fascist officers to be abroad after dark.

The CVL and its politically controlling body the CLNAI (Committee of National Liberation for North Italy) established an effective system of taxation on industry and commerce to support their vast invisible government and their not-so-invisible military organization. Even the most pro-Nazi and pro-Fascist manufacturers paid their taxes – if for no other reason than as a form of health, life insurance! The GAP's enforced this simple tax system.

The GAP's also collected arms by waylaying small groups of enemy soldiers and by raiding arsenals and barracks. They rescued their fellow-partisans by other raids on hospitals and prisons.

The weapons and uniform shortage was acute. This had been due to Field-Marshal 'Jumbo' Wilson's orders sometime in the winter of 1943–44 to deliver a minimum of supplies to north Italian partisans lest 'they become politically too important'. Again, later in 1944, supplies had been cut off, diverted, along with the planes to deliver them, to the ill-timed and ill-fated Warsaw insurrection, which the Russians betrayed to wipe out non-Communist resistance.

When on 26 April word came over the Milan radio that more than half the city was in CVL's hands and that Mussolini and his German staff had fled, I wanted badly to go to Milan – but our front was still far away from the city. It did not seem possible.

My friends in G2 Fifteenth Army Group promised to put me on the first contact plane to take off for Milan. That long day was a slow wait. Finally, Colonel Blom sent for me. A plane was to take off with a few correspondents and a G2 representative the next morning, but orders were that the press had to return the same night. But Blom added, 'If you disappear, you'll be there. No one will make a fuss about it.'

'Sometime today,' he added, 'and this is top-extra-special secret, the first German delegate will fly over here on his way to Caserta to sign the armistice. So maybe this is the end.'

'Glad?'

'Sure, I'm glad. I'll get back to Seattle...'

We took off with a very tight pilot. Out over enemy territory there didn't seem to be any Luftwaffe to worry about – and no ack-ack opened up from below.

What worried us much more than the Nazi air force was that the upper Po Valley around Milan was in its usual fog. Added to the cognac haze of the pilot, it was too thick for him to spot Milan. So we cruised around about an hour east of the fog, between the Alps and the Ligurian Apennines, watching German columns worming along the flat Lombard plain. The spring crops were well up between the scars across the landscape left by the defensive works of the Todt organization.

Trying again, through one hole in the fog we saw an airport along a canal – Milan! Our pilot's fog lifted too, and we wheeled down to land. Some partisans in uniform ran out into the grass runway and, with the palms of their hands turned up, tried to lift us with a signal not to land. Either the pilot didn't see it or else he just decided that he needed a rest, or a drink, or both. We landed.

The partisans crowded around us and asked who we were and why we had landed in a mine field. Then I saw the signs: *Achtung*: *Minen*. The partisans – they jumped about like children – knew a safe path off the grassy runway and we made friends by lighting our cigarettes in their mouths.

In the hangar they showed us a British plane in which some liaison officer had arrived a few hours ago. Beside it was an elegant, spick-and-span, trimotored Savoia-Marchetti.

'That,' said the leader, 'is Mussolini's plane. It is full of petrol and was ready to take him to Spain. But we got the airport before he could get here. They say he has fled to Switzerland, but we also heard this morning he is dead and his body will arrive today in Milan.'

'Can I go into town?'

'Surely, you may get sniped at, there are Fascists and ss holding out in some of the apartment houses. But there is no car out here to take you in.'

I saw a few bicycles parked outside the hangar. 'How about one of those?'

'Certainly, *signore*. But I'd better send a couple of *ragazzi* with tommy-guns along with you.'

So we set off on three bikes, myself and two Garibaldini partisans. I hadn't ridden a bike for twenty years and, with my knapsack and the tommy-gun I had been given, wasn't at all sure of myself. We passed the last partisan sentry at the end of the long road which leads from a railway bridge at the edge of the town out to the airport.

183

'From here on to the centre of the city it is no-man's-land,' said the older partisan. 'We've got the centre itself except for the Hotel Regina where the Gestapo have sealed themselves in behind cemented-up windows and kilometres of barbed wire. I heard they had flame-throwers too, but I don't see why we don't blow them up – hotel and all, the pigs.'

Just after the railway underpass a car with partisan insignia and two tommy-gunners seated like Buddhas on the roof come into the square. It curved over and signalled us to stop. A man in Alpini uniform with a long eagle feather in his hat jumped out.

'Isn't that an American officer?' he asked my escort. 'Yes,' I replied, 'but only a war correspondent. Can you direct me to CVL Headquarters?'

'Why, yes, I'm going there. Come in my car with me. I am Major Superti of the Brigade of Valdossola.'

'My name is Downes. Do you know if Ferruccio Parri is in the city?'

'Yes, it is to him I go now.'

So I thanked my escort and entered the major's car. I asked him rapid questions about the situation in Milan, but got no real answers as he himself had just arrived from the mountains.

'We'll get all the latest news at CVL,' he said.

At CVL Headquarters we were told 'Maurizio' had gone to the Hotel Milano, OSS Headquarters. Captain Dadario, one of Dulles' men from Switzerland, was already in the city and probably at the hotel now with Parri.

Outside the Hotel Milano four partisans of the *Partito d'Azione* stood at attention with American sten-guns across their chests. A *P.d'A.* partisan officer was passing on credentials of those who wanted to enter. Captain Dadario was in the bar-lounge talking to a man I saw only from the back – a shock of white hair and a shabby, worn-out, almost white raincoat. I introduced myself to Dadario.

'Signor Parri, may I introduce Mr Downes?'

Parri turned. In his saint-like face, tired, lined, pale and determined, I saw that intellectual strength that made a Nazi-Fascist conquest of Europe only a veneer – Parri was the perfect symbol of the resistance to police-ism, state-ism, and brutality, from Norway to Greece.

'I have heard of you often, Signor Parri, since "Mondo" Craveri first used your name as the centre of the movement when we were still at Salerno.'

'Yes, he spoke of you to me. You are our friend, I am told.'

'I hope so. I am proud to be a friend of the Italy you and the CVL represent.

'I am not in OSS any longer. I am now a newspaper correspondent. May I have an appointment, if you aren't too busy, to write a story about the Resistance?'

'Yes, indeed, come back now to CVL with me. You can have whatever information you want, and I shall give you a special pass to move freely in the territory we hold.'

In the car I asked him if there were any news of Mussolini.

'He is dead. He and the principal Gerarchs rounded up escaping to Switzerland were shot yesterday at Dongo on Lake Como. *Nostro Duce* was wearing the uniform of a German soldier, and was hiding under a pile of overcoats in the back of a German truck heading for Switzerland when he was captured.'

'Was he shot trying to escape?'

'No fear! He was shot by a firing-squad sent out by our headquarters.'

'Was he given some sort of trial?' I asked.

'No – and yes, he was tried by the Italian people in a trial which lasted twenty-three years.'

There was a moment's silence. Parri went on: 'I suppose you Americans wanted to try him as a war criminal. That he was, too, but it did not seem to us just that he be tried by foreigners; his gravest offences were against us. We like to clean our own house when it is dirty. And, besides, most important of all, a trial by you of Mussolini would be, not a trial of Mussolini, but a trial of forty-five million Italians. We hope to spare them that humiliation. The actual orders were given the unanimous approval of the delegates of all six parties in the CLNAI, Socialists, Communists, Labour Democrats, Liberals, Christian Democrats, and the Action Party.

'If you want, for your newspaper article, to see Mussolini – his, *la Petacci's*, and the captured Gerarch's bodies are now on display to the people he so abused, the people of Milan, in Piazza Loreto.'

At CVL Parri introduced me to Signor Ricardo Lombardi and asked him to tell me the story of the fruitless negotiations for the surrender of the Fascists to the partisans.

185

'When Mussolini saw the game was up, that his "betters", the Germans, were beaten and every day becoming more afraid of us, he, the Great Infallible who boasted for twenty years, and had written on tens of thousands of Italian walls, "*Mussolini ha sempre ragione*" (Mussolini is always right), he tried to desert his German patrons, and join the Socialist partisans – of course, providing he could be chief.

'Imagine, he who left Socialism nearly thirty years ago to hound it, persecute it, denounce it, and send the leaders to prison and exile wanted to come back – to save his own cowardly skin.

'Of course they refused him.

'Then the CLNAI received through his fellow, the Cardinal Schuster, an offer to treat for the surrender of the whole puppet Fascist republic. We accepted.

'The meeting took place in the Archepiscopal Palace. I was one of the delegates from CLNAI. There we met Mussolini, Graziani, and some lesser swine.

'They were only interested in their own sacred hides. They asked for no general terms for the rank and file of their little henchmen, but insisted on promises of safey for the big names of Fascism.

'We replied that we were authorized by the CLNAI to accept their surrender unconditionally, that we could and would give them no promises whatsoever. We reminded him of the unconditional surrender statement of Roosevelt and Churchill, and that Italy was an occupied country.

'They argued, they pleaded with the aid of their friend the Cardinal. We would not budge.

'Then Mussolini suddenly agreed, "I accept your terms. But I must inform the Germans, it would not be *honourable* to desert them without letting them know. I give you my word that if your partisans allow my car to pass unmolested to tell the Germans, I shall return, *on my honour!*"

'His honour! His Excellency's Honour! His honour was that he fled using this as a means to get safely out of Milano, to don a German uniform, and flee towards Switzerland to save his honourable hide!'

'It is nice,' I suggested, 'that he made the case so clear for historians by departing on a broken word of honour in a German uniform. That should label him precisely for future generations of Italians.'

186

'Don't be too sure. *We Italians soon forget.* His uniforms, his tinsel empire, and his big words may outlive his essential falsity, shallowness, dishonour.'

As I write this, seven years later, Lombardi's words have more meaning. The MSI (*Movimento Sociale Italiano*) is the fastest growing political party in Italy – undistinguishable from Fascism, it welcomes through its leader, a rabble-raiser named Augusto de Marsonich, full responsibility for the acts of the former régime.

'*We Italians soon forget!*'

Lombardi himself has been beguiled by phrases into the Communist front, which would saddle Italy with all the trimmings, suppression, and police control he so hated in Fascism – '*We Italians soon forget*'!

The CVL found me a car with the inevitable armed kids perched on the running-boards, and I was driven out to Piazza Loreto. It is a big, irregularly shaped square formed, as if by accident, when a lot of broad streets met; the buildings are ugly and the air is of a poor section of town. This square was packed with people and partisan police.

Inside this vast jam of people a stream, like an ocean current, flowed toward a large petrol station on the far side, flowed between lines of armed partisans. Because our car bore the sticker of the CVL, it was passed half-way through the crowd. From there my two guards with CVL Headquarters' passes led me afoot toward the filling station. Suddenly I realized what set this crowd aside from all other crowds I had ever seen. One was its almost deadly silence. The other was the look of quiet satisfaction on its faces.

Eight bodies hung by thongs, tying their feet together, from the iron parquet put up over the pumps to protect the customers in inclement weather. There hung a half-dozen of the big-wigs and bully-boys who had become Gerarchs. In the middle was the dictator's mistress, lovely Clara Petacci, whose family had used the relationship for extra-legal financial gain. Beside her the puffy little dictator himself dressed in a T-shirt, riding trousers, and high German black military boots. Mussolini's arms were outstretched towards the crowd, pulled down by their own weight against the *rigor-mortis* which had set in when the body was in a horizontal position.

The faces were scarcely above the level of the heads of the crowd, and were separated only by a single file of partisan police, preventing

187

physical contact with the bodies. As I passed I noticed that those next to me usually nodded, as if saying something to themselves, closing some old account.

I wanted to ask my guardians some questions – but I could not bring myself to break the almost religious silence of the great square. Even the partisan police gave their orders in husky whispers.

Back at the car one of my guards said, 'A couple of hours ago an old woman pulled a revolver out of her bag and shot him twice in the head. Her son, they said, was one of the boys of Piazza Loreto.'

'What are the boys of Piazza Loreto?' I asked.

'A month or so ago the local *Decima Mas** brought twelve boys to this square accused of being partisans and shot them. It was not so much the shooting which enraged the Milanesi, for that is war, but the fact that they left the bodies under armed guard here in the square where a hundred thousand people pass every day going to and from work. They left them until they swelled up and stank, until their faces turned blue and blew up like grotesque masks of monkeys. They left them until the putrescence of their rotting bodies ran out of their clothes, a liquid. That is why it is just that he, that they, should be hanging here like swine in a pig-butcher's shop.' He spat.

Less than five years later I was to sit in a Roman court room and see Prince Valerio Borghese, head of the *Decima Mas* in Milan, whitewashed. When the anniversary of some brave deed he had performed in the war fell during his trial, the proceedings were interrupted, with the permission of the judge, for his admirers to present him with a bunch of white roses. I remembered Piazza Loreto, and also my friends of the CVL who had been unwilling guests of the *Decima Mas* in their torture office in Milan.

*   *   *

We climbed into the car and went back to CVL Headquarters. Inside I was astonished at the calm and efficient deliberation of this headquarters. Until a couple of days before it had functioned in bits and pieces, hidden away in a dozen different parts of Milan and nearby cities. It now compared favourably with AFHQ in Algiers.

---

* Originally motor torpedo boat crews. Under the Fascist Republic of Salo, the *Decima Mas* commanded by Prince Valerio Borghese became notorious in Milan where it functioned as a political police.

It was still conducting a large-scale war, and was, in addition, facing all the bitter problems of civil strife and revolutionary administration.

In those four or five days before the arrival of the American forces and Allied Military Government, the astonishing fact in Milan was the moderation and human generosity of the partisan revolutionary government. On orders of the CLNAI and the CVL most of the people accused of war crimes and collaboration with the Germans were held for trial by later and calmer courts, set up by Allied Military Government.

An instance of this was the case of Marshal Graziani. The Allies had informed the CVL that high military personages who surrendered should be considered Allied POW's. When Captain Dadario was the only American uniform in Milan, the Marshal was captured. He was considered as the prisoner of Dadario and kept in the Hotel Milano, OSS Headquarters, until he could be delivered to G2 Fifteenth Army Group. Technically, the CVL could have shot him, as they did the other Gerarchs of the Fascist puppet Republic, since he held a political post, Minister of War, and as such issued the orders for summary execution of partisans, in or out of uniform.

*　　*　　*

The Gestapo under Colonel Rauf – mentioned earlier in this story for his special tortures – was still defending the Hotel Regina, a stone's throw from Piazza del Duomo, the very centre of Milan. The CVL left them alone, officially on the ground that they could not escape and it was useless to expend partisan lives to take such a strong position. An assistant of Parri told me the real reason: the crowd would unquestionably lynch them all, and, torturers though they were, they were all in uniform and came under the AFHQ instructions as Allied POW's. 'We cannot be responsible for the lives of those beasts. The Milanesi would tear them limb from limb.'

Two days before the first Allied forces arrived, the bane of the generals, Bill Mauldin, *The Stars and Stripes*' cartoonist, shot into Milan by jeep. In some miraculous fashion, aided by the speed at which he habitually travelled, he had passed the German lines. 'Just didn't see any Krauts except at a distance,' he said, casually.

Two days later at the bar of the Hotel Milano we were discussing the Gestapo in the Regina.

189

'Let's go visit them,' he said.

'I hear they are looking for some Americans to surrender to, maybe we could get in.'

'I think we need about four or five more of those torpedo cocktails before we stick our heads in the Gestapo's mouth – bartender, eight more torpedoes!'

A half-hour later we set out in Bill's jeep which we parked just before the Regina would come into sight around the corner. There were partisan sentries to warn civilians not to go down the street. They warned us too: '*Non andare, tedeschi, pericoloso, tedeschi.*'

We stopped on the corner. My knees were shaking an eccentric tattoo, and it wasn't from the torpedoes – equal parts of vermouth, grappa and Campari bitters served in a water tumbler – my tattoo was purely Gestapo – the word had so long symbolized horror and fear that I was automatically averse to seeing it in flesh and blood and a uniform, especially when I was half-tight, and hopelessly in the minority. But I was ashamed to suggest turning back.

'Let's take a peek around the corner?'

We did: there, less than fifty yards away, was the fortress-hotel Regina, apparently deserted behind its massive defences. The street was empty and all the shutters were closed on both sides and in all buildings. Only a black cat, doubly bad omen when in front of a Gestapo headquarters, peacefully washed her face near the wire.

We pulled back for a conference. I suggested waving a white handkerchief.

'At whom?' said Bill, 'there's no one to see it. The bastards are out to lunch, I think.'

I eased my chest and head around the corner and self-consciously held up a limp, used, white handkerchief. I gave it a few half-hearted waves, hoping no one would see it.

Then I saw a head with binoculars at its eyes in the slit of one of the pill-boxes inside the wire. In a minute it went away and reappeared around the side of the pill-box with the rest of the body. He beckoned us to approach. With what small dignity we could muster (my scalp prickled fiercely) we walked towards what proved to be a lieutenant of ss; coming closer, we saw we were covered by two gun barrels in two slots of the next pill-box.

When we reached the wire the lieutenant said in English:

'Americans?'

'Yes.'

'Has a column arrived to take us out?'

No answer from us.

'Will you come in?'

'Yes, is Colonel Rauf there?'

'Yes.'

At a command four ss soldiers appeared and began to move the big carpenter's horses spun around with wire, which closed the entrance gap in the defences.

We entered and followed the lieutenant into the lobby of the hotel. There were a half-dozen big automobiles parked in the lobby itself, Mercedes and Alfa Romeos.

'The colonel is here. Follow me.' We followed him into the dining-room. The far wall was covered with a huge swastika banner, on which were large photographs of Hitler and Himmler. A few officers were still eating. At one table were a dozen French prostitutes.

Colonel Rauf was giving orders to several officers who stood by. Seeing us he dismissed them, rose from his seat, clicked his heels and introduced himself. He spoke French.

'You are authorized to take our surrender and take us back to the American lines? So our people let you pass; General Wolf promised they would. Have you enough force to protect us from that murderous red crowd?'

'I'm not authorized to take your surrender. I know nothing about it. I am a war correspondent and so is my companion. We have heard nothing of any American column coming to take your surrender.'

'General Wolf wirelessed us that you Americans had promised to come and our troops would let you pass. Why isn't the column here?' The colonel was losing his nerve. '*Sauvez-nous. Sauvez-nous de cette foule rouge.*'

Bill Mauldin asked what he had said. I explained. Bill's comment was, 'Tell him for Christ's sake he should have thought of that twelve years ago. I personally hope the "red" crowd pulls him into little pieces.'

'You will stay in, won't you? You're in American uniform. They won't dare come while you are here.'

His fear gave me too much pleasure for me to tell him that Ferruccio Parri, whom he had 'questioned' upstairs in this hotel, had decided not to attack. It was one of the real satisfactions of the war to see Rauf suffer.

191

Mauldin had disappeared. I saw him using a major of Gestapo as model – he was doing a cartoon, one of his most famous ones, *The Last Roundup*, which showed the vicious face of the German being brought in by bearded, bedraggled GI's. It was the face of the SS major. With utter disdain for the Nazis looking over his shoulder, Bill gave him an expression of extreme bestiality.

I returned to Rauf to try to get an interview that would make a story, in addition to his terror. But he continued to plead with me not to leave until the column arrived. Screwing up my courage on Mauldin's example I finally, said:

'I am not authorized to interest myself in your situation. Nor do I desire to intercede in any way.' He glared and after a moment's silence said, 'You are mistaken to charge us with the excesses of the band of Pietro Kock at the Villa Trieste. They are a den of sexual sadists not worthy to wear a uniform.' It was true that in the last few weeks in Milan the Resistance preferred to be captured by the Germans than by the Kock band, the *Decima Mas*, or the *Muti*. But it was hateful to hear Rauf calling the kettle black, after what had gone on in his own Hotel Regina.

A terrific rumble from the street announced the arrival of the American tanks, far behind the German lines, to rescue these Gestapo and their friends. Everyone piled out into the little alley behind the fortifications. The barbed wire was opened. Three American officers, one a colonel, entered. None spoke German and Rauf didn't speak English. As bad as my German is he asked me to interpret.

'What the hell are you doing here in American uniform?' the colonel asked us. I recognized a pre-war U.S. Military Attaché in Rome.

'We just dropped in for lunch, Colonel,' replied Bill Mauldin in his best deadpan.

'Well, tell him, Colonel Rauf, we are authorized to accept his surrender. Are they ready to go in custody of this tank column to a POW cage? How soon can they start? Tell him to stack all their arms inside the hotel. They'll have to go out of here absolutely unarmed'.

I stumbled clumsily through a translation: Rauf flatly refused to disarm his men. 'That red mob will destroy us. I cannot disarm my men.'

I told the American colonel. 'Oh, my God, tell him he'll have to leave his arms. We will be responsible for their safety. Doesn't he see a dozen Sherman tanks?'

Rauf refused again.

'For God's sake get this thing over. This place is probably mined. It may go up *any minute*. But they will have to be unarmed.'

Rauf finally gave in and our colonel, nervous as an old spinster, begged us again to convince Rauf to hurry.

Finally ready, the German cars were brought out and loaded with baggage, officers, batmen, and the French whores.

In the meantime a crowd had come into the formerly empty street and the American soldiers had come out of their tanks to exchange cigarettes for wine; a general festa resulted in the street with half the crowd, while the other half screamed insults and spat at the German officers.

'Don't you think you'd better put a guard over the hotel? There may be valuable documents here,' I suggested.

'I guess you're right. But I'm not authorized to leave troops here.' He ran off to talk with his major.

By this time confusion was complete. Someone in the crowd was beating an ss officer over the head with a wine bottle. The baggage was being looted, wine was being drunk, some Milanesi were singing, others crying. At this moment the tanks were ordered to turn around and the uproar was deafening.

In the smoke of tank exhaust the column set off. The crowd began throwing bottles and anything else loose and at hand, stones and shoes.

An American NCO and a soldier had been left to guard the building. In an hour's time they had disappeared to drink or make love or both, and the looting of the hotel began. Money chests were broken open, liquor carted away, and a big Alfa Romeo disappeared from the lobby.

It was the only disorder I saw in the Milan insurrection. The Gestapo had made a sufficiently inglorious exit from the city to please everyone, and no one seemed to care what happened at the hotel.

Here, in Milan, was none of the tired cynicism and worldliness of Rome, none of the pitiful exhaustion and petty corruption of Naples, none of the damaged museum air of Florence. Milan, burned and bombed as she was, with youth and confidence planned a better future for herself and Italy. 'Our *wind of the north* will blow a new fresh energy and spirit down the full length of the Peninsula.'

But Milan planned without realising that the Allied Commission had a horror of change; without considering the layer upon unnecessary layer of idle and bakshish-ridden bureaucracy which made up the government in Rome; without, in fact, remembering that the Vatican, the oldest and most cynical totalitarian government in the world, would set itself firmly against 'the wind of the north.'

There were foreigners other than myself into whom that wind blew a something that will never come out. There were Alexander Timoschenko – Russian, Rudi Eggen – German, and 'Martino' – Dutch.

*　　*　　*

On 1 May Major Corvo of the OSS Italian Desk, who had arrived that day, said to me, 'Downes, we have a bird here in the hotel who will make a good story for you. He is the son of the Russian Marshal Timoschenko. In some crazy way he was with the Christian Democrat partisans. I'll send him up to see you. I'm afraid to get mixed up with him.'

A few minutes later he came to my room, a fine looking boy in his early twenties. He clicked his heels, and said, 'Timoschenko'. I seated him and poured a generous, Russian-sized glass of grappa.

'To President Roosevelt and the American Army,' he toasted.

So I returned, 'Marshal Stalin and the Red Army.'

'They said you might be able to help me. I do not want to go back to Russia just now. They have sent a colonel from our mission in Rome to take me back. Maybe they will not permit me to marry her. And I intend to join her church. She gave me this.' He brought out of the neck of his shirt a medal of the Virgin Mary. 'It has saved my life.'

'I'm not quite sure what you mean. Would you begin at the beginning of your story and explain to me how you happen to be here.' I poured him a third grappa.

'To the Italian partisans, my dear brothers in arms.' He settled down to his story. 'My father is General of Aviation Timoschenko, not Marshal Timoschenko, as the Americans downstairs thought.

'I went from school to war when the Germans invaded Russia. Soon after I was captured in White Russia and sent to a camp not far from Berlin. In November 1943 I escaped and hid in the fields for over a week.

'Then one night I saw a German soldier going towards the railway station. He was about my size so I crept up behind him and hit him with a big stone I picked up in the field. He was dead so I carried him into the woods and took his uniform and papers. One, I knew, was orders and these were good for railway travel.

'The orders took me to a station in Berlin where we were put on another train. I only said "Ja" or "Nein" as my accent was certain to give me away.

'Well, that train did not take me to the Eastern front, as I had hoped it would, so I could cross the lines and get back to Russia. It went to Italy. I recognized it was Italy when I saw a sign on a station, "Bolzano".'

I interrupted, 'No one picked up your accent on the train?'

'No, because I moved into a car sending Ukrainians in the German Army to the Italian front. We had many traitors among the Ukrainians.

'When the train stopped for an air-raid alert about thirty kilometres south of Bolzano, I jumped off with the others to take cover in the woods, but I did not return to the train after the planes had passed.

'I walked on for a whole day, through deep snow, hoping to find the Swiss frontier. I was not sure of the geography. That night I stopped at a peasant's house for food. I could not speak any Italian, but they brought the landowner's son from nearby. He could speak German. He was a boy of sixteen years, no more.

'"What are you, a German soldier, doing alone in the country?" I could see he hated my uniform, me, as a German, and everything German. You could see it in his eyes, in his doubled-up fists as he talked.

'" Because I am a deserter", I told him.

'"For punishment?" he asked

'"No, for politics," I replied.

'"Why?" I could see he still did not trust me.

'"I lied. I am really a Russian escaped from the Germans." He was astonished, but he took me to his father. His father offered to hide me until there should be an opportunity to pass the Swiss frontier, sixty kilometres away.

'These kind people, richer than the peasants around them but really sort of peasants themselves, fed me and kept me hidden in their house. It was dangerous for them, because the Germans and Fascists were looking everywhere for officers of the Italian Army who had fled on 9 September when the Germans began to take over. They were like my own family to me. The *Mamma* called me Sandro, my name is Alexander, and she made me new socks by hand.

'One night the other son, in his twenties, returned. He was a corporal in the army. He told how the Germans had shipped most of his regiment off as prisoners to Germany, but a few of them had escaped. They dared not stay home for certainly the Germans would go to every house looking for them.

'Five of the deserters had promised their lieutenant, who had escaped with them, to meet him in a village in the mountains in two weeks. He was going to Milan to make arrangements for them to join a new movement of resistance.

'The father sent for the priest and they talked late that night. In the morning the priest returned. He was very excited. The new Fascist Government was sending searchers for ex-soldiers, and were forcing even boys of sixteen and seventeen to join their new army.

'So with packs of food and clothing, I set off for the hideout in the mountains with the two sons of my host. They gave me everything as they gave their own sons. We had an address from the priest, where to spend the first and second nights. It was very cold in the mountains.

'Then after four or five days of hiking, we came up with the brother's lieutenant and started for the mountain town from which we, as a part of the Christian Democratic partisans, were to operate.'

He handed me a document. It was from his partisan commander, full of such phrases as *extraordinary bravery...disregard for his own safety and life ... the best machine-gunner in our brigade ... wish him all good fortune with the deepest affection of all his comrades and his Commanding Officer....*

'But how did you get your medal of the Virgin?' I asked.

'Oh, Maria gave it to me. If she believed, why should not I believe? We are not a godless people, we Russians, and after this war you will see a great revival of Christian faith in Russia.

'Somehow, I shall take Maria back to Russia. But we shall often visit Italy, I am sure. For while my duty is in Russia, my heart, a great part of me, will always be in Italy.'

He took from his pocket a red kerchief, 'I had this in case our Russian colonel catches me,' he laughed.

I gave him a few thousand lire to get back to Maria in the mountains. He autographed his red handkerchief and gave it to me.

196

'When I get back to Russia, I shall tell everyone, my father, Stalin himself if I see him, that Americans are kindly people and good soldiers. I shall say that some of the *dolcezza* of Italy is what we Russians need.'

I handed him a last drink. 'To Russia, my father, to America, my friend, and to Italy, my new mother.'

'To the wind of the north,' I replied.

He saluted and left.

*　　*　　*

Rudi Eggen, a boy of nineteen, a member of the Gestapo detail of the Nazi ss, was a guard over the political prisoners in San Vittore prison in Milan in 1944–45.

One of Ferruccio Parri's secretaries asked me to help Rudi. 'Parri is hiding him from the Americans. We have heard that the ss prisoners are being treated pretty badly (as they should be) and may be held in labour camps for years.

'Rudi, soon after he was sent to Milan, became disgusted with the brutality of the ss. Little by little he began to do favours for the prisoners in San Vittore – and not for money – he never accepted a *soldo*; from this he drifted into active participation in the resistance. He carried our letters in and out of the prison.

'He smuggled food to the Jewish children who were given sub-starvation rations.

'Finally, just before the insurrection he even stole arms and smuggled them to prisoners. You can imagine what would have happened to him if his sadistic superiors had discovered him.

'When the insurrection finally came, he opened cells, liberated prisoners, and was an active participant in the capture of the prison.

'Parri wants to know if you can possibly get him back to Germany. And not via a prison camp. Some German might recognize him for his part in the insurrection.'

I went to G2 IV Corps in Milan. The reply was 'no', not just 'no', but a rude 'no' with a threat of the jug for me if I continued 'to be a party to harbouring an unsurrendered Kraut'. I hurried down the eighty miles to Fifteenth Army Group Headquarters on Lake Garda, hoping that my old boss, General Howard, would react differently. He did.

'Well, Downes, I can't very well reverse IV Corps G2. But if you smuggle him out of IV Corps territory and get him down here, I'll see he gets on the first train over the Brenner for Germany.'

Rudi, with the tell-tale tattoo of the SS under his left arm, dressed as a GI, was passed through the IV Corps' road-blocks the next day. I pretended to be in a hurry and used once my old pass from 1943, which said, *Do not question either the holder of this pass or persons for whom he vouches.*

As we bumped along the autostrada, badly pitted from long Allied bombing and straffing, Rudi began to talk.

'Now that I can go home, I don't really want to. I don't want to leave Italy ... the Italians.'

'What's wrong? Have you got an Italian girl?'

'No, it's not that. They saved me. They cured me, the Italians. I was only really a baby in 1933 when HE came to power. I never knew any different. I believed what THEY told me, believed THEM more than my mother, who tried in her way, I think, to plant doubts in my head.

'But THEY had me all day in school, after school in the *Hitlerjugend*. The books in school, the teachers, the youth leaders, the story-books, the radio, THEY all said HE was right.

'Here, in Italy, I learned, mostly from the prisoners, but also from the townspeople, that HE was wrong, that I was only educated in brutality and hatred.

'I learned what kindness was, what tolerance and patience were; I learned that how you do something is often more important than what you do.

'What I may find at home frightens me. Maybe we Germans have not learned we were wrong but only think we have lost a war.

'I must go home. My mother is a widow. Our house has been destroyed; she is not well. I must return, *but I shall never forget these people*, these kind people who saved me from those things I was taught and which I believed when I put on that uniform of the SS.'

'Your country needs you, too, Rudi.'

'These Italians are old and they have learned how not to hate. They are maybe tired, or lazy, or dreamy, but if I could carry their civilization, their heart to Germany, maybe in some way I could help...'

We pulled up before the hotel on Lake Garda, which served as headquarters for Fifteenth Army Group. General Howard and Colonel Blom were as good as their word. Rudi left the next day with a special pass for his home in the British Zone of Germany.

Rudi has often written me, when he built a house for his mother, when he got a job with the British, and later when he became a travelling salesman for a petrol company.

'... to dear Italy,' said his last letter in 1951, 'at last I shall be able to return on a vacation; return to breathe her civilized air and try to see some of those people from the Prison of St. Vittore who saved me my self-respect and my belief in goodness. I hope Signor Parri will not be too busy to see me for a moment.'

* * *

The third foreigner was Martino, but his name isn't really Martino – he is Dutch with a flat Dutch name, yellow hair and pale-blue eyes. He was personal secretary and almost the adopted son of Ferruccio Parri when I first met him in Milan in April 1945.

But Martino's story begins in 1936 when he lived in Spain. His mother had run away with an intellectual Spanish Anarchist and taken her four children with her. They had settled, in near poverty, in a little Catalonian town.

The mother's lover had taught the children philosophy and languages. Martino's memory of those days is happy. He and the other children did not miss the stuffy, middle-class, Dutch household with its starched antimacassars. They had their mother, Spain's sunshine, and their exciting new father.

But then the civil war broke out in Spain; the foster-father casually said 'good-bye' and went off to fight against Fascism. The mother and children were stranded. Finally, a British warship evacuated the Dutch along with the British and Martino was back in Holland in the stuffy home in the Hague.

'I was eleven when we arrived back in Holland,' Martino told me in the little black market restaurant in Milan, where we were celebrating the German surrender with *prosciutto* and wine and illegal white bread.

'My life really began with a letter. I said in it, *I know what you call Communism, although in Spain it was not Communism. They say you wish to substitute Fascism. I do not know what Fascism is. Please write to me and tell me what it is.* I signed my name, addressed it to *Benito Mussolini, Rome, Italy*, and dropped it in a post box.'

199

Two weeks later a big black Fiat from the Italian Embassy drew up at Martino's house. A secretary of embassy carried an invitation from the Fascist Party for the boy 'to come to Italy as our guest and see what Fascism is.'

He went. Two months with Gerarchs for duennas, up and down the peninsula. 'There were reviews of the *Figli della Lupa*, the *Balilla*, tots like myself or a little bigger carrying wooden guns and daggers: individually trying to look like desperadoes, collectively like a Roman Legion.'

Back in the Hague, Martino's father died. The family wanted nothing to do with the runaway daughter-in-law. She took her children and left their house. That meant a job, not only for her but for all the children. The three boys went into a chocolate factory.

This family disaster reached the ears of the Italian diplomats in the Hague. The big car returned when Martino had barely passed his twelfth birthday. Would Mrs "Martino" allow the Fascist Party to educate little Martino? He would go to the best schools, to the university, be clothed and housed as befitted the son of a Gerarch of the party. No doubt the Ministry of Propaganda had its eyes open to publicity values: 'Fascist Party educates blond nordic child.'

It was against the mother's and the children's anarchist puritanism...but an education instead of the chocolate factory for the brightest of the children...it was a temptation not to be resisted. Besides, the consul promised they would also send a small allowance to the mother.

Martino returned to Italy. The *Collegio* was full of the children of aristocrats (*Princepi* and *Marchesi* and *Conti*) and the children of the new aristocrats, the Fascist Gerarchs. The tow-headed angel from the Lowlands soon found out what Fascism was. It contradicted all the anarchist philosophy he had learned and must be false.

Within six months there was a cell of anti-Fascist children in the elegant boarding school – and Martino was its Capo. At night they scaled the walls after the *professori* were asleep and made contact with the children of a *Giustizia e Libertà* cell in the nearby city.

How to avoid the oath to Fascism and the Duce? The brains, anarchist trained, behind the innocent eyes of the northern child found a way. The long oath was read out by the professor. Each boy standing at attention was supposed to raise his right hand in Fascist salute and say '*Lo Giuro*' (I swear it) – instead, coached by

Martino, each angelic little face said, *'L'ho duro'* – which is too pornographic to translate!

Over the *prosciutto* and wine it was like pulling teeth to get this part of the story out of Martino. His later exploits as a celebrated triggerman, as a member of a GAP and, finally, as Parri's secretary, I already knew from others. The earlier story seemed babyish and unimportant to this twenty-year-old tommy-gunner and escaped prisoner of the Gestapo.

'In 1941 I came up to Milan to the university. My vacations were still spent with this or that Gerarch or his family. But in Milan I soon had contacts with *Giustizia e Libertà*... in those first war years we had to be careful.

'Came 1943 and the Duce fell. *G. e L.* came out in the open as the Party of Action. Then the armistice, and the Germans occupied northern Italy and formed the Fascist Republic.

'I had less and less university and more and more resistance. They put me in a GAP and gave me the name of "Martino". We raided arsenals, we liberated some partisans held in a hospital; at night we would put our sawed-off guns under our raincoats and hunt groups or individuals, Fascist or Nazi officers, preferably armed.'

In the dim light of the black market restaurant this baby-face was talking as casually of killing men as if they were quail. For a group of two or three children to wander around a blacked-out metropolis at night, on and off street-cars, in and out of cafés, seeking humans to kill, and to tell of it casually, over ham and wine (still a well-mannered and well-behaved child), that is a new product of this war.

'Then I was sent to Parri when he took over the new command of the *Corpo Volontari della Libertà*. He was surprised that they sent a foreigner and that I was so young. He didn't seem at all like the fierce leader of a great armed conspiracy. He was the perfect, quiet, and kindly *paterfamilias*, and I felt soon like a son.'

Martino and Parri were both captured by the Germans on New Year's eve, 1944. They were given the treatment at the Hotel Regina and then sent to St. Vittore Prison to 'await disposition' – the last trip to the Mauthausen gas chambers.

But weeks passed in St. Vittore without the liquidation of the prisoners because Allen Dulles was already in contact with General Wolff of the SS and talking of eventual surrender. As a show of good faith Wolff released Parri* and delivered him across the Swiss frontier to Dulles. So the machine of liquidation could proceed with Martino.

Packed with forty or fifty others in a sealed freight car, he began the trip to Mauthausen over the Brenner Pass covered with the Alpine snows of late January.

'They took our shoes and stockings and jackets away to prevent escapes. As the train climbed higher and higher we huddled together to keep warm.

'After we left Bolzano I was glad it was dark. I was in a rage of tears. Not because I was to die when the train arrived in Mauthausen, but because I was to die outside Italy. All the kindnesses and *camaraderie* of those in the resistance came back to me.

'I began to think of the Italians, especially the northerners with whom I had been friends and how they liked a soft bourgeois life: their wine, their business, their arguments, their reading, but above all their family, children, the roof over their heads and their matrimonial beds. They had given up all this.

'This was not the Italy which I had been shown in 1937 and 1938 and 1939 – cynical and corrupted and false and covered with silly uniforms and sillier catch-phrases.

'This was the fire of the Risorgimento which for a moment had relit the lamps of hope for half of Europe. This was the Italy of Garibaldi and Mazzini, not of D'Annunzio and Badoglio.'

He leaned toward me over the table and lowered his voice.

'Sacrifice and faith have replaced selfishness and cynicism. *I was fortunate to have been even a little piece of it and I wanted to die with it*, not killed machine-like by mystic nordics far away.

'Like a crazy person I began to batter the freight car with my fists. The others tried to persuade me not to try to escape. They pleaded that the war would soon be over, maybe before we were killed. To jump out into the snow with no shoes, no coat, was sure death.

'But using for leverage the little air-hole window covered with bars, I tore out a few boards. It was narrow, but I squeezed through and fell into the darkness.

* Parri refused liberty without the others arrested with him. He had to be liberated by force.

'I don't remember much more that night. I saw the train, like a dream, disappear into a tunnel. Then I must have fainted. My face was bleeding when I awoke – this scar by my mouth and this by my ear. Somehow I got up and trudged through the snow, in places up to my waist.

'I came to a little house. I knocked. It was opened by a priest. He spoke German.

'"You have escaped from the train. You are a criminal. I shall have to call the police."'

Martino argued with him; the priest found a compromise as he heated the soup.

'"I shall shelter you until you are well again, until your injuries are healed; then I shall give you a four-hour start after which time I shall notify the German police in the village."'

The priest was a good nurse and Martino was fed well. In two weeks his host declared him cured and ready to travel. Providing him with a work-jacket, socks, and shoes and a little money, the priest said good-bye, and warned Martino that he would carry out his compromise to the letter. 'It is now 10.30, at 2.30 I shall alert the police.'

Hitch-hiking on a German convoy – without even documents – Martino arrived at Verona, where the trucks stopped to give the soldiers a chance to get a hot drink. The Fascist police came through, examining documents. Martino left by the back window in the W.C. and hitched another ride with the same German trucks to Milan.

'It is an ugly city at best, this Milan, but it seemed heaven to me. Parri was back from Switzerland. We picked up where we had left off on New Year's eve.

'I expect most of the others on the train were killed. They had made the safer choice but had lost. I have learned that in Italy it is often more prudent to follow the heart than the head.'

'What will you do now?' I asked.

'I don't know. I will stay with Maurizio as long as he can use me. I'd like to see our "Wind of the North" blow Rome clean. To Holland I shall never return. *Italy will always be my country.* After these years I should be a foreigner anywhere else, that is a foreigner in my own heart.'

I drove him back to Parri's house and said good night. 'May I write your story?' I asked.

'Promise me you won't. It would embarrass me here. And maybe

I have told too much and made myself seem heroic and ridiculous. More important it might embarrass Maurizio...at least not for now, don't write about me, please.'

Ferruccio Parri went to Rome, too good to succeed in his post as Prime Minister. Among his personal secretaries in the Viminale Palace was installed, much to the horror of the Roman bureaucrats and the secret security police, a Dutch boy, only twenty years old; a foreigner with access to the most secret state documents! But Parri knew the measure of Martino's loyalty to Italy.

Little by little the 'Wind of the North' blew itself out in the *anticameras* of the Allied Commission on Via Veneto, in the councils of the Vatican, in far distant Moscow, and under the languid sunlight of Rome. But those of us who felt it, even as outsiders, in the spring of 1945, will remain under its spell for a lifetime. It was, as it were, a fleeting glimpse of the world millions hoped would come after the war. But it was only a glimpse and of a world essentially too clean and too good for habitation by man.

> Open my heart and you will see
> Graved inside of it, 'Italy'.
> Such lovers old are I and she:
> So it always was, so shall ever be!

ROBERT BROWNING

CHAPTER SIXTEEN

CONCLUSION-RAHAB AND UNCLE SAM

> Blessed with victory and peace
> May the Heavens rescue the land.
>
> FRANCIS SCOTT KEY

Looking backwards to the years 1940–45 when I was a sort of small-fry - Admiral - Canaris - from - the - sticks, a schoolteacher trying to master-mind spy rings, I think I gave my government more enthusiasm and effort than I have ever given to anything else in my life, and, somewhat ashamedly, I admit I liked it.

But what of all those who worked for us? How did they come out? How does Uncle Sam stack up against Joshua's Israel? The reply is '*Poorly*'.

'Rahab, ... and all that she had, ... and all her kindred ...' were saved at the annihilation of Jericho, and 'she dwelleth in Israel *even* unto this day.'

A considerable proportion of our recruits, young men and women (and sometimes old ones), were to die; the more fortunate ones quickly by the enemies' guns or by means of the little pills they carried for that purpose; the less fortunate ones in the hands of the Vichy Police or Militia, the *Muti* or the *Decima Mas*, the *Falangiste* or *Sicherheitsdienst*. These are the unavoidable casualties of the work; our volunteers did not shrink from this prospect, and if they lost, the vast majority paid without a whimper and without giving away any secrets.

But we made a good many promises to these men and the organizations they represented; we told them to 'bind this line of scarlet thread' to their window and after our victory we would look after them. In few cases were these promises kept; in many cases they were broken, and unnecessarily broken.

An example is the Italian partisan movement in northern Italy (CVL and its governing body CLNAI). This organization put 130,000 armed men in the field many months before the war was over, not including its sabotage and terror cells. It suffered casualties of approximately 35,000 dead. It was never controlled, either in numbers or in direction, by the Communists.

205

We gave it a niggardly supply of arms and ammunition and in the last six months of the war some $8,000,000 in cash – both Britain and America together. Then, after the armistice, we cracked down through Allied Commission, AFHQ, and our diplomatic missions; we were afraid to undermine the Communists because Russia was our great ally and the Communists had her protection; but the non-Communist parties of the Resistance were allowed to wither for lack of help and Allied backing. The result is that Italy finds herself today with no real democratic party – a country split between the undemocratic Christian Democrats and the undemocratic Communists.

This failure to recognize 'the scarlet thread' of our promises applied not only to political parties, but also to individuals. We in the field were instructed by Washington to offer our agents a salary and a type of life-insurance (a flat sum to be paid to their dependants if they lost their lives). We were authorized to make these 'employment contracts' in U.S. dollars payable either in the U.S. or in Europe, at the desire of the 'employee'.

Men do not do espionage well for money. The best, and I might say nearly a hundred per cent of those I had occasion to use, ran the high risk of torture and death and the certainty of terror only for an ideal, or an emotional reason, like love or hate. As a result we set our salaries low to sift out those whose chief motive might be gain: $100 or $150 a month and $5,000 life insurance to the widow or mother.

Our contract read:

...The employer shall pay the employee the sum of _ dollars in the currency of the United States of America each month while said contract is in force...and further that this contract is a voluntary act of employee undertaken without duress.

Most of our recruits refused at first to sign such a contract; they said they did not wish to work for money. We were instructed to convince them that it was little enough to offer and might come in handy after the war, especially if there were an inflation of the lira.

Thus, as for instance in the case of Gianni, the former artillery lieutenant from Trieste, there might be a tidy, small sum at the end of the war: Gianni worked for us, crossing the lines with a radio six times, from September 1943 to April 1945, nineteen months, or $1,900.

After the armistice, Gianni was told, in effect, that Uncle Sam's contract was 'only a scrap of paper'. 'Policy has changed. You will be paid in lire at 225 to each dollar.' The free market lira was worth 450 to the dollar. Gianni's nest egg was cut by American fiat from $1,900 to $950. Worse yet, the value of the word of the U.S. Government was cut close to zero.

'Do you consider it honourable?' asked Gianni. 'In my case, I don't care. I shall just refuse to accept it. But some of the others need it badly. And poor Salvatore's mother is penniless. For her it is most serious – she has no one to look after her.'

There were hundreds of these cases. Those who stayed behind our lines were paid each month in U.S. currency as the contracts specified. Those who risked their lives behind the enemy lines, leaving their miserable stipend to accumulate, were short-changed by the greatest and richest country in the world.

The Russians may bump off their ex-agents who know too much, but they aren't dumb enough to cheat them and then leave them in circulation to talk badly about the contractual word and the gratitude of the Cominform. Even a semi-civilized Semite King, Joshua, leader of a nomadic tribe, knew better than that 3404 years ago!

I was told it was 'orders of the War Department', which took over oss responsibilities after the close of hostilities. I am sure it was a willing decision neither of Donovan nor of his chief finance officer Lane Rehm.

For Uncle Sam, as represented by Bill Donovan's oss, let it be said that it was the least cynical of the big Allied Secret Intelligence organizations, and most of its personnel leaned over rather too far backwards in not making promises. I have said and I have heard a good many others say:

'I think we can promise. But don't count too much on any Government's word. At least you and your organization will live in a better, freer world if we win than if Hitler wins.'

As compared to any other big country, I think Uncle Sam made a greater and more real effort to live up to Joshua's standard – but he failed.

Printed in Great Britain
by Amazon

34160932R00128